Land of Our Lady Series

Founders of Freedom
by
Sister M. Benedict Joseph, S.H.N.
Los Angeles, Calif.

Bearers of Freedom
by
Sister M. Veronica, S.P.B.V.
Central Falls, R. I.

Leaders of Freedom
by
Sister M. Clarita, O.P.
Watertown, Mass.

Challenge of Freedom
by
Sister M. Theresine, S.N.D.
Cleveland, Ohio

Guardian of Freedom
by
Sister M. Augusta, H.H.M.
Akron, Ohio

The Hail Mary

HISTORY. The first part of the Hail Mary was spoken by the Angel Gabriel at the Annunciation, when he addressed Mary with the words: "Hail, full of grace, the Lord is with thee" (*Luke 1:28*). Then, at the Visitation, Mary's cousin Elizabeth said to her: "Blessed art thou among women and blessed is the fruit of thy womb" (*Luke 1:42*). The Holy Ghost guided the Church in making the second part of the prayer.

Catholics began to use the first part of the hail Mary as a prayer in the eleventh century. Mary has always encouraged the use of the Hail Mary by granting many graces to those who pray to her in this way.

THE DEVOTION. The Hail Mary has two parts, a prayer of praise and a prayer of petition. In the first part we honor the Mother and her Son; we honor Mary for all the graces and privileges God has conferred on her; we honor Jesus as the Saviour of all. In the second part we ask Mary to pray for us sinners and obtain for us all the blessings we need both for this life and for the life to come.

Prayer

HAIL MARY, full of grace! the Lord is with thee; blessed art thou among women, and blessed is the fruit of thy womb, Jesus. Holy Mary, Mother of God, pray for us sinners, now and at the hour of our death. Amen.

DEVOTIONAL GIFTS OF MARY. The Hail Mary is one of seven great devotions given to us through Mary. The other great devotions are the Rosary, the Miraculous Medal, the Scapular, the First Saturday Devotion, the Little Office of the Blessed Virgin Mary, and the Angelus. Through these devotions you appeal to Mary for the graces which, as Mother of God, she obtains to help you save your soul.

Courtesy of Rev. J. B. Carol, O. F. M.

Land of Our Lady Series

Challenge of Freedom

by Sister M. Theresine, S.N.D.

EDITOR-IN-CHIEF:
Rev. Timothy F. O'Leary, Ph.D.
Assistant Superintendent of Schools
Archdiocese of Boston

ASSISTANT EDITOR-IN-CHIEF:
Sister M. Veronica, S.P.B.V.

CO-EDITORS:
Rt. Rev. Clarence E. Elwell, Ph.D.
Superintendent of Schools
Diocese of Cleveland

Rev. Patrick J. Roche, Ph.D.
Assistant Superintendent of Schools
Archdiocese of Los Angeles

Neumann Press
Charlotte, North Carolina

Land of Our Lady Series—Book One
Challenge of Freedom

Published by Neumann Press, an imprint of TAN Books. Originally published as: "Land of Our Lady Series"—Challenge of Freedom, Benziger Brothers, Inc., 1953. Revised edition with color corrections, cover design copyright © Neumann Press.

ISBN: 978-0-911845-56-3

Printed and bound in the United States of America.

Neumann Press
Charlotte, North Carolina
www.NeumannPress.com
2014

EDITORS' INTRODUCTION

THE TEXT, CHALLENGE OF FREEDOM, covers the period of American history in which the United States was breaking loose from Old World customs and traditions and developing a way of life all its own.

This change in American life, known to us by the name of Jacksonian Democracy, is handled in the first Unit. In this and the following Unit the pupils are made acquainted not only with the westward extension and development of the American frontiers, but also with the establishment and growth of the Catholic Church in these new territories.

In the third Unit slavery is taken up from many different points of view, including the attitude of various churchmen on the slavery problem. This phase of American history has unusual interest because it so often has been neglected. Along with the many problems of the Reconstruction period, pupils are made aware of the work of the Church in establishing religious Communities of men and women to aid the Negroes after the Civil War. The Unit on immigration deals with the main features of a topic which again became important after World War II. Proper emphasis is given to the contribution which immigrants have made to American culture and progress as well as to the development of the Catholic Church in the United States.

While every text of the series contains American Catholic history, CHALLENGE OF FREEDOM holds the honor of focusing attention on the dedication of the United States to the Immaculate Conception of Our Lady which was one of the chief reasons for choosing the title of the Series, *Land of Our Lady.*

Before the doctrine of the Immaculate Conception of Mary was officially defined by the Church, the bishops of the United States wished to give Mary special honor through this title. At the Sixth Provincial Council of Baltimore in 1846, they unanimously determined "to place ourselves and all entrusted to our charge throughout the United States, under the special patronage of the Holy Mother of God, whose Immaculate Conception is venerated by the piety of the faithful throughout the United States." By this act, the United States became Mary's land, dedicated as it was to her Immaculate Conception.

7

Further tribute was rendered Our Lady by the bishops of the United States in 1849. In that year they petitioned Pope Pius IX to proclaim the Immaculate Conception a dogma of the Universal Church. In accordance with this request, and after consultation with the Catholic bishops throughout the world, Pope Pius IX solemnly proclaimed the dogma of the Immaculate Conception on December 8, 1854.

Four short years later Our Lady appeared at Lourdes. The words of the Blessed Virgin at this time, "I am the Immaculate Conception," gave her faithful children the assurance that she approved of this title and was pleased with the honor rendered to her by the promulgation of this dogma.

We Catholics of the United States should prove by our lives that we are grateful to Mary Immaculate for the constant, loving protection, under God, which she has given to the people of this great nation, the *Land of Our Lady*.

THE EDITORS

CONTENTS

UNIT ONE

THE COMMON MAN COMES TO POWER

UNIT TWO

THE CROSS AND THE FLAG REACH THE PACIFIC

UNIT THREE

SLAVERY—A BLOT ON AMERICAN HISTORY

UNIT FOUR

BINDING UP THE NATION'S WOUNDS

UNIT FIVE

AMERICA—ONE FAMILY FORMED FROM MANY

UNIT SIX

SELFLESS COURAGE—PRICE OF PROGRESS

LIST OF MAPS

FOREWORD

THE publication of the "Land of Our Lady" Series marks a notable advancement in the field of history textbooks for Catholic elementary schools. The Series fulfills very effectively the need for history textbooks that are devoid of secularistic and materialistic tendencies and based on the sound principles of Christianity and therefore, a Christian philosophy of history.

This Series includes not only the factual data that comprise the history of America as a nation, but it incorporates also those elements of American Catholic history that can be assimilated by pupils of the elementary school level. The growth and development of the Catholic Church in the United States parallels the content of American history in each textbook of the Series.

The greatest contribution of these texts to the training and schooling of young American Catholic boys and girls is the manner in which Christian social principles are woven in the texts. As the various events of history are taken up for study, the textbooks point out the positive or negative correlation of the factual data to the principles of Christian social living.

We are grateful to the firm of Benziger Brothers, and to the competent Board of Editors and Authors for the task they have successfully accomplished in producing this American Catholic Series, "Land of Our Lady."

RT. REV. FREDERICK G. HOCHWALT, PH.D.
SECRETARY GENERAL, N.C.E.A.

Mary's Rosary

HISTORY. The Blessed Mother inspired St. Dominic to urge Catholics to practise the devotion of the Rosary. As a result of St. Dominic's preaching, the Rosary devotion spread rapidly throughout the world. Our Blessed Lady herself has encouraged this devotion by her apparitions at Lourdes, and more recently at Fatima, where she urged the daily recitation of the Rosary.

THE DEVOTION. In saying the Rosary, we meditate on fifteen events in the life of Christ and the Blessed Virgin. We think of one of these events or Mysteries while we recite a decade of Hail Marys.

Prayer

Saying The Rosary

Bless yourself, and begin.

THE CRUCIFIX
Pray: 1 Apostles' Creed

THE FIRST LARGE BEAD
Pray: 1 Our Father

THE THREE SMALL BEADS
Pray: 3 Hail Marys, 1 Glory

Start 1st decade, thinking of 1st Mystery.

THE LARGE BEAD
Pray: 1 Our Father

THE TEN SMALL BEADS
Pray: 10 Hail Marys, 1 Glory

Recite rest of five decades in same way, meditating on Mysteries in order shown.

THE END OF THE ROSARY
Pray: 1 Hail, Holy Queen

THE JOYFUL MYSTERIES	**THE SORROWFUL MYSTERIES**	**THE GLORIOUS MYSTERIES**
1. ANNUNCIATION	**1.** AGONY	**1.** RESURRECTION
Pray to be meek.	Pray for love of prayer.	Pray for hope.
Pray: 1 Our Father, 10 Hail Marys, 1 Glory	Pray: 1 Our Father, 10 Hail Marys, 1 Glory	Pray: 1 Our Father, 10 Hail Marys, 1 Glory
2. VISITATION	**2.** SCOURGING	**2.** ASCENSION
Pray for love for others.	Pray for sorrow for sin.	Pray for love.
Pray: 1 Our Father, 10 Hail Marys, 1 Glory	Pray: 1 Our Father, 10 Hail Marys, 1 Glory	Pray: 1 Our Father, 10 Hail Marys, 1 Glory
3. NATIVITY	**3.** CROWNING	**3.** PENTECOST
Pray for avoiding pride.	Pray for courage.	Pray for love for Mary.
Pray: 1 Our Father, 10 Hail Marys, 1 Glory	Pray: 1 Our Father, 10 Hail Marys, 1 Glory	Pray: 1 Our Father, 10 Hail Marys, 1 Glory
4. PRESENTATION	**4.** CARRYING CROSS	**4.** ASSUMPTION
Pray for obedience.	Pray for self-sacrifice.	Pray for life of grace.
Pray: 1 Our Father, 10 Hail Marys, 1 Glory	Pray: 1 Our Father, 10 Hail Marys, 1 Glory	Pray: 1 Our Father, 10 Hail Marys, 1 Glory
5. FINDING	**5.** CRUCIFIXION	**5.** CORONATION
Pray for love of Jesus.	Pray for faith.	Pray for patience.
Pray: 1 Our Father, 10 Hail Marys, 1 Glory	Pray: 1 Our Father, 10 Hail Marys, 1 Glory	Pray: 1 Our Father, 10 Hail Marys, 1 Glory

Indulgences, Partial: For each recitation, 5 years; if said with others, 10 years. During October, 7 years each day. Plenary: Requiring Confession, Communion, and Visit: On last Sunday of each month if said on three days of each preceding week. On feast of Holy Rosary, and during Octave (see "The Raccolta," the official book of indulgenced prayers, page 287).

DEVOTIONAL GIFTS OF MARY. The Rosary is one of seven great devotions given to us through Mary. The other great devotions are the Hail Mary, the Miraculous Medal, the Scapular the First Saturday Devotion, the Little Office of the Blessed Virgin Mary, and the Angelus. Through these devotions you appeal to Mary for the graces which, as Mother of God, she obtains to help you save your soul.

Courtesy of Rev. J. B. Carol, O. F. M.

UNIT ONE

THE COMMON MAN COMES TO POWER

UNIT ONE

THE COMMON MAN COMES TO POWER

A NEW NATION was born, grew, and developed. That nation was the United States of America. It came into being with the signing of the Declaration of Independence. Then followed years of struggle and strife, for the new nation had many problems to solve before it could take its place among the family of nations.

Shortly after 1800 three distinct areas developed in the United States: the North, the South, and the West. At this time the West, or the new frontier region, took in the land which lay between the Appalachian Mountains and the Mississippi River.

In the older states in the East, few people had the right to vote. In most of these states a man had to be a property owner before he could vote. There was still a distinction made between "gentle folk" and "common folk."

As new states were created, they allowed more freedom. Vermont and Kentucky were the first states admitted which did not require a property qualification for voting.

As homes began to multiply and new territories were organized and states were admitted to the Union, an enthusiasm for government "by the people" developed. Soon this democratic spirit began to influence people of the East. Gradually the older states, one by one, followed the example of the frontier and allowed all free men to vote.

Many leaders of the West believed that most Americans would be happier if men trusted by the common people were placed in high government positions. Chief among these champions of the common people was Andrew Jackson.

In this Unit and in the Units that follow, we shall see that the many problems which the new nation had to face were a real CHALLENGE TO FREEDOM.

13

CHAPTER I

VICTORY FOR THE COMMON MAN

Getting started. Monroe's years as President were called the "Era of Good Feeling." By 1824, however, things had changed. All three sections of our country had become strong. With strength, came selfishness. Each section began to think only of itself. The industrial and commercial North, the agricultural South, and the new West all had interests of their own. For that reason each region was anxious to place its man in the White House. This fact became very clear during the presidential campaign of 1824.

In this chapter we shall see how (1) Sectional Jealousies Gave Rise to Favorite Sons and (2) the Triumph of the Common Man.

1. Sectional Jealousies Gave Rise to Favorite Sons

As our country grew larger and stronger, different interests developed in the North, the South, and the West. The North was interested in manufacturing and shipping. Its chief concern was to obtain high prices for manufactured articles and to secure raw materials at low cost. The South, on the other hand, was fast becoming the Cotton Kingdom. It sought high prices for its cotton, and at the same time it endeavored to purchase manufactured goods as cheaply as possible. The West was interested in the development of its territory. Therefore, it wanted cheap land for settlers and good transportation for its products.

Soon each section became jealous of the others and wanted the government to pass laws that would favor its interests. The side a section took on any question depended upon its interests. Often the members of Congress were so concerned with the interests of their own sections that they thought little of the welfare of the nation as a whole.

The election of 1824. As Monroe's second term drew to a close, each section of the country had its leader and wished to see him made President. For this reason, the presidential campaign of 1824 had four candidates, all members of the same party. John Quincy Adams was the choice of the Northeast. The South supported William Crawford of Georgia, while the favorite sons of the West were Andrew Jackson and Henry Clay.

When the votes were counted, no one received a *majority* of the elec-

John Quincy Adams

William Crawford

toral votes, that is, more than half of all the votes. Andrew Jackson had received more electoral votes than anyone else, but not the required majority. Adams was second. Crawford came next and Clay followed him. In such a case, the Twelfth Amendment of the Constitution provides that the House of Representatives shall elect a President from the three candidates who have received the most electoral votes. Clay, seeing that he had no chance of winning, used his influence as Speaker of the House to bring about the election of Adams.

What is an electoral vote?

2. Triumph of the Common Man

Jackson's followers did not take the results of the election with good grace. They declared that Jackson was cheated of the Presidency.

When Adams appointed Clay to be Secretary of State, they became bitter because they felt Adams rewarded Clay for his support. They declared that Andrew Jackson would be put in the White House at the next election.

The result of this dissatisfaction was the formation of two political parties. The supporters of Adams were known as the National-Republicans, and the followers of Jackson called themselves the Democratic-Republicans. Both parties started at once to prepare for the next election.

Adams was able, honest, and patriotic. Yet, as President, he was unpopular. He was cold and reserved. He could neither arouse enthusiasm nor make friends. The people did not understand him. They felt that he was not one of them. Although

Henry Clay

Andrew Jackson

the circumstances surrounding Adams' election injured him, he worked hard at being President. He made plans for the betterment of the nation, but at every turn Congress opposed him. Adams' term of office was a continual warfare between his friends and the followers of Jackson. The "Era of Good Feeling" had come to an end.

The Democratic-Republicans were determined to make the next campaign a triumph for Jackson. So well did they work, and so cleverly did they lay their plans, that Jackson won an easy victory over Adams in 1828.

One of the reasons why Jackson won the election was due to the support given him by the pioneers who had settled in the West.

These rugged frontiersmen had a strong sense of equality. In their eyes one man was as good as another and had as good a chance to succeed. This feeling of equality caused a strong democratic spirit to develop in regard to government. The pioneers insisted upon being equal in government. They believed that all men should have a right to vote and a right to hold even the highest government positions. Because of this great faith in the common man, the people of the frontier communities followed the example of Vermont and Kentucky in permitting all free men over twenty-one years of age to vote.

After the election of Jefferson in 1800, democratic views spread throughout our country. Jefferson was not a Federalist. He was the leader of the Democratic-Republican party. The members of this party believed that all men should be allowed to share in the government and that all should have a chance to be educated. To them, the rights of men were very important. Nevertheless, even in Jefferson's time the people as a whole were not permitted to take a direct part in government affairs.

Jackson's election as President of the United States in 1828 marked the triumph of the common people. Jackson's greatest contribution to American democracy was the principle that government should give due consideration to the rights and wishes of the great group of ordinary men.

Do you think Americans still feel that the ordinary men should have a voice in government?

Are you familiar with these terms?

majority
electoral votes
the masses
common man
challenge
presidential campaign

frontier communities
sectional jealousies
raw material

Study exercise

1. Locate each of the three major sections of our country at the time Jackson was elected President. What were the chief interests of each section? Should these sections have thought more of their own interests or of the good of the nation as a whole?

2. Why was President John Quincy Adams unpopular with the people? Do you think he was a good President? What makes a good President?

Test yourself

Make each of the untrue statements below true.

1. Civil authority comes from God to the person or persons designated by the people as rulers of the country.

2. "Created equal" means that all men are created by God and have certain God-given rights that no one can take from them.

3. The West of this time was the land west of the Mississippi River.

4. Massachusetts and Kentucky were the first states to permit all free men over twenty-one years of age to vote.

5. Andrew Jackson believed that government should recognize the common man.

6. The North, the South, and the West thought more of their own selfish interests than of the good of the nation as a whole.

7. The followers of Jackson were known as National-Republicans.

8. John Quincy Adams was an honest and capable man, but as President he was unpopular.

9. In the early days our government was ruled by the Federalists.

10. John Quincy Adams was elected President in 1824 by a large majority of electoral votes.

CHAPTER II

ANDREW JACKSON, A REAL MAN OF THE PEOPLE

Getting our bearings. The first six Presidents of the United States had all belonged to old *aristocratic*, or high-ranking families. Washington, Jefferson, Madison, and Monroe had been wealthy Virginia planters. The two Adamses had represented the rich merchants of New England. All had had experience in political affairs.

Jackson, as we shall see in this chapter, was the first President who did not belong to this group of aristocrats. To understand better how Jackson was a real man of the people, we shall see how (1) Jackson Becomes a Popular Hero, (2) Jackson Champions the Cause of the Common People, (3) Jackson Handles the Problems of the Nation, and (4) the Panic of 1837.

1. Jackson Becomes a Popular Hero

The frontiersmen of the West, the working men of the city, and the small farmers of the country all felt that Andrew Jackson was one of them.

Early life of Jackson. Andrew Jackson was a true son of the soil. Born of poor parents on a frontier farm of South Carolina, he had to face hardship, poverty, and danger. When still a boy he was left an orphan and had to make his way in life by hard work. At the age of fourteen, he was captured by the British during the Revolutionary War. To his dying day he carried on his scalp the scar of a saber. This he received for refusing to black the boots of a British officer.

As a young man, Jackson moved to the frontier country of Tennessee. Here he practiced law and became a judge. Did a man have to graduate from a law school to practice law or to be judge in those days?

Jackson rises to leadership. Although Jackson was not wealthy, he soon rose to leadership. He understood the common people because he was one of them. In the early days of Tennessee, he won a name for himself as an Indian fighter. Later, when Tennessee became a state, he helped to draw up its constitution and was sent to Washington as its first representative in Congress.

During the War of 1812, Jackson's victory over the British at New Orleans made him known to

Andrew Jackson wins the Battle of New Orleans

the nation as a whole. Later his work of subduing the Florida Indians won for him the governorship of that newly-acquired territory. Always and everywhere he endeared himself to the men who served under him. He was simple and lived like the private soldiers of his army. In the camp and on the march, he shared their hardships and their food.

Jackson was a soldier and a man of action. He was bold, courageous, and determined. But at the same time he was honest, frank, and hard-working. He was as bitter to his enemies as he was loyal to his friends. He never hesitated to stand up for what he thought was right.

Because of these qualities, the people called him "Old Hickory." He shared the western belief that the common people had the right and ability to rule. Because of his lack of schooling and his fiery temper he often made mistakes. But in spite of these weaknesses, he became the idol of the people.

The hardy frontiersmen thought the election of 1824 should have gone to Jackson and, therefore, considered him a martyr as well as a hero. In all sections of the nation, Jackson came to be looked upon as the champion of the common man. In 1828 the frontiersmen of the West united with the immigrants and mechanics of the East and

Brown Brothers

Jackson's inauguration

many Southern farmers to elect him President.

Jackson is inaugurated. On March 4, 1829, the city of Washington was tense with excitement. The hero of the common people was to be inaugurated. Crowds flocked to Washington to see Jackson take office. During the inaugural address and the taking of the oath, they stood silent.

After the ceremony, however, they swarmed into the White House and the surrounding grounds shouting for "Old Hickory." They were so anxious to shake hands with the new President that chairs were overturned in the rush to get to him. The crowds pushed so frantically that bowls of punch were upset and glasses were broken. Those who could not get near the President stood with muddy boots on the satin-covered chairs in order to see him. All was in a state of confusion.

Many people were shocked and felt that the government would "go to pieces" with this "crude" Westerner as President. They did not realize that Jackson was a gentleman. The celebration simply meant that Andrew Jackson was the hero of the common people. He was their President. His election was their triumph, and now they were celebrating it with him.

2. Jackson, Champion of the Common People

Democracy has meant different things at different times. Jefferson thought "government for the people" to be democracy. Jackson believed it to be of the people, for the people, but especially *by* the people. As President, Jackson felt that it was his duty to carry out the will of the people who had elected him. He had definite ideas of what a President should and should not do. He was not afraid to tell anyone that he knew what was best for the nation. This often caused him, as we shall see, to make enemies as well as friends.

The "Spoils System." During the days before and after Jackson's inauguration, Washington was thronged with people from every section of the country, and the new President was besieged by office seekers.

During the first days of his administration, Jackson dismissed many experienced government officials. He believed that any honest man could hold a government position. He also wanted to appoint members of his own party to take the place of the officials he had dismissed. Since his friends had worked hard to get him elected, he thought that giving them government positions was one way of rewarding them for their help and their loyalty.

This practice of giving government positions to faithful party workers, without considering their ability to fill the office or to do the work, is called the "Spoils System." Although such a practice seems unwise to us today, Jackson was sincere in his purpose. He mistrusted the members of the opposing party because he thought they were his personal enemies. He did not care to have them help him in the management of the government. He was also of the opinion that any man who holds an office for a long period of time may become careless. Furthermore, Jackson was convinced that the "Spoils System" was one way of giving the people their will.

The "Spoils System" was not a new idea. Jackson did not begin it. Pennsylvania and New York had used it locally since 1800. Jackson merely applied it to the national government. It had always been

A cartoon against the spoils system. Jackson is master of the ship "Experiment." Spoils System rats on the deck, and "pork barrels" are on the mastheads

customary for the new President to appoint, with the consent of the Senate, the members of the Cabinet, the ministers to foreign countries, the federal judges, and the minor officials, such as postmasters and revenue collectors. Jackson, however, used his appointing power in a new way. He removed officials who disagreed with him and filled their places with his own supporters. Other Presidents had waited until vacancies occurred, or until they found it necessary to remove an official who was not faithful to his duty.

The "Spoils System," even though approved by many at the time, was not a good thing for the nation. Offices were not given to men who could best fill them, but to those who had helped to elect the President. Officials chosen in this way often did poor work. Nevertheless, this system was used by the Presidents following Jackson for more than a half century.

As time went on, the problems of the government became more and more complex. Then it was that the "Spoils System" began to be a hardship not only on the men who were put out of office, but also on those who, without ability or previous training, had to fill the office. Despite its many weaknesses, however, the "Spoils System" was not brought to an end until the passage of the Civil Service Act in 1883.

3. Jackson Handles the Problems of the Nation

When Jackson became President, the country was buzzing with discussions about the Constitution. Everywhere men tried to determine whether the national government or the individual states were sovereign, whether a state could nullify, or declare void, an act of Congress, and whether a state could secede, or leave the Union. These problems were not new. As we have seen before, the Constitution meant different things to different people. There were those who, like Hamilton, believed in "broad construction" of the Constitution, that is, in giving a great deal of power to the federal government. Such persons thought that the Constitution expressed only *some* powers of the President, of Congress, and of the Supreme Court; but left them free to do many other things not mentioned.

Others, like Jefferson, believed in "strict construction," or that the Constitution meant exactly what it said. Accordingly, the President, Congress, and the Supreme Court had only a few general powers which they could exercise. The states themselves were to carry on most of the business of government.

Tariff and Nullification. Even before Jackson became President, there had been trouble over the tariff. Many Northern people had invested the little money they had in factories. During the War of 1812 they had prospered. After the war, however, there was much suffering in the towns. Factories were closed and people were out of work.

England, hoping to wipe out the infant industries of America, flood-

Interior of a Northern factory in the nineteenth century

ed the markets of the United States with cheap goods. This convinced Northern manufacturers that protection was necessary.

In 1816 the United States government placed a tax, known as a *tariff*, on goods brought into the United States from other countries. The purpose of the tax was to obtain money to support the government and to keep England from underselling American-made articles, and thus to limit the domestic market to American manufacturers.

The tariff had helped to some extent, but the Northern manufacturers kept demanding higher protective tariffs. Accordingly, the tariff was raised in 1819 and again in 1824. Finally, when a higher tariff law was passed in 1828, trouble arose. This tariff was hated by so many people that it came to be known as the "Tariff of Abominations."

The people living in the agricultural regions of our country, especially in the South where there were practically no factories, were opposed to a high tariff. They were farmers and naturally had to buy whatever manufactured products they needed. The tariff raised the price of these products. This caused much suffering. Furthermore, the Southerners could not understand why they should be taxed to help the Northern manufacturers.

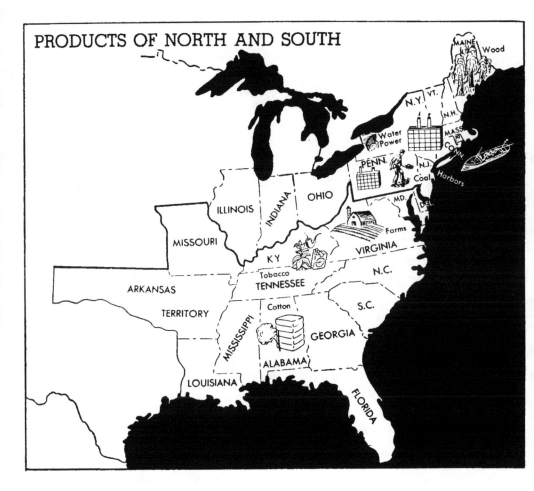

PRODUCTS OF NORTH AND SOUTH

Wood · MAINE · N.Y. · VT. · N.H. · MASS · CONN. · Water Power · PENN. · N.J. · Coal · Harbors · ILLINOIS · INDIANA · OHIO · MD. · DEL. · MISSOURI · Farms · K Y · VIRGINIA · Tobacco · N.C. · ARKANSAS · TENNESSEE · TERRITORY · Cotton · S.C. · MISSISSIPPI · GEORGIA · ALABAMA · LOUISIANA · FLORIDA

National Government or States' Rights. The people of the South clung to the belief of Jefferson that the individual state had certain rights which could not be taken from it. These people declared that since a state is supreme within its own boundaries, it has the right to *nullify*, that is, to keep from being enforced within its boundaries, a law which it considered unfair. Some people even maintained that a state had the right to secede from the Union. These rights were supposed to be based on the Declara-

tion of Independence. This document declares that whenever a government ceases to respect the rights of the people "it is the right of the people to abolish it and to institute a new government." Besides they argued that since the states freely joined the Union, they could freely leave.

The North at this time claimed that a state had not the right to secede. It upheld that part of the Constitution which reads, "The Constitution and the laws of the United States shall be the supreme

A Southern cotton plantation. While the North manufactured goods,
the South grew cotton

law of the land, . . . anything in the constitution or laws of any state to the contrary notwithstanding."

The South, however, was not alone in defending States' Rights, Nullification, and Secession. In 1798 and 1799 Virginia and Kentucky declared the Alien and Sedition Laws null and void within their boundaries. Pennsylvania, in 1811, announced that the bill to re-charter the First United States Bank was unconstitutional. Furthermore, during the War of 1812, New England and New York, embittered by the Embargo Act, talked seriously of seceding from the Union.

The Webster-Hayne Debate. In 1830, however, the question whether a state had the right to nullify an act of Congress was hotly debated in the Senate. Calhoun, a staunch defender of the South and a believer in States' Rights, was Vice-President, and so could not participate in the debate. He worked out arguments in favor of States' Rights and gave them to Senator Hayne of South Carolina. Senator Hayne used Calhoun's arguments in the debate. He explained the Doctrine of Nullification as the South saw it so well that Calhoun listened with rapt attention to the arguments which he himself had worked out.

Just as Hayne began to speak,

Daniel Webster stepped casually inside the Senate chamber. At the time, Webster was deep in thought about certain cases which were coming up before the Supreme Court. But as soon as he heard Hayne, he forgot his perplexing problems. He felt that New England was being derided and the Constitution was under attack. He felt that he must refute Hayne's arguments.

Calhoun's arguments as explained by Hayne were: The states in joining the Union had given certain powers to the national government. The states themselves had kept the supreme power. The national government had gone beyond its power when it levied the protective tariff at the expense of the South. In such a case, a state had the right to nullify the law. The state had the right to secede from the Union if it felt that it had been unjustly treated.

Webster replied to Hayne as follows: After defending his own state of Massachusetts, he declared that the people of the United States, rather than the states themselves, had framed the Constitution, which provided for an inseparable Union. He declared that although the states had entered the Union of their own free will, they had no right to secede because the Constitution could not grant a right that would lead to

Webster's reply to Hayne. What were the differences between their views?

its own destruction; and that the Constitution had provided for a Supreme Court to define the powers of the national government and of the states. After holding his listeners spellbound for three hours, Webster ended his great speech with the widely quoted words: "Liberty and union, now and forever, one and inseparable."

Jackson's attitude towards Nullification. No one knew exactly where President Jackson stood on the doctrine of Nullification. He was a Southerner and a cotton planter. Yet he gave no sign of approval or disapproval. He awaited the right moment to speak.

That opportunity came in April, 1830. At a banquet held in honor of Jefferson's birthday, Jackson was asked to give a toast. This was his chance to express himself *for* or *against* Nullification. Jackson rose and, drawing himself to his full height, looked straight at Calhoun. Then amid breathless silence, he exclaimed, "Our federal Union! It must be preserved!"

In a few words, Jackson showed that as President he intended to fulfill his oath to enforce the national laws and to preserve the Union. The men who upheld States' Rights were dumbfounded. After a few minutes, Calhoun, who knew that the President's words were a challenge to him, slowly and hesitatingly, offered the second toast: "The Union! Next to our liberty most dear!" There was a pause for a minute, and Calhoun added, "May we all remember that it can only be

Bettmann Archive

"Our federal Union—it must be preserved"

preserved by respecting the rights of the states and by distributing equally the benefits and burdens of the Union."

South Carolina and Nullification. In 1832 the "Tariff of Abominations" was repealed and a new bill passed which lowered the tariff somewhat. This law did not lower the tariff enough, however, in the eyes of South Carolina, to relieve the sufferings of the South. On this account, and in spite of Jackson's warning, South Carolina decided to act. A convention was held in Columbia, South Carolina, which declared that the Tariff Acts of 1828 and 1832 were "null, void, and no law." The people were told that after February 1, 1833, they were not to pay duties required by these laws. At the same time, the Convention members boldly declared that any attempt of Congress to enforce the hateful tariff would cause South Carolina to secede from the Union.

Jackson upholds the Union. All eyes were immediately turned upon Jackson. His native state, South Carolina, had threatened the existence of the Union. What would he do?

Jackson was angry, and rightfully so. To a Congressman preparing for a trip home to South Carolina, he said: "Tell them from me that they can talk and write resolutions and print threats to their hearts' content. But if one drop of blood is shed there in defiance of the laws of the United States, I will hang the first man of them that I can get my hands on to the first tree that I can find."

Hayne expressed his doubt that Jackson would really hang anybody. A Missouri Congressman who heard him, replied, "I tell you, Hayne, when Jackson begins to talk about hanging, they can begin to look for the ropes."

Jackson acted promptly. He sent a *proclamation*, or a message, to the people of South Carolina in which he told them that if a state could withdraw from the Union at pleasure, the United States would not be a nation. Furthermore, he warned that he would use the Army, if necessary, to enforce the tariff law. He called upon the people of South Carolina to obey.

Upon the request of the President, Congress passed the Force Bill, which authorized Jackson to use the Army and the Navy to enforce the tariff law. Ships were sent to Charleston Harbor, Fort Moultrie was strengthened, and General Scott was sent to the scene of the trouble. To the customs officer at Charleston, Jackson wrote, "I will meet treason at the threshold . . . In forty days I will have 50,000 men in South Carolina to enforce the law."

In his message to Congress, Jackson used gentler words. He suggested that Congress revise the objectionable tariff. Henry Clay came to the rescue with a compromise tariff. Clay's bill provided that the tariff should be lowered year by year until in 1842 it would reach the level of the 1816 tariff.

Fortunately, both sides were satisfied with the compromise tariff bill, often known as the Tariff of 1833. Clay's efforts at peace-making were successful. South Carolina repealed the Act of Nullification and war was avoided. However, the question of whether a state could secede from the Union was not settled. Thirty years later the same question of States' Rights caused the whole South to take up arms in a Civil War.

Jackson destroys the bank. The First United States Bank, as we have learned, was established by Hamilton in 1791. At this time, many people were opposed to the bank. They did not think that the Constitution gave Congress the power to establish a bank. Washington was puzzled and asked the advice of his Cabinet. Hamilton and

Jefferson could not agree on the question. Hamilton and the Federalists thought the bank useful and proper. Jefferson and the Democratic-Republicans said that the bank was not necessary and the Constitution did not permit it. Finally, after listening to both sides, Washington accepted Hamilton's advice and signed the Bank Bill. Thus the First United States Bank came into existence with a charter for twenty years.

When the charter expired, or ran out, in 1811, Jefferson and his party were in power and they refused to renew it. After some time, men found out that a bank is a very useful institution. Therefore, in 1816, the Second United States Bank was set up and given a charter for twenty years. Its power over state banks and over money in general, together with a feeling that it favored the East and injured the West, made it very unpopular in the West and the South. Jackson shared this feeling. From the very beginning he declared that it was unconstitutional.

Besides, the bank had become wealthy and powerful. For this reason, Jackson distrusted it. He felt that such a powerful institution was not democratic. He believed it was an enemy of the common people because it placed too much power in the hands of a few wealthy persons. He was also of the opinion that the bank could use the money in its possession to help elect persons to office and to influence officials to pass certain laws. In other

The First U. S. Bank

words, it could control government, money, and business. There was, however, only one way in which Jackson could put an end to the bank and that was by not renewing its charter in 1836.

As time for election drew near, Clay persuaded the friends of the bank that now would be a good time to ask for a renewal of the charter. Clay was running against Jackson. He felt that this would be a good way of ruining Jackson's chance of being reelected. He figured that Jackson would not dare to veto the renewal bill before the election, and if he did the bank would surely become a campaign issue.

Jackson saw the trick and vetoed the bill. It was a brave act, for it could have cost him the Presidency.

The friends of the bank received

the news of the veto very calmly. They felt that the veto would work against Jackson in the coming campaign. They were confident that if Clay were elected and Jackson defeated, the bank's charter would be renewed in 1836. Therefore, they felt there was no reason to become excited.

The bank becomes the leading issue. Events, however, did not turn out as Clay's followers expected. True, the bank did become the leading issue during the Presidential campaign of 1832. Clay and the National-Republicans defended the bank and spoke against the veto. Jackson and his party denounced the bank at every opportunity. Jackson himself appealed to the people to support him in his war against the Second Bank of the United States.

In November the issue was definitely decided by the people. Jackson was reelected with an overwhelming majority of votes. This convinced Jackson that the people wished him to get rid of the bank at once.

The bank was entitled to four more years of life, and its friends still hoped to turn defeat into victory. They felt that business would be severely crippled in 1836, when all loans would have to be called in, in order to close the bank. This they hoped would cause so much dissatisfaction that Congress would be forced to approve the charter and give the bank a new lease of life.

Jackson, too, realized that to withdraw all funds at once or to close the bank suddenly would be tragic to business. Under such circumstances, he knew that a charter might be obtained from Congress in spite of his veto.

However, Jackson did not intend to wait until the charter ran out. Neither did he intend to cripple business by suddenly closing the bank. Instead, he intended to cut off gradually the activities of the bank until it would cease to exist without a shock to the country. Accordingly, he instructed the Secretary of the Treasury not to deposit any more government funds in the National Bank, but to deposit them in certain selected state banks. These banks were often called "pet banks" by Jackson's enemies. As bills came due they were to be paid with money drawn from the National Bank. Thus, when the charter expired in 1836, the bank went out of existence. It later became a state bank with a charter from Pennsylvania.

All debts paid. During Jackson's second term, the Democrats worked hard to pay off the national debt. The high protective tariff, our foreign trade, the collection of money owed the United States by foreign countries, and the sale of public lands in the West helped to increase the wealth of the government. At the close of 1834 the last dollar of the national debt was paid off and there was still a large surplus in the Treasury.

It was not fair to continue to tax the people when the government had so much money. Some thought

Cartoon showing confusion created by withdrawal of public funds from the U. S. Bank

the surplus should be used for national improvements, such as the building of railroads, canals, and roads. Jackson was not sure that such work was permitted by the Constitution. In 1836 Congress decided the matter by passing a bill stating that the money should be divided among the states. Before this could be carried out, a depression descended upon the country. Never since has there been a surplus in the Treasury to distribute among the states.

Van Buren becomes President. As Jackson's second term drew to a close, the Democratic party followed his suggestion and nominated Martin Van Buren to run for President. Jackson, in spite of his many mistakes, was still the idol of the people. His support caused Van Buren to be elected in 1836.

Wild speculation. Not all "pet banks" were well managed. Some of them, as well as the "wildcat" banks which sprang up, acted rashly. They issued paper money without gold or silver in the bank to back it up. They also loaned a great deal of money on very poor security. Do you know what security is?

Since it was so easy to borrow money, people began to speculate; that is, they bought land in the West with the intention of selling it later at a profit. They bought land, manufactured articles and other neces-

31

Brown Brothers
Martin Van Buren

General Harrison leads the attack on Tecumseh's warriors

government money was kept in the Treasury Building at Washington and in specially built vaults, known as *sub-treasuries*, in the larger cities of the country.

Nevertheless, the people blamed Van Buren and his administration for the panic of 1837. As a result the Democrats were voted out of office in the election of 1840. The Whig Party, whose members were all anti-Jackson men, succeeded in electing another Western President, William H. Harrison, of Ohio.

Jacksonian Democracy. The term "Jacksonian Democracy" applies not only to the two terms of Jackson as President, but also to the term of Van Buren. Since "Little Van," as he was often called, tried so faithfully to carry out the aims of Jackson, his term of office is frequently referred to as Jackson's third term. The election of Harrison by the Whigs, in 1840, did not cause much change in the democratic idea of government. The principles of Jacksonian Democracy were too firmly established to be overthrown by mere party changes.

Words to know

aristocratic	secede
frontiersman	proclamation
inaugurated	security
"Spoils System"	tariff
nullify	panic
veto	specie

"Tariff of Abominations"
Independent Treasury
sub-treasuries
Jacksonian Democracy
Nullification   States' Rights
speculate   tradition

To test your knowledge

1. Discuss the advantages and disadvantages of the Spoils System.
2. What is free trade? What is a protective tariff? Which do you think is more in accord with Christian principles? Why?
3. Prove that South Carolina was not the first to believe in States' Rights.
4. Show how the doctrine of Nullification would result in the breakup of the Union.
5. Was Jackson's action towards the National Bank justified?

How well do you remember?

On a sheet of paper write the items in Column A. Next to each copy the item in Column B which best matches it.

Column A	*Column B*
1. "Spoils System"	a. was an order which demanded that government lands be paid for in gold or silver.
2. "Pet banks"	b. meant government not only "of the people" and "for the people" but "*by* the people."
3. Jeffersonian Democracy	c. was the practice of giving government positions to faithful party workers.
4. Jacksonian Democracy	d. was looked upon by Jackson as a dangerous money power.
5. National Bank	e. were the state banks favored by Jackson.
	f. meant government "for the people."
6. Specie Circular	g. revised the tariff to satisfy the South.

REVIEW OF UNIT ONE

Minimum essentials

1. All men have an equal right to life, to liberty, and to the pursuit of happiness.
2. All men do not have the same gifts and talents.
3. All authority comes from God.
4. As the United States grew stronger, selfishness developed and each section began to think more of its own interests than of the nation as a whole.
5. Andrew Jackson was the first President from the West and the first President chosen from among the common people.
6. The old National-Republican party divided into two parties: National-Republicans and Democratic-Republicans. In 1832 the Democratic-Republicans came to be known as the "Democrats," while the National-Republicans became the "Whigs."
7. Jefferson believed in government "*for* the people," that is, capable representatives should rule the people. (Representative government.)
8. Jackson believed in government "*by* the people," that is, the people, themselves, should guide the actions of the officials whom they elect. (Direct government.)

34

9. Jackson nationalized the "Spoils System."

10. Development of democracy during the administration of Jackson:
    a. Property qualifications for voting were gradually abolished.
    b. The right to vote was extended to all free men over twenty-one years of age.
    c. The idea of equality of all men spread with the development of the West.

11. Three outstanding issues during Jackson's administration were: (1) Tariff, (2) Nullification, and (3) the Second United States Bank.

12. North, South, and West thought differently about:
    a. Political issues, such as States' Rights, Nullification, and strict construction.
    b. Economic issues, such as tariff, the Second United States Bank, internal improvements, and slavery.

13. The panic of 1837 was caused by: (1) business depression in Great Britain, (2) poor crops in the West, (3) destruction of the National Bank, (4) unsound paper money, (5) wild speculation, and (6) Jackson's Specie Circular.

14. The Independent Treasury System was established as a result of the panic of 1837.

15. Important definitions:
    a. A tariff is a tax on goods imported into the country.
    b. A protective tariff is a tax to protect manufacturers in this country against lower priced goods from abroad.

c. The Force Act was a law passed by Congress which gave the President the power to use the Army and Navy to collect duties.

d. The Specie Circular was an order which stated that payment for all Western lands was to be made in gold and silver.

e. The States' Rights doctrine was the belief that each state had a right to decide for itself whether or not a law was constitutional and should be obeyed.

f. Nullification was the action of a state to prevent a new law passed by the federal government from being enforced within its territory.

Things to do

1. Prepare and present a panel discussion in which you compare Jacksonian Democracy with Jeffersonian Democracy. Be sure to make clear the difference between government "for the people" and government "by the people."

2. Prepare a report about Jackson's election and inauguration. Write it as a modern newspaper man might do. Give the article an interesting headline.

3. Make an interesting time-line of the events of this Unit. Be sure to include the following: Tariff of Abominations; Compromise Tariff; Independent Treasury System; Destruction of the United States Bank; Inaugurations of Jefferson, Madison, Monroe, J. Q. Adams, Jackson, and Van Buren; Webster-Hayne debate; Panic of 1837; and and Specie Circular.

4. Make a map showing the North, South, and West of 1830. In some manner indicate the interests of each section and the reason for them.

5. Collect poems, pictures, graphs, or stories illustrating the events of this Unit.

I. Matching Test

On a separate paper copy the names in Column I. Behind each name write the letter found before the phrase in Column II that is related to it.

Column I	Column II
1. Andrew Jackson	A. used his influence to bring about the election of Adams.
2. John Quincy Adams	B. was President during the "Era of Good Feeling."
3. Thomas Jefferson	C. was a defender of the South and believed in the doctrine of States' Rights.
4. William Crawford	D. believed that the common people have the right and the ability to rule.
5. Henry Clay	E. opposed the plans Adams made for the betterment of the nation.
6. James Monroe	F. was honest, able, and patriotic.
	G. believed in representative government.
7. Martin Van Buren	H. said, "Liberty and union, now and forever, one and inseparable."
8. Congress	I. was the candidate of the South in the presidential election of 1824.
9. Daniel Webster	J. carried out the aims of Jackson during his term of office.
10. John C. Calhoun	K. desired to purchase manufactured goods cheaply.

II. Multiple Choice Test

Check the item or items in each statement that will make that statement correct.

1. President Jackson gave government jobs to his
   . . .a. friends
   . . .b. enemies
   . . .c. sons
   . . .d. relatives
   . . .e. brothers

2. South Carolina's refusal to obey a law of the Federal Government is known as
   . . .a. States' Rights
   . . .b. tariff
   . . .c. Nullification

. . .d. veto
. . .e. Spoils System

3. The practice of giving government positions to faithful party workers is called the
   . . .a. tariff
   . . .b. Spoils System
   . . .c. Specie Circular
   . . .d. Force Act
   . . .e. States' Rights

4. State banks favored by Jackson were called
   . . .a. city banks

36

...b. National Banks
...c. local banks
...d. "pet banks"
...e. federal banks
5. Created equal means that
    ...a. all men have the same gifts and talents
    ...b. all men are capable of doing the same kind of work.
    ...c. all men have a right "to life. liberty, and happiness."
    ...d. all men are capable of holding office.
6. Rulers get their authority
    ...a. directly from God.
    ...b. from God through the people.
    ...c. through an act of their own.
    ...d. directly from the government.
7. Jackson believed in emphasizing government
    ...a. "for the people"
    ...b. "of the people"
    ...c. "by the people"
    ...d. "for the people and of the people."
8-11. The issues on which the North,
South, and West could not agree were
    ...a. Spoils System
    ...b. tariff
    ...c. Specie Circular
    ...d. Nullification
    ...e. States' Rights
    ...f. United States Bank
12. A tax on goods imported into the country is a
    ...a. reward
    ...b. tariff
    ...c. spoils
    ...d. veto
    ...e. circular
13-14. Andrew Jackson was a President chosen from the
    ...a. North
    ...b. South
    ...c. West
    ...d. common people
    ...e. privileged class
15. The Independent Treasury System was established by
    ...a. Jackson
    ...b. Jefferson
    ...c. Van Buren
    ...d. Madison
    ...e. Monroe

III. Essay Test

1. Between the years 1828 and 1840 the population of the United States increased 50% while the number of voters increased 100%. What reason can you give for this difference?
2. What advantages and what disadvantages came from the destruction of the National Bank?

IV. Sequence Test

Arrange the following events in the order in which they took place.

...Nullification Act of South Carolina
...Era of Good Feeling
...Spoils System

...Second United States Bank
...Clay made Secretary of State
...Tariff of Abominations

Do the same with these.

...Panic of 1837
..."pet banks"
...Jackson's victory at New Orleans
...Inauguration of Jackson

...Specie Circular
...Independent Treasury System
...Jackson elected President

Mary's Miraculous Medal

HISTORY. In 1830, at Paris, Our Blessed Lady appeared to Catherine Labouré, a novice of the Sisters of Charity, and showed her the pattern of the Medal now known as the "Miraculous Medal." The Blessed Virgin appeared as if standing on a globe and holding in her hands another small globe which she said represents the entire world and each person in particular. Her fingers were filled with rings and precious stones emitting brilliant rays of light. These rays, she said, are a symbol of the graces she obtains for those who ask for them.

Then the globe disappeared and the Blessed Virgin extended her arms. Around the figure of the Virgin there appeared an oval frame bearing in golden letters the words: "O Mary, conceived without sin, pray for us who have recourse to thee." Then a voice was heard saying: "Have a medal struck after this model. Those who wear it will receive great blessings."

Then the oval frame seemed to turn around and the reverse of the Medal was shown; there appeared the letter M surmounted by a cross having a bar at its base; beneath the monogram of Mary there were figures of the Sacred Hearts of Jesus and Mary, the former encircled by a crown of thorns, the latter pierced with a dagger; the monogram and the two Hearts were surrounded by twelve stars.

With the distribution of the Medal, the devotion spread rapidly. The wonders which Almightly God has worked by its means gave rise to the name "Miraculous Medal."

THE DEVOTION. The Miraculous Medal is a sacramental, that is, an object blessed by the Church to obtain temporal and especially spiritual favors. In the blessing of the Miraculous Medal the Church prays that the wearers of this medal may enjoy the protection of Mary. We therefore honor the Mother of God by wearing the Miraculous Medal as a token of our devotion, respect, and confidence towards her.

Prayer

O MARY, conceived without sin,
Pray for us who have recourse to thee.

An indulgence of 300 days, each time. Plenary, once a month on the usual conditions, for the daily repetition of this prayer (see "The Raccolta," the official book of indulgenced prayers, page 259).

DEVOTIONAL GIFTS OF MARY. The Miraculous Medal is one of seven great devotions given to us through Mary. The other great devotions are the Hail Mary, the Rosary, the Scapular, the First Saturday Devotion, the Little Office of the Blessed Virgin Mary, and the Angelus. Through these devotions you appeal to Mary for the graces which, as Mother of God, she obtains to help you save your soul.

Courtesy of Rev. J. B. Carol, O. F. M.

UNIT TWO

THE CROSS AND THE FLAG REACH THE PACIFIC

UNIT TWO

THE CROSS AND THE FLAG REACH THE PACIFIC

THE EARLY HISTORY of the United States is a story of frontier life. From the settlement of Jamestown in 1607 until almost the close of the nineteenth century, the wilderness attracted the pioneer. Courageous men and women constantly pushed onward to settle and to establish homes on the wild and unclaimed land that stretched to the Pacific. As one part of the country was settled, the uninhabited regions just beyond were called "the West."

Dense forests, mountain barriers, and danger from the Indians could not still "the call of the West." Mile by mile the frontiersmen cut their way over the Alleghenies into the lands east of the Mississippi. On they pushed—down rivers, across plains, over mountains — into Texas, Oregon, and on into California.

In the 1830's the freedom and promise of the vast unsettled regions across the Mississippi beckoned adventurous men.

In our previous Unit we spoke of Jackson as the first President from the West. But the West of Jackson's day was not the West beyond the Mississippi that we shall study about in this Unit.

To the scattered communities of pioneers, religion was of vital importance. Men felt that God watched over their every movement—rewarding, punishing, directing, and guiding them.

It took courage, faith, and strong will on the part of the Catholic pioneers to preserve the Faith. At first there were no churches, no priests, no Sisters. However, as the number of Catholic settlers increased, missionary priests and Sisters were sent from Europe and from the Eastern states to care for the spiritual needs of these people.

Then after years of self-sacrifice, courage, and perseverance, the Cross and the Flag were firmly planted in every region of THE LAND OF OUR LADY.

CHAPTER I

EXPLORING THE FAR WEST

The beginning of the Far West. In FOUNDERS OF FREEDOM we learned how the desire of the pioneers to control the Mississippi River led to the purchase of the Louisiana Territory. This changed the whole future of the United States. It not only doubled the territory of the young nation, but it settled for all time the control of the Mississippi, removed the possibility of an unfriendly neighbor, and opened a vast and fertile land to American settlers. Later, almost a dozen states were to be carved from this huge territory.

President Jefferson had long wanted to explore the land west of the Mississippi. He wondered what that part of the country was like—what soil, minerals, plant and animal life were found there. Furthermore, along with other people, Jefferson thought that if the source of the Missouri River were explored a water route to the Pacific might be discovered. The old idea of a short cut through the continent to the ocean on the west was still in the minds of many people.

How Jefferson satisfied his curiosity and how he and the people learned more about the country west of the Mississippi is the exciting story of this chapter. We shall study the following points: (1) Lewis and Clark Explore the Northwest, (2) Zebulon Pike Explores the Southwest.

1. Lewis and Clark Explore the Northwest

While Louisiana was still French territory, American hunters and trappers had crossed the Mississippi and established a thriving fur-trading post at St. Louis. Jefferson, always interested in science and exploration, was eager to send an exploring party across the Mississippi. Shortly before the purchase of the Louisiana Territory, Congress had given permission to organize such an expedition. However, before permission was secured from the French government, Louisiana was purchased by the United States. Now exploration could go ahead freely.

Preparation for the expedition. As soon as the Louisiana Territory had been bought, Jefferson went ahead with his plans of exploration so that we might know the resources of the new land and perhaps discover a water route to the Pacific. For this purpose, he chose Meriwether Lewis and William Clark.

Lewis was the private secretary of Jefferson, and William Clark was a young brother of George Rogers Clark, the famous conqueror of Vincennes. Both were captains in the Army. As leaders they were well chosen. Both were daring, resolute, wise, tactful, and keen observers. Both had spent their youth in hunting and trapping, they were expert woodsmen, and understood the Indians.

From the large number who volunteered to join the expedition, they carefully chose a small group of young and hardy men. Sturdy boats were built and loaded with necessary equipment: food, camp equipment, powder and lead, and many trinkets and gifts for the In-

dian tribes they would encounter. **Into the wilderness.** Finally in May, 1804, all was in readiness. With Jefferson's parting words in mind, "Keep peace and good will with the savages," Lewis and Clark and their daring companions proceeded up the Missouri River.

They traveled slowly, making maps of the country as they went. On these maps they indicated the location of mountains, streams, and navigable rivers. They also noted the climate, soil, plants, animals, and minerals of the region, and the character of the Indians.

By the end of October, they had traveled sixteen hundred strenuous miles up the Missouri to what is now the Dakotas. They found the Indians friendly; and since it was too dangerous to venture into the mountains during the winter, they accepted the invitation of these In-

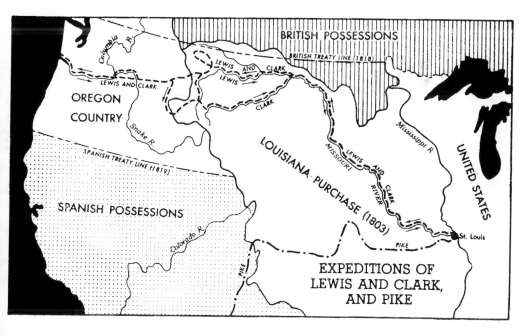

EXPEDITIONS OF
LEWIS AND CLARK,
AND PIKE

dians to camp among them until spring. Here they met a young Catholic Indian woman named Sacajawea (sak-aja-we'-a), which means "Bird Woman," and her husband, a French fur-trapper. These two proved to be most helpful.

Expert guides. When the explorers set out again early in spring, Sacajawea and her husband consented to guide the party. As a child, Sacajawea lived west of the Rocky Mountains and could, therefore, be of great assistance to Lewis and Clark. For weeks the explorers traveled the upper valley of the Missouri River and its branches. Frequently they encountered forks in the rivers. Which should they take? It was then that Sacajawea always came to their rescue and decided which was the main stream.

As they drew near the high and rugged Rocky Mountains, the way became more and more difficult. Again it was the help of Sacajawea that saved the day. They obtained horses from the Indians to use in the trail over the mountains. With her papoose on her back, that brave Indian woman led them through passes in the mountains until they reached the navigable waters of a river flowing westward. Imagine how happy they must have been. They had crossed the Great Divide, that ridge or spine of mountains in the West which runs from north to

Sacajawea guiding the Lewis and Clark Expedition through the Rocky Mountains

south. After a brief rest, they built canoes and paddled down the broad Columbia River.

Perseverance rewarded. For eighteen long months Lewis and Clark and their courageous men had overcome untold difficulties and endured indescribable hardships. But their perseverance was finally rewarded. On November 7, 1805, they caught their first glimpse of the Pacific Ocean. On reaching the mouth of the Columbia River, they built a fort and encamped for the winter.

The next spring the explorers started to retrace their course. After an absence of two and a half years, they reached St. Louis on September 23, 1806.

Lewis and Clark had earned a right to the admiration and gratitude of the people of the United States. They had accomplished a great task. They had traced the Missouri to its source; they had crossed the great western mountains; they had found the Columbia River and paddled down it to the Pacific Ocean. In all, they had pushed their way through some four thousand miles of wild, uncharted country and back. They had blazed the trail to the Pacific; they had established the northwest boundary of the Louisiana Territory; they had brought back much valuable information about the wilderness of the great Northwest; and they had helped to strengthen the claim of the United States to the Oregon country.

Results of the expedition. The ex-

Brown Brothers
Lewis and Clark on the Columbia River

pedition of Lewis and Clark also started a marvelous development. Their glowing report of the western country aroused much interest. Soon trappers, Indian traders, and settlers were trekking westward.

Today the territory through which Lewis and Clark traveled is part of nine states. Missouri became a state in 1821, Iowa in 1846, Oregon in 1859, and Nebraska in 1867. Twenty-two years later, in 1889, North Dakota, South Dakota, Montana, and Washington came into the Union. In 1890, Idaho was admitted as a state. Cattle raising, mining, lumbering, farming, and commerce are some of the flourishing industries of this region.

2. Zebulon Pike Explores the Southwest

While Lewis and Clark were pushing westward across the Rocky

Mountains, another exploring party was sent to trace the Mississippi to its source and then to explore the southwest boundary of the Louisiana Purchase. This expedition was headed by a young army officer, Lieutenant Zebulon (zeb'-you-lun) Pike.

In August, 1805, Pike with his party of twenty men set out from St. Louis to search for the source of the Mississippi River. After nine months they reached what is now the southern part of the state of Minnesota. Here they built a camp and spent the winter. During this time the party tried to win the friendship of the Indians while continuing their search for the headwaters or source of the Mississippi.

In this region Pike found a cluster of beautiful lakes. The ground around was covered with snow, and the lakes and streams with ice. After exploring the area, Pike thought Red Cedar Lake to be the source of the great Mississippi. Although he was mistaken, he learned a great deal about the region of the upper Mississippi River.

In spite of his error, Pike's search for the source of the Father of Waters was splendid training for the difficult and dangerous expedition through the Southwest.

Pioneer missionaries. Then, too, just east of Minnesota, in Wisconsin and the region of the upper Mississippi, Father Mazzuchelli (mats-soo-kel'-li), O.P., ministered to the Indians. Later he took care of the lead miners, and finally after the wilderness had been conquered

Brown Brothers

Zebulon Pike

largely, he became a teacher in the College of Sinsinawa (sin-sin-ah'-wah), which he founded. Today, this college is a school for young women under the direction of the Dominican Sisters, known as the Dominican Sisters of the Most Holy Rosary of Sinsinawa, Wisconsin. This Congregation was founded by Father Mazzuchelli.

After years of suffering, hardships, and difficulties as missionary to savages and settlers of the West, Father Mazzuchelli died as a parish priest at Benton, a village near Sinsinawa, Wisconsin. Although most of his missionary career was spent traveling among savage Indians and rough miners, it is said that his refinement, his friendliness, and his holiness always made Father Mazzuchelli a welcome visitor wherever he went.

Another zealous pioneer missionary, who spent his life for the conversion and civilization of this region, was Bishop Matthias Loras. In 1837, he became the first Bishop of Dubuque, Iowa. His cathedral was the Church of Saint Raphael, the Archangel. This church, erected by Father Mazzuchelli in 1835, was the first church to be built in this region.

Like Father Mazzuchelli, it was said of Bishop Loras that his fine manners remained as fine as ever in the backwoods. It was the lives of refined people like Father Mazzuchelli and Bishop Loras that helped to give culture to the growing West.

Early explorers. Little did Pike realize that one hundred thirty years before Columbus discovered America, Catholic explorers, Scandinavians, had penetrated the heart of the "North Star State." Nor did he ever dream that the first recorded prayer that sped heavenward was uttered on Minnesota soil. It was in 1898, forty years after Minnesota had been admitted as a state, that a Swedish farmer unearthed a stone on which was found an inscription in runic characters, or lettering, of the fourteenth century. The inscription is translated as follows:

Eight Goths (Swedes) and twenty-two Norwegians on an exploring journey from Vinland very far west. We have a camp by two skerries [rocks in the water] one day's journey from this stone. We were out fishing one day. When we returned home we found ten men red with blood and dead. A V M [*Ave Maria* or *Ave Virgo Maria*]. Save us from evil.

We have ten men by the sea to look after our vessel, fourteen [forty-one?] days' journey from this island. Year 1362.

Pike's second expedition. In the summer of 1806, Pike left St. Louis again. This time he was to trace the Arkansas and Red Rivers to their sources, to explore the Louisiana Territory south of the route taken by Lewis and Clark, and to gather information about the Spanish settlements in New Mexico.

Across the Great Plains. Pike and his party of twenty-three followed the Arkansas River westward across the Great Plains into Colorado. There in the tall, snow-capped Rockies, Pike discovered the high mountain which now bears the name Pike's Peak.

Cold, tired, and hungry, the men struggled on for days through deep snow. They followed streams and climbed rugged mountains until they found a pass across a low range of mountains. This pass led to the valley of the Rio Grande. Here Pike and his men built a fort and established winter quarters on land which was at that time Spanish territory. Soon after, the Spaniards, thinking the explorers intended to seize their lands, arrested them. When the Spaniards learned, however, from Pike that they were only exploring, they sent them back to the border of the United States and then set them free. While exploring the Southwest, Pike traveled through what are today the states of Arkansas, which was admitted to the Union in 1836, Kansas (1861), Colorado (1876), and Oklahoma (1907).

The Sante Fe Trail. Upon his return from exploring the Southwest, Zebulon Pike told about the rich gold, silver, and copper mines in the region around Santa Fe (san'-ta fay). He also reported that trade with the Mexican town of Santa Fe would yield good profits. But nothing could be done about Pike's suggestion so long as Spain held Mexico. The Spanish government had forbidden anyone to trade with Mexico.

It was not until 1821 that Mexico became independent. Shortly after, ambitious American traders began to make regular trips to Santa Fe. Every spring parties of traders and merchants met in Independence, Missouri. There was much excitement. Men hurried about loading wagons with dry goods, notions, glassware, tools, and hardware. Soon, all was ready to set out for Santa Fe. Do you recall any recent prominent American who came from Independence?

The route which the traders followed was called the Santa Fe Trail. It stretched for over eight hundred miles across prairies and sunbaked treeless plains. Day and night the traders were forced to be on the

Preparing for an Indian attack on the Santa Fe Trail

Brown Brothers

lookout, for the wagon trains were in constant danger of attack from savage and unfriendly Indians.

After weeks of travel, the traders came in sight of Santa Fe, resting snugly at the foot of the mountains. Great rejoicing broke out as the men, tired and dusty, stopped long enough to clean up and to put on their Sunday suits. Then they hurried down the mountain into the town.

The wagons groaned under their heavy loads, as they lumbered through the streets of the quaint old town. Soon they were surrounded by Mexicans, eager to make a bargain. Ribbons, shawls, cloth, glassware, needles, pins, tools, and many other articles were exchanged for furs, gold, and silver. The traders sold their articles for twice their value. Wagons which they purchased for a little over a hundred dollars in Missouri were sold for five or six times that amount in Santa Fe.

The traders made so much profit that they continued to make the trip year after year in spite of the dangers. So many wagon trains followed the path that in time there came to be a well-beaten trail from Missouri to Santa Fe.

Define these words

headwaters	expedition
Christian lives	trekking
blazed	frontier

49

Discuss these points

1. Discuss the meaning of "they blazed the trail to the Pacific."
2. Compare Lewis and Clarks' expedition to the West with a tourist trip through the same region today.
3. Discuss Jefferson's reasons for sending Lewis and Clark to explore the Louisiana Territory. Also discuss his reason for sending Zebulon Pike on an exploring expedition.
4. Discuss how the ownership of the Louisiana Territory strengthened the power of the federal government.

Choose the correct ending

1. Louisiana Territory was purchased in
   ...a. 1800   ...c. 1803
   ...b. 1787   ...d. 1801
           ...e. 1783
2. The desire of the western pioneers to ship goods down the Mississippi River led to
   ...a. annexation of Texas
   ...b. purchase of Louisiana
   ...c. purchase of Florida
   ...d. purchase of California
3. Lewis and Clark were sent to explore the Louisiana Territory by
   ...a. President Jefferson
   ...b. President Jackson
   ...c. President Monroe
   ...d. President Adams
   ...e. President Madison
4. The expedition which explored the southwest boundary of the Louisiana Territory was led by
   ...a. Lewis and Clark
   ...b. Zebulon Pike
   ...c. President Jefferson
   ...d. Andrew Jackson
   ...e. Pike and Clark
5. The exploration of Lewis and Clark helped to strengthen the claims of the United States to
   ...a. Texas
   ...b. Louisiana Territory
   ...c. Oregon country
   ...d. California
   ...e. Florida
6. The early pioneers
   ...a. had no religion
   ...b. depended upon God
   ...c. thought little of God
   ...d. rejected God
   ...e. hated God
7. After the purchase of the Louisiana Territory the western boundary of the United States was the
   ...a. Mississippi River
   ...b. Appalachian Mountains
   ...c. Rocky Mountains
   ...d. Pacific Ocean
   ...e. Western Reserve
8. At the time of Zebulon Pike's expedition, the land southwest of the Louisiana Territory was held by
   ...a. Spain
   ...b. England
   ...c. France
   ...d. United States
   ...e. Canada
9. The number of states carved from the Louisana Territory was about
   ...a. 15   ...c. 12
   ...b. 9   ...d. 5
           ...e. 20
10. Pike's Peak was discovered by
   ...a. Lewis and Clark
   ...b. Zebulon Pike
   ...c. Sacajawea
   ...d. Rogers Clark
   ...e. Daniel Boone

CHAPTER II

WINNING AND SETTLING THE WEST

Looking backward and forward. At the time of the explorations of Lewis and Clark, and of Pike, the boundaries of the United States west of the Mississippi River were very uncertain. In LEADERS OF FREEDOM, we learned that when Spain ceded Florida to the United States, the Sabine River was chosen as the line between the Louisiana Purchase and the Spanish Territory. The pioneers found the fertile land across the river very inviting. Thousands of them soon crossed the border and established homes on Spanish soil. As the region became populated, Americans manifested a strong desire to have this land annexed to the United States.

Our northern boundary also was not definitely settled. In 1818, England and the United States fixed the northern boundary of the Louisiana Purchase at forty-nine degrees north latitude. At that time the United States and England could not come to a decision about the ownership of the Oregon Territory. They agreed, therefore, upon joint occupation for a period of ten years. This opened the Oregon Territory to traders and settlers from both England and the United States.

When the United States purchased Florida in 1819, Spain, England, and Russia claimed land between the Mississippi River and the Pacific Ocean. By treaty, by purchase, and sometimes by war, we excluded these nations. Then all the country between the Atlantic and Pacific, from Canada on the north to Mexico on the south, was ours.

In this chapter we shall learn the story of the westward march of explorers, missionaries, fur-traders, gold seekers, and settlers. We shall see how the United States, through the efforts of these groups, acquired and settled Texas, the Southwest, and Oregon. We shall study: (1) American Interest in Texas Leads to Annexation; (2) Black Clouds Gather over the Rio Grande.

1. American Interest in Texas Leads to Annexation

The history of Texas and the Southwest cannot be told without mentioning the work of the missionaries in that area. Almost a century before the colonists fought the Revolutionary War, missionaries planted the Cross in many parts of what is today the southwestern and western United States.

Coronado, a Spaniard who explored the Southwest in 1541, was accompanied by several priests. While trying to spread the Faith in this region both priests were martyred by the Indians.

Over a century later, La Salle, although intending to form a French colony at the mouth of the Mississippi, landed instead on the coast of Texas. With La Salle there were also missionary priests.

As early as 1690, Spain sent Franciscan missionaries to East Texas at the request of the chief of the Tejas Indians. Besides trying to please the Indians, Spain was eager to protect her frontier. She had learned about La Salle's expedition landing on the coast of Texas.

The mission to the Tejas tribe lasted only three years, but the Franciscans never forgot the virtue of these Indians. These good Fathers, therefore, in 1716 established anew the missions in East Texas. Many other flourishing missions were found in the Southwest.

In 1821, Mexico revolted from Spain and established an independent republic. With the passing of Spanish rule, the day of the missions in California and the Southwest came to an end. The Christian spirit which Catholic Spain had shown in the conversion and civilization of the pagan Indians gave way to a spirit of greed. In time the new Mexican Republic plundered the missions, sold the property, and disbanded the priests. As a result of such action on the part of the Mexican government, the Indians were abandoned and all the work of the missionaries, which we read about in LEADERS OF FREEDOM, was brought to an end.

By the time the settlers from the Eastern states came into this territory, the Indians were scattered and the buildings erected by the missionaries were in ruins. Evidence of Spanish culture is still found in the Southwest. It can be seen in the names of the cities and in the style of architecture. Many of the customs of the natives also show traces of this culture.

Americans settle in Texas. When the United States purchased the Louisiana Territory in 1803, there was still disagreement between France and Spain over the ownership of Texas. France claimed that it was part of her colony of Louisiana. Spain, however, declared that

An old Spanish mission

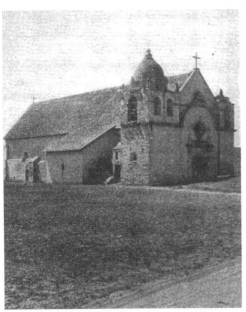

it was within her province of Mexico, and refused to admit that the United States had any right to Texas.

In 1819, to make sure of our claim to Florida, we accepted the Sabine River as our western boundary and surrendered our claim to Texas. Many Americans were displeased with President Monroe for giving up Texas. American settlers, however, were not much concerned. Hard times had gripped the United States, and a large number of families had lost their homes. The cotton planters of the South were also in need of more land. To people such as these, Spanish ownership seemed an advantage, for the Spanish government was giving away land or selling it for almost nothing to anyone who would settle in Texas.

When Mexico won her independence from Spain in 1821, she not only permitted but even invited Americans to settle in Texas. Moses Austin in 1820 received permission to settle three hundred families in Texas. The only conditions were that the settlers be Catholic and respectable people. Before he could carry out his plan, Moses Austin died, and the task of actually making a settlement fell to his son Stephen F. Austin. Stephen went about the unfinished work of his father with such interest, energy, and courage that he is often called the "Father of Texas." He and his first immigrants reached Texas in 1821, shortly after Mexico became an independent republic. They

Brown Brothers
Stephen Austin

found the new Mexican government just as eager as Spain to have Texas developed.

Relations between Americans and Mexico. To these settlers it did not make much difference whether the government was Spanish, Mexican, or American. They were more concerned in developing homes. This they could do because the soil was fertile and they could open up farms or ranches and get a new start in Texas. They introduced the English language and American ideas and ways of living. Many brought their slaves, and all lived as they had in the United States.

At first Mexico welcomed American settlers to Texas. By 1830, however, the attitude of the Mexican government changed. Over twenty thousand Americans had settled in Texas. Twice the United States had

53

made an attempt to purchase Texas. The Mexican government became alarmed. It now realized that Americans in Texas did not regard themselves as Mexican citizens. The seat of the Mexican government was in far-away Mexico City. The Texans, therefore, did as they pleased. Mexico abolished slavery in 1829, but the Texans ignored the law and kept their slaves. Although Mexican authorities said that no more Americans could enter Texas, they kept on coming.

Revolt of the Texans. Texas belonged to Mexico, and the Mexican government had a right to enforce its laws. But the Texans had no intention of changing their way of living. They became angry and re-volted when Mexico tried to enforce her laws.

The Mexican government took immediate steps to compel obedience. But the Texans were not to be frightened. They organized a government and declared themselves an independent nation. A Mexican army under Santa Anna marched into Texas to put down the rebellion. With some five thousand men he laid siege to the Alamo (al'-a-moe), an old monastery in San Antonio, used as a fort by the Texans. Almost two hundred soldiers were surrounded and trapped within the walls of this old monastery.

Defense of the Alamo. The Texans were determined to die rather than surrender. For days Santa Anna

The defense of the Alamo

54

Santa Anna is captured and brought before the wounded General Sam Houston

kept up a steady cannonade until, on March 6, 1836, the walls of the Alamo were battered down. Then Santa Anna and his men rushed into the fort. The Texans would not give up but fought bravely until the last man was killed.

This heroism of the Texans aroused so much sympathy among the people of the United States that many went to aid the Texans in their fight for independence while others sent money and supplies.

Sam Houston takes the Lead. The Texans did not lose heart after this defeat. Instead, "Remember the Alamo" became their battle cry. Sam Houston (hews'-ton), who had once been governor of Tennessee,

was made commander-in-chief of the Texan army. With his small force of Texans and the men who had arrived from the United States to help them, he took his stand against the Mexicans. For a time, Houston misled Santa Anna and his Mexican soldiers by retreating. On April 20, 1836, Houston with an army of about seven hundred eighty men encamped near San Jacinto (san ja-sin'-toe) in an oak grove overlooking a stretch of prairie. Later in the day, Santa Anna and his army arrived and attempted to draw Houston into the open. When this failed, Santa Anna pitched camp about a thousand yards from the woods in which lay the Texans.

The next day Houston's army began quietly to prepare for battle, but not a single demonstration took place on either side. Still unaware of the plans of Houston, Santa Anna with little precaution went to sleep. Suddenly a line of Houston's men appeared on the edge of the woods. The fifer struck up the tune, "Will you come to the bower I have shaded for you?" The Mexicans were awakened from their *siesta*, or nap, to find the Texan army rushing upon them. Most of the Mexicans broke into a run and fled, while the Texans shot them down. This sudden attack so surprised and confused the Mexican soldiers that the battle was over in twenty minutes. Of Santa Anna's army of over a thousand men, scarcely forty escaped. Over six hundred were killed and the rest were wounded or captured. The loss of the Texans was small. Two were killed and twenty-three were wounded.

Santa Anna was captured the next day. He agreed to withdraw his troops from Texas, but the Mexican government refused to acknowledge the independence of Texas. Nevertheless, the people of Texas proclaimed themselves an independent republic. They adopted a flag with a white star in the field of blue. Because of the lone star in her flag Texas was known for the next nine years as the "Lone Star Republic."

Soon after, the United States, Great Britain, and France recognized the independence of the new republic.

Texas becomes a State. In September, 1836, Sam Houston was elected President of the "Lone Star Republic." The majority of the Texans were Americans in blood, language, and traditions. Once free from Mexico, they wanted Texas to become a part of the United States. Texas, however, had to wait nine years before it could be annexed to the United States. Since Mexico had not recognized the independence of Texas, some people in the United States feared its annexation would cause war. They remembered the statement which Henry Clay had made in a speech: "Annex Texas, and you annex a war with Mexico." Another reason for the delay was that the growing feeling against slavery led many Northern members of Congress to oppose the acquisition of more slave territory.

Expansion. The Democratic party, in 1844, decided to make expansion an issue of the presidential campaign. The cry throughout the campaign was "reoccupation of Oregon and reannexation of Texas."

Polk, the Democratic candidate, won the election. President Tyler, who was still in office, regarded the victory of Polk to mean that the nation was in favor of the annexation of Texas. He therefore asked Congress to admit Texas by a "joint resolution." The "joint resolution," which required only a majority vote in each house instead of a two-thirds vote in the Senate, was passed. President Tyler signed it just three days before President Polk was inaugurated. Before the

President Polk

close of 1845 the "Lone Star Republic" became the twenty-eighth state in the Union.

2. Black Clouds Gather over the Rio Grande

Everything seemed to point to a clash with Mexico. The annexation of Texas was the signal for war. Mexico had never acknowledged the independence of Texas and had, therefore, recalled her minister to the United States. A boundary dispute which arose shortly after the annexation of Texas only added to the tenseness of the situation. Texans claimed that their southwestern boundary was the Rio Grande. Mexico insisted that Texas extended only as far as the Nueces (noo-ay'-ses) River. President Polk supported the claims of Texas.

Another source of dissatisfaction was the repeated refusal of the Mexican authorities to settle for the damages done to American property in wars and revolutions that occurred during the early days of the Mexican Republic. Probably the strongest of all reasons, however, was the fact that President Polk was desirous for expansion and had his eye on the Mexican territory of California.

In order to adjust these issues, President Polk sent John Slidell (sli-dell') to Mexico. He was to offer to cancel the claims against Mexico if that country would agree to the Rio Grande boundary line. Slidell was also to attempt to purchase California and New Mexico. The Mexicans were indignant and refused to listen to any of President Polk's proposals. They demanded that the United States first settle with Mexico for taking Texas before they would consider settling damage claims of the Americans.

Steps towards war. President Polk, seeing that he was unable to accomplish his aim in this manner, began to prepare for war. He drew up a message to Congress asking that war be declared because Mexico refused to settle the damage claims. He also sent troops into the disputed territory between the Nueces and Rio Grande Rivers.

Mexico considered this an invasion of her property and asked General Taylor, who was in command, to withdraw his troops within twenty-four hours. When Taylor refused, the Mexican soldiers attacked the Americans.

President Polk, upon receiving

the word, declared in his message to Congress that American blood had been shed upon American soil; therefore, a state of war existed between the United States and Mexico by an act of Mexico. People knew that blood had been shed, not on American soil, but on disputed soil and were opposed to war with Mexico. A young Whig representative from Illinois, Abraham Lincoln, offered a resolution in the House asking an investigation to show on whose territory the incident had taken place. Only after considerable debate did Congress yield to the President and vote for war on May 12, 1846.

The Mexican War. The war lasted less than two years and was carried on in three important campaigns. General Zachary Taylor, known to his men as "Old Rough and Ready," was given the task of conquering northern Mexico. He led an army southward into Texas. After defeating the Mexicans in two battles, he crossed the Rio Grande and successfully stormed the important city of Monterey (mon-ta-ray'). This victory brought Taylor before the public eye and later helped to bring him to the presidency. After the victory of Monterey, Taylor proceeded to Buena Vista (bway'-na vees'-ta), where he dealt the Mexicans a crushing defeat. His triumph at Buena Vista brought un-

General Zachary Taylor directs the action of the Battle of Buena Vista

der American control all of northeastern Mexico.

The war in California. Meantime, General Stephen Kearny marched across the plains and took New Mexico and Arizona. Then he pushed on to California. Before Kearny reached California, the combined naval and land forces had taken California.

When the Mexican War broke out, the American settlers in California proclaimed their independence and adopted a flag on which were a bear and a lone star. Some think that the settlers were aided in this revolt by John C. Fremont, a famous American explorer. Two naval commanders, Commodore John C. Sloat and his successor, Commodore R. P. Stockton, acquired control of the western coast of California. When Kearny and his army reached California, they were most welcome. The Bear Flag was replaced by the Stars and Stripes, and California came entirely under the control of the United States.

End of the Mexican War. In order to end the war more quickly, an army under General Winfield Scott was sent to capture Mexico City. Early in 1847, he landed his army at Vera Cruz (vay'-ra croos), which he attacked and captured. Then for a distance of two hundred and fifty miles, he fought his way to Mexico City. The Mexicans put up a stubborn resistance, but Scott won every battle. On September 4, 1847, at sunrise, Scott's worn and torn regiments swept into the beautiful streets of Mexico City. At

THE MEXICAN WAR

seven o'clock, the flag of the United States was raised, and the Americans were in possession of Mexico City. Scott's capture of the seat of the Mexican government brought the war to an end.

On February 2, 1848, the treaty of peace was signed at Guadalupe Hidalgo (gwa-da-loo'-pay ee-dal'-go). As a result of the war with Mexico, the Rio Grande became the boundary between the United States and Mexico. Mexico ceded the territory between the Nueces and Rio Grande Rivers and also ceded New Mexico and California to the United States. In return, our country paid Mexico $15,000,000 and agreed to pay the debts which Mexico owed our citizens.

General Scott and his troops enter Mexico City

Gadsden Purchase. The Gadsden Purchase of 1853 completed the southwestern boundary of the United States. About five years after the Mexican Cession a strip of land south of the Gila River was needed for a projected railroad route to the Pacific. James Gadsden, our ambassador to Mexico at the time, negotiated with the Mexican government and obtained this land for $10,000,000.

From the lands acquired from Mexico were formed the states of California, admitted in 1850; Nevada in 1864; Utah in 1896, and Arizona and New Mexico in 1912.

How just was the Mexican War? Many people have questioned the justice of the Mexican War. "Manifest Destiny," or the belief that the United States was clearly destined to extend to the Pacific, had become the slogan of the day. President Polk, by sending troops into the disputed area, created a situation which made war unavoidable. To many, the Mexican War was just another instance of our attempt to reach the Pacific regardless of justice to our neighbors. At the time, the true destiny of the United States as the guardian of liberty and justice was lost sight of.

The Mexican War served to arouse suspicion in Canada and in the Latin American countries to the south. The people in these countries believed that the war was unjust and they feared that the desire of the United States for expansion might threaten their very existence. Although we gained a vast territory, we lost the respect of these nations.

The Church and Annexation. After the disbanding of the missionaries, the Church in Texas was neglected. During the nine years that Texas was a republic there were only two priests laboring in this vast territory. When John Odin, a Vincentian missionary priest, was appointed Vicar Apostolic of Texas in 1841, he discovered that thousands of Catholics in Texas had not seen a priest since they had come West.

A little over two years after the United States annexed the "Lone Star Republic," the whole of Texas was placed under the care of Reverend John Timon. His position as provincial superior of the Missouri Province of the Vincentians in America, would not allow him to undertake the work in person. He did, however, make an exploratory visit of the entire area. After that, he saw to it that priests of his Congregation, as well as volunteer priests from established dioceses in the East, kept up the work of firmly reestablishing the Church in Texas. Much of the credit for the sturdy growth of the Church in this part of the Southwest belongs to these two priests, Reverend John Timon, C.M., and Reverend John Odin, C.M., his helper who later became the first Bishop of Galveston.

John Baptist Lamy. New Mexico also benefited by passing under new ecclesiastical authority. John Baptist Lamy, who was named Vicar Apostolic of New Mexico in 1850, found that his first duty was to build up a neglected diocese. The area committed to his care was very large, and the Catholics widely scattered. This zealous prelate succeeded in bringing to his mission field heroic priests and Sisters to help him in his work of putting the Church in that region on a firm foundation. With these self-sacrificing souls, he worked untiringly to bring Christ's Church to this portion of His fold and to better the lives of the people.

In 1875, John Baptist Lamy was made Archbishop of the Diocese of Santa Fe. The work of this simple, self-sacrificing and zealous prelate

Bishop Lamy

is immortalized in *Death Comes for the Archbishop,* by Willa Cather.

Mary, Patroness of the United States. Already in the very earliest days of its discovery the United States had been chosen as the Land of Our Lady. As early as 1791, the feast of the Assumption of the Blessed Virgin had been chosen as the patronal feast for the United States. When the Spaniards had explored and settled most of the southwestern part of our country, Spanish missionaries erected missions and dedicated each region to the Immaculate Conception.

Later, in 1846, our armies invaded New Mexico and California, and we were about to take over some of this land at the same time that the Sixth Provincial Council, a group of bishops, met in Baltimore. The Council sent a petition to Rome asking that the United States be dedicated to the Immaculate Conception of Mary, the Virgin conceived without sin, and that she mght be officially appointed as the patroness of this nation. This petition was granted, and Mary Immaculate became the Patroness of our land.

When the Seventh Provincial Council was held in 1850, a petition was again sent to Rome. This time the Council asked the Holy Father to declare the Immaculate Conception of the Blessed Virgin a dogma of the Church. In 1854 the petition was granted when the Pope, to the joy of all Catholics, defined as a doctrine always taught and held by the Church, that Mary was never touched by the stain of sin, not even by original sin. That year the feast of the Immaculate Conception was celebrated with greatest joy here in the beloved Land of Our Lady.

The settlement of Utah. While the Mexican War was still in progress, settlers were making their way westward. Among these settlers was a strange religious group known as the Mormons or Latter-Day Saints. This new religion was founded in New York during Jackson's first term of office by Joseph Smith, a native of Vermont. He claimed to have had visions and to have received revelations from God.

Although Smith had many followers, there was strong opposition to the new religion. Wherever the Mormons went, they came into conflict with their neighbors and the local authorities because of their peculiar practices and customs. This constant hostility of their neighbors forced the Mormons to migrate from place to place. They left New York and went to Missouri. Not being wanted there, they moved to Illinois where they lived quietly for a few years. After a time, the people of Illinois also demanded that they be driven from the state. It was here in Nauvoo that Joseph Smith was killed by a mob.

Brigham Young becomes leader. After the death of Smith, Brigham Young, a shrewd and practical man who knew how to manage people, led the Mormons westward. Young and his followers trekked across plains and mountains to find a place

An early Mormon home in Utah

outside the United States where they could live and worship in their own way. Their choice fell upon an isolated spot in the beautiful valley of the Great Salt Lake.

The Mormons were an industrious people. Under the leadership of Brigham Young, Salt Lake City was firmly established.

When the Mormons went West, they intended to settle outside the United States. They did so, but as a result of the Mexican War, the property on which they settled became part of the United States.

At this time, the Mormons drew up a constitution and sent it to Washington with the request to be admitted as the state of "Deseret."

Because of their unusual idea of marriage, which permitted a man to have many wives, there was considerable opposition to them. Congress, therefore, refused their application for statehood. Instead a territorial government was organized for the settlement. The new territory was called Utah, with Brigham Young as territorial governor.

Although Utah grew great and wealthy, it had to wait many years to be admitted as a state. It was not until the Mormon Church changed its teachings and strictly prohibited polygamy, or the practice of having many wives, that Congress, in 1896, permitted Utah to become a state of the Union.

How well have you read?

manifested

reoccupation

reannexation

provincial superior

ambassador

"Manifest Destiny"

vicar apostolic

Mormons

polygamy

How many of these terms do you know?

1. Discuss reasons for and against the annexation of Texas by the United States.
2. Discuss the question: "How just was the Mexican War?"
3. Discuss the advantages and disadvantages of life on the frontier.
4. Why were the annexation of Texas and the Mexican Cession a blessing for the Church in the Southwest?
5. Who were the Mormons and why was there so much opposition to them?
6. What states were formed from the Lone Star Republic and from the Mexican Cession? When was each state admitted to the Union?

Test yourself

Each of the following names is related to one or more of the phrases listed below. Copy the names on a sheet of paper. Behind each name write the number found before the phrase which best matches it. There are nineteen phrases. Your best score is 20, therefore in only one instance is a phrase used more than once.

Texans . . . .

Mexican Republic . . .

Santa Anna . . . .

Zachary Taylor . . . . .

Stephen Kearny . . . .

James Gadsden . . . . .

Sam Houston . . . . . .

Stephen Austin . . . . .

President Polk . . . . . .

President Tyler . . . . .

Winfield Scott . . . . . .

Commodore Sloat

and Commodore

Stockton . . . .

Phrases Related to the Names Listed Above

1. started a settlement of American families in Texas
2. captured Mexico City
3. was United States ambassador to Mexico in 1853
4. known as "Old Rough and Ready"
5. refused to obey the laws of Mexico
6. plundered the missions
7. was president of the Lone Star Republic
8. was the democratic candidate for President in the election of 1844
9. took New Mexico and Arizona
10. destroyed the work of the missionaries among the Indians
11. laid siege to the Alamo
12. was commander-in-chief of the Texan army
13. brought northern Mexico under American control through his victories at Monterey and Buena Vista
14. helped to bring California under control of the United States
15. established the Lone Star Republic
16. was captured by the Texans and forced to surrender
17. was President of the United States in 1845 when Texas was annexed to the United States
18. adopted a flag with one star
19. favored the expansion of the United States to the Pacific

64

3. The Oregon Country Becomes a Part of the United States

Texas and the Southwest were not the only lands that lured the settlers westward. Oregon, that beautiful country which then included the whole Pacific coast from California to Alaska, attracted many. Its southern portion was also destined to become a part of the United States.

At various times this entire region had been claimed by five different nations: Spain, France, Russia, England, and the United States. One by one these nations surrendered their claims until England and the United States were the only rivals left.

The claim of England. England's claim to this vast territory was well established. Discovery, exploration, and settlement — all helped to strengthen her rights to the Oregon country.

Francis Drake, during his voyage around the world had taken possession of Oregon in the name of Queen Elizabeth. About two hundred years later Captain Cook explored the same territory. Besides, England could base her claim upon the early explorations of the French Canadian fur-traders and missionaries and the well organized fur-trading posts and forts of the Hudson Bay Company.

Most important of all, England started first in the race for Oregon. Mackenzie, an English explorer, crossed the continent over a decade before Lewis and Clark made their famous trip. The agents of the Northwestern Company, which later united with the Hudson Bay Company, visited lakes and rivers of the region in their search for the fur of the beaver. Their trappers and fur-traders were in the valley of the Columbia long before Astor established the American fur-trading post of Astoria in 1811.

The claim of the United States. The United States could also point to discovery, exploration, and settlement as proof of her right to Oregon. Captain Robert Gray, a Boston trader, had discovered the Columbia River in 1791 and explored it almost to its source. Lewis and Clark, while exploring the Louisiana Purchase lands, had reached the headwaters of the Columbia

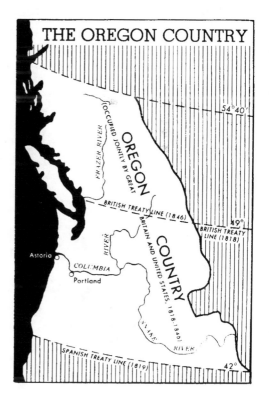

THE OREGON COUNTRY

River and had followed it to the Pacific Ocean.

Under the leadership of John Jacob Astor, the American Fur Trading Company had erected fur-trading posts in Oregon. Astoria, the most important of these posts, was established at the mouth of the Columbia in 1811.

The United States also fell heir to the claims of France and Spain. France relinquished, or gave up her claim to Oregon in 1803, when she sold the Louisiana Territory to us. Spain in 1819 ceded to the United States her right to Oregon in the treaty for the purchase of Florida. Four years later Russia agreed not to colonize south of 50° and 40′ if the United States would not colonize north of that latitude.

Both England and the United States could claim ownership on the basis of exploration, discovery, and settlement. Each country recognized the foundation for the other's claim.

Joint occupation. To prevent a clash, Great Britain and the United States agreed in 1818 to hold the territory jointly for ten years. Under this treaty, subjects of both nations were permitted to settle in Oregon. At the end of ten years the two nations agreed to continue joint occupation indefinitely. Each nation had the privilege of ending the agreement at any time, provided it would give the other nation one year's notice.

Joint occupation remained in effect for almost thirty years. During all that time the Oregon Country had no established government, nevertheless there was law and order.

"Father of Oregon." When the Northwestern Company and the Hudson Bay Company combined in 1821, John C. McLoughlin was placed in charge of the Oregon Territory. Some ten years before, he had gone West as the official physician of the Northwestern Company. He knew the country well and proved himself a worthy and capable leader and organizer.

Dr. McLoughlin was a born leader. Everything about him commanded respect, obedience, and love. He was a man about six feet four inches in height, broad-shouldered, and of striking appearance. His upright character, his kindly manner, his dignity, his mass of white hair, his shaggy eye-

John Jacob Astor

The first settlement at Astoria, Oregon

brows, and his piercing eyes caused the Indians to call him "White Eagle."

On reaching the Oregon Country, Dr. McLoughlin found it a forlorn and dangerous place. The Indians had been mistreated and were eager for revenge. There were few ways of making a living, and the forts were in a miserable condition. Soon, however, all this was changed.

Improvements in Oregon. With his characteristic energy and foresight, Dr. McLoughlin abandoned the old fort which had been his headquarters. Further up the Columbia River in the Willamette Valley, he started a new settlement which he named Fort Vancouver.

At the fort itself and on the land along the Columbia, McLoughlin established farms on which were grown vegetables and grain. Later, he imported cattle from California. He always encouraged retired employees of the Hudson Bay Company to farm, because he realized that forts so far away from the settled regions could not rely upon transportation of food by land or sea.

Near the fort he built a flour mill, a granary, and a saw mill. These new industries, together with salmon-catching, fruit-raising, and fur-trading helped to make this region one of the most prosperous

Fort Vancouver, the end of the Oregon Trail. Who founded this fort?

in North America. In this manner the settlement of Oregon was begun years before covered wagons crossed the plains.

McLoughlin and the Indians. There was no more trouble with the Indians after Dr. McLoughlin took charge. He put a stop to the sale of intoxicants to the Indians. He treated them justly and kindly and saw to it that others did the same. Under his rule the white man and the red man were treated alike in the fur-trading business. The Indians responded eagerly to fair treatment and in a short time became very friendly. They trusted McLoughlin and looked upon him as the great white chief.

Dr. McLoughlin ruled wisely. Under his command there was no lawlessness, for he would tolerate no wrong. Drunkenness was unknown. Although the men worked hard all week, Sunday was religiously observed.

During the whole time McLoughlin was in charge, there was not a single Indian war or uprising in Oregon. Life was safe and happy for both the red men and the white men. The Indians trusted Dr. McLoughlin; the trappers and settlers looked upon him as a true friend and leader.

The American settlers who later came over the Oregon Trail found in this big-hearted Canadian a wise guide and a friendly helper. Even after the Hudson Bay Company disapproved of his friendly relations with the American settlers, he continued to help them. He gave them seeds and supplies. He tended their sick. He prevented the Indians, who resented the coming of so many American settlers, from rising against them. When a person was in need, Dr. McLoughlin, true to the teachings of his Catholic Faith, never let nationality, creed, or anything else stand in the way. Can you learn any lessons from this man's life?

The request of the Flathead Indians. Hunters, trappers, fur-traders and a few French Canadian settlers reached Oregon before 1830. Up to that time, however, no missionary had ventured into the Rocky Mountain region of the far Northwest. The first call from the Far West for missionaries, strange as it may seem, came not from the white settlers, but from the Indians.

Years before, a band of Iroquois Indians left the valley of the St. Lawrence, crossed the plains, and settled among the Flathead Indians of the West. These Iroquois were descendants of the Indians for whom Father Isaac Jogues had died in 1646.

Old Ignace, their leader, was a fervent Catholic. He told the Flatheads about the God of the Christians and how the "black robes," as the Indians called the priests, had taught his people to pray to the Great Spirit. The Flatheads listened eagerly to all that Old Ignace taught them.

They, too, wanted the missionaries to come and teach them about the Great Spirit. In 1832, therefore, a little band of Indians made a two-thousand-mile journey to St. Louis to ask for a "black robe." At the time it was impossible for the Jesuits to spare a single priest. The Indians, however, did not give up hope. Repeatedly during the next eight years they renewed their petition.

Others answer the call. The news of the petition of the Flathead Indians soon reached the Protestant missionary bodies in the East. This started a movement to Christianize the Indians. In 1834, the Methodist Church sent Jason Lee to establish a mission in the Willamette Valley. The Presbyterian Church sent Marcus Whitman, a young doctor, to select a place for a mission. After finding his way across the Rocky Mountains, he returned to New York to report. In 1836, he and his wife, accompanied by Henry Spalding, a Presbyterian minister, and his wife set out for Oregon. Part of the way they traveled with a large party of fur-traders who were going to the Rocky Mountains.

Both the Methodist and Presbyterian ministers intended to work among the Flatheads. They had no success, however, because these Indians were expecting the "black robes." Then the missionaries endeavored to work among the French Canadians, but McLoughlin, who was a Catholic, forestalled the efforts of the Protestant missionaries among the French Canadians until the coming of Catholic priests in 1837.

Upon McLoughlin's advice Whitman and Spalding labored among the Cayuse (kye-use') Indians at Walla Walla and among the Nez Percés (nay per-say') Indians on the Clearwater River.

The great migration. After six years among the Indians, Whitman went East on business for his mission. By the time Whitman was ready to return, people had caught the "Oregon Fever." In the spring of 1843 a caravan of hundreds of adventurous settlers was ready to cross the plains and mountains.

Whitman joined this group and led the way to Oregon.

The settlers in Oregon wrote glowing letters to their friends back East. They told about the forests, the beautiful hills and mountains, the navigable rivers and, above all, the rich soil.

Along the Oregon Trail. Every year large wagon trains of settlers followed the trail to Oregon. The route was generally that followed by Lewis and Clark. The "Oregon Trail," as this route came to be called, stretched for two thousand miles over plains, deserts, and mountains. Long trains of wagons, each drawn by six or eight oxen, jolted along from early morn until

A wagon train beats off an Indian attack on the Oregon Trail

just before sundown. Sometimes the wagons had to be floated across the streams. At other times the precipices were so steep that there was no path for a wagon. The wagons were then taken apart and lowered by means of ropes to another path below.

Each day shortly before sunset a corral was formed. The wagons were driven in a circle, with the tongue of one at the tail gate of the next, and chained together. Camp was pitched inside this circle. Then all were busy. Fires had to be made, the meal cooked, and the cattle cared for. There was no time to lose as all fires had to be out before dark. The feet of the horses were hobbled, that is, tied together, so that they could not get away, and all was ready for the night. Some of the men stood guard while the weary travelers slept.

A corral was also formed whenever a war party of Indians was sighted. At such times the live stock was quickly driven within the circle of wagons. From behind the corral the men with their rifles could beat off Indian attacks.

After six months of thrilling experiences, hardships, and dangers, the long journey of the pioneers ended in the beautiful Willamette Valley of western Oregon.

Request of the French Canadians. The Catholics among the pioneers of Oregon found Canadian priests already there. In 1834, two years after the Flatheads petitioned for a "black robe," the Catholic traders in Oregon sent a similar plea.

Early in the Spring of 1838 the Bishop of Quebec appointed Father Francis Blanchet (blan-shay') his Vicar General or personal representative for the Oregon Country. Father Demers was named his companion.

These two missionaries arrived at Fort Vancouver on Mary's day, Saturday, November 24, 1838. The next day Father Blanchet celebrated the first Mass ever offered in the Oregon Territory. The Catholic settlers were overjoyed to once again assist at Holy Mass after having been so long denied that privilege.

Father de Smet. In the spring of 1840, the Flathead Indians received an answer to their repeated petition for a "black robe" in the person of Father de Smet. Great was the joy of the Flathead Indians when they heard that Father de Smet was coming to them. Over a thousand of their number traveled some eight hundred miles to meet him. Then began one of the most unusual careers in American history. At one and the same time Father de Smet was priest, missionary, explorer, historian, and diplomat.

Father de Smet preached to the Indians, taught them, and cared for them. He shared in every way their wandering life. He ate their food. Like them, he slept under the stars, wrapped in a blanket with a buffalo hide for a bed. The Indians loved and trusted him. From the Rocky Mountains to the Pacific Ocean he was known as "the only white man who never talked to them with a forked (lying) tongue."

So eagerly did the Flatheads accept the teachings of the Catholic Faith that Father de Smet found it necessary to appeal for help. Within the next year, several other Jesuit priests and lay brothers from St. Louis joined him in his work. With their aid, he founded the mission of St. Mary. This was the first Catholic mission to be established among the Indian tribes of Oregon. **Helping the Indians.** As still more help was necessary Father de Smet left for Europe. So well did he plead the cause of the Indians and so impressed were those who heard him that he returned to Oregon with four priests, several lay brothers, and six Sisters of Notre Dame de Namur. From Father de Smet's diary we learn that he crossed the ocean nineteen times to beg for his Indian missions. We also learn that his trail-blazing in the wilderness for the good of his Indians totaled over 180,000 miles. The numerous descriptions in his diary of every phase of the early West, and his maps and charts were an aid to other missionaries, pioneers, and historians.

The missionaries, under the guidance of Father Blanchet and Father de Smet, not only Christianized the Indians, but they also civilized and educated them. Captain Wilkes,

A Catholic mission for the Oregon Indians

Bettmann Archive

who had been sent to Oregon for research purposes, was enthusiastic in his praise of the Catholic missions. After visiting Penn Cove Mission he wrote: "It is in possession of the Sackett Tribe. This whole tribe are Catholics and have much affection and reverence for their instructors. Besides inculcating good morals and peace, the priests are inducing the Indians to cultivate the soil."

So zealously did the missionaries labor and so rapid was the progress of the mission that in 1846 three dioceses were erected in the Oregon Territory. Father Blanchet, now Archbishop Francis Norbert Blanchet, was placed over the newly-erected Archdiocese of Oregon City. Walla Walla was alloted to his brother, Augustine M. Blanchet, and Vancouver Island to Father Demers.

Father de Smet the diplomat. The United States government realized the great influence Father de Smet had over the Indians. It was well known that he was the only white man who was always welcome in their lodges and was loved and respected by every Indian tribe in the West. He alone could pass through the territory of hostile Indians without fear of harm. The government, therefore, in its difficulties with the Indians, turned to Father de Smet for help. He was invited to attend the Grand Council of the prairie and mountain tribes which was held at Fort Laramie in 1850. Father de Smet took no active part in the decisions of the council. Nevertheless, his influence and his conversation with the Indians of the various tribes contributed much to the success of the council and to the peaceful relations that existed during this time among so many hostile tribes.

Later, trouble arose with the Indians of the Northwest over the invasion of their territory by the pioneers. The government ordered General Harvey to put an end to the trouble. General Harvey knew the power of Father de Smet over the Indians, and asked to have the missionary appointed chaplain to the troops. In this capacity Father de Smet accompanied the army. Through his kindness he was able to pacify the Indians and turn them from the warpath.

Time and time again this gentle missionary was far more successful than thousands of soldiers in restoring peace among the Indians.

No one has a greater claim to a prominent place in the frontier history of the West than Father de Smet. He was first and foremost a missionary. Besides, he was an invaluable agent of peace between the United States government and the Indians. Furthermore, he was a writer on every phase of frontier life west of the Mississippi.

The Oregon boundary. The year after the annexation of Texas and two years before the acquisition of New Mexico and California, the Oregon boundary was settled.

As early as 1838, settlers in Oregon had asked Congress to establish a territorial government for their protection, but their request was refused. Repeatedly these same settlers discussed the matter of setting up a provisional government. Finally, in 1843 something had to be done. The American settlers, although befriended and protected by McLoughlin, did not understand the "White Eagle." They were unwilling to acknowledge his authority; therefore they held a convention and set up their own government. Two years later, they drew up a constitution and appointed a governor.

Soon the troublesome matter of settling the Oregon boundary came to the front. A year before the settlers had set up their own government, President Polk was elected on the slogan: "Fifty-four Forty or Fight."

This meant that if Great Britain did not recognize our claim to all of Oregon from California to Alaska, we would declare war.

At the time a war with Mexico was pending. To fight Great Britain at the same time would have been very unwise. Therefore, in 1846, England and the United States arranged a compromise. By the terms of the Oregon Treaty the forty-ninth parallel was fixed as the boundary between the territories of England and those of the United States.

In the settlement of the Oregon Question we have an example of the use of arbitration rather than war as a means of adjusting disputes between nations. Which is better, war or arbitration?

4. California is Settled

Just two years after the American flag was raised in California, that territory had a population of over one hundred thousand inhabitants. No other region had grown so rapidly. This remarkable growth was the result of an accidental discovery. A little over a year had elapsed since the settlement of the Oregon Question when an event occurred in California that spread excitement throughout the world.

Many Americans had drifted into California during the days when it was held by Mexico. One of these, John A. Sutter, a Swiss by birth, had obtained from the Mexican government in 1841 a large tract of land along the American River. This was a branch of the Sacramento River. Here he built a fort and established an American settlement.

Gold in California. In 1847, Sutter found it necessary to build a new saw mill. He charged James Marshall to locate a suitable site and build the mill. After examining several possibilities, Marshall decided to build the mill on the American River, a swift mountain stream about forty-five miles from the fort. The men first cut a narrow channel to obtain a swift current of water to turn the wheel, and then set to work to build the mill.

One day in January, 1848, Marshall decided that the mill was far enough along to test it. As he sat watching the mill in operation, he noticed shining yellow particles in the newly dug earth. Upon further

Sutter's Mill, where gold was discovered in 1848

search, other particles were found. Marshall took them to Sutter. The two men tested the particles and found that they were gold.

This discovery was made just nine days before the signing of the treaty of peace with Mexico. Sutter tried to keep the discovery a secret. But a few months later the news leaked out and spread rapidly through all of California. Soon the magic words "Gold in California" leaped across the United States and across the Atlantic and Pacific Oceans.

The Forty-niners. By the spring of 1849 many were seized with the gold fever. Men closed their stores and offices, sailors left their ships,

carpenters their benches, and farmers their fields. Business and professions of all types were abandoned as men rushed eagerly towards the land of gold.

The "forty-niners," as the thousands of adventurers were called, had a choice of several routes. All were long and dangerous.

Routes to California. Most of the forty-niners followed the Oregon Trail as far as Great Salt Lake. Here they turned southwest and traveled the California Trail across the deserts of Nevada and over the Sierra Nevada Mountains to northern California. This route took five months. The latter part of it was attended by many hardships. The fierce sun, the drifting desert sand, and the lack of water destroyed many men and oxen. Those who survived these perils hastened to cross the mountains before the heavy snows blocked the passes. Other forty-niners took the Santa Fe Trail and continued across the deserts of Arizona, New Mexico, and California. This route took over two months. Those who followed it suffered from heat and thirst.

The safest way was around Cape Horn and north to San Francisco. But it was long, and the sailing ships were too slow for most of the eager gold seekers. These preferred a shorter though more dangerous route. They went by sea to the Isth-mus of Panama. Then they made their way through swamps and jungles across the Isthmus of Panama to the Pacific Ocean. Here they took ship to San Francisco. Although short, this route was expensive and perilous. It was not easy to travel through the tropical jungle. Furthermore, the deadly climate of Panama caused many to die of fever and cholera.

Life was rough. Once in California, the gold seekers staked out their claims and started to dig and wash gravel for gold. For a time, there was much disorder and crime. Many of the treasure hunters were rough and lawless men. But there were also enough honest and cour-

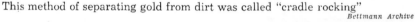

This method of separating gold from dirt was called "cradle rocking"

Bettmann Archive

A "gold town" in the early days

Brown Brothers

ageous men in California to change such conditions. As the territory at the time had no strong government, groups of citizens organized themselves as Vigilance Committees for the preservation of law and order. These committees, seized, tried, and punished all offenders against public peace and safety. Some offenders ended their careers at the end of a rope, while others were deported, that is, sent out of the territory.

Gradually, law and order were restored. By the end of 1849, California had grown so tremendously that the people drew up a state constitution. A year later, September, 1850, California was admitted to the Union as a free state.

5. Growth of the Church in the West

The rapid growth of the city of San Francisco, due to the gold rush, made necessary the establishment of another diocese in the West. On July 27, 1853, three years after California was admitted as a state, the Archdiocese of San Francisco was created.

Into every region acquired by the United States went zealous missionary priests and Sisters. In some areas, like those of Texas and California, the Church was there in advance of the frontiersmen. These missionaries labored unselfishly among the Indians and the pioneers.

Work of priests and Sisters. Foremost among the orders of religious

77

men to endeavor to spread the Faith west of the Mississippi were the Franciscans, the Jesuits, and the Fathers of the Mission, sometimes known as the Vincentian Fathers.

Father de Smet, S.J., brought the Sisters of Notre Dame de Namur into the Oregon Country, as we have seen, in the 1840's. Archbishop Blanchet a little later secured another group of this same Community to labor in his diocese. The prosperity of their schools, however, did not continue very long. The discovery of gold in California in 1848 attracted so many families from Oregon that the Sisters found it necessary to close their schools a few years later. Religious education in Oregon was given a new start in 1859. In that year the Sisters of the Holy Names came from Montreal and founded St. Mary's Academy, on the site of what is now St. Mary's College, in Portland, Oregon.

As early as 1818, the Ladies of the Sacred Heart, under the guidance of Mother Philippine Duchesne, opened the first free school west of the Mississippi, about fifteen miles north of St. Louis. Later, in 1825, Mother Duchesne began the work for which she came to America, a school for Indian children.

The Ursuline Sisters settled in New Orleans in 1727. Soon they conducted an academy, an orphanage, a free school, and held instruction classes for the colored children. Just as the Ursulines were the first to establish schools and orphanages in New Orleans and Texas, so the Sisters of Charity from Cincinnati and the Sisters of Loretto were among the first to open schools, hospitals, and orphanages in New Mexico and Arizona.

So rapidly did the West develop and so zealously and untiringly did the missionaries labor that between 1840 and 1860 the Church found it necessary to establish almost a dozen new dioceses west of the Mississippi.

Make sure that you understand these terms

lured	decade	civilized
relinquished	covered wagon	Grand Council
latitude	lawlessness	frontier

How well have you read

1. Discuss the influence of the missionaries upon frontier life.
2. Why is Dr. John McLoughlin known as the "Father of Oregon"?
3. What is meant by "joint occupation" of Oregon? How was it ended?
4. Why is Father de Smet called the "Apostle of the Rockies"?
5. Discuss the work of Archbishop Blanchet and Father de Smet.
6. Prove that Dr. McLoughlin and Father de Smet accomplished more through their practice of justice and charity and their belief in the dignity of man than others did through the use of force.

How good is your sense of time?

Arrange the following in the order in which they came to Oregon. Score: 20 points for entire test.

...Fathers Blanchet and Demers

...Sisters of the Holy Names

...Dr. John McLoughlin

...Father de Smet

...Marcus Whitman

...Sisters of Notre Dame de Namur

Arrange the following events in the order in which they took place.

...gold discovered in California

...annexation of Texas

...forty-niners

...California becomes a State

...Lone Star Republic

...Mexican Cession

Do the same with these.

...Archdiocese of San Francisco established

...Immaculate Conception made patroness of the United States

...Flathead Indians petition for a "black robe"

...Mother Duchesne opens first free school west of the Mississippi

...Ursulines come to New Orleans

...Assumption chosen as patronal feast of the United States

REVIEW OF UNIT TWO

Minimum Essentials

1. In many parts of the West and Southwest the Cross preceded the Flag.

2. Self-sacrificing missionaries endured hardships and privations to bring the Faith to all regions west of the Mississippi.

3. It took courage, faith, and strong will on the part of the Catholic pioneers to preserve the Faith.

4. The frontier offered greater freedom. The pioneers treasured and sought social equality and complete religious freedom.

5. The missionary priests and Sisters contributed to the cultural development of the West.

6. The idea that the United States was bound to expand to its natural boundaries was known as "Manifest Destiny."

7. Territories added to the United States during the first half of the nineteenth century were: Louisiana Purchase, Florida, Oregon Territory, Texas, Mexican Cession, and the Gadsden Purchase.

8. Lewis and Clark explored the upper Missouri region of the Louisiana Purchase in 1804.

9. Zebulon Pike in 1805 headed an expedition to trace the Mississippi to its source. In 1806 he explored the southwest boundary of the Louisiana Territory.

10. The rapid settlement of California was due to the discovery of gold in 1848.

11. The two land routes west were the Oregon Trail and the Santa Fe Trail.

12. Those who went to California in 1849 in search of gold are known as the "forty-niners."

13. Texas and California were independent republics before they became states of the Union.

14. Make sure that you know the meaning of all terms listed in the chapters and the location of all places mentioned in this Unit.

Suggested Activities

1. Continue the illustrated time-line begun in Unit One.

2. Make a disjointed map showing the successive additions of territory to the United States.

3. On an outline map of the United States show the Oregon Trail, the Santa Fe Trail, and the routes to California during the Gold Rush. Use a different color for each route. Be sure to label each route.

4. Make a chart to show the territories acquired by the United States from 1800 to 1853. Show on the chart when, from whom, and how each territory was acquired.

5. Make a series of slides to depict the territorial expansion of the United States from the Mississippi to the Pacific.

6. Make a map of the United States showing the date on which each state was admitted to the Union.

TEST ON THE ENTIRE UNIT

Copy and fill in the following form

Territory	When Acquired	How Acquired	From Whom
Texas			
Oregon			
Mexican Cession			
Gadsden Purchase			

Identification Test

Number your test paper from 1 to 15. Behind each number write the name or names which correctly complete the statement to which the number corresponds.

1. ......a leader of the Texans in their struggle for independence.

2. ......explored the Louisiana Territory.

3. ......established a fur-trading post at the mouth of the Columbia River.

4. ......led the Mexican attack on the Alamo.

5. ......are two states of the Union that were at one time republics.

6. ......was sent as missionary to the Flathead Indians.

7. ......was President of the United States at the close of the Mexican War.

8. ......was nicknamed "Old Rough and Ready."

9. ......captured the City of Mexico.

10. ......purchased from Mexico a strip of land at the southwestern boundary of the United States.

11. ......were French Canadians and the first priests to labor in the Oregon Territory.

12. ......was the owner of the land in California on which gold was first discovered.

13. ......were people who went West in the rush for gold in 1849.

14. ......is called the "Father of Oregon."

15. ......discovered gold at Sutter's mill in 1848.

True - False Test

Number your paper from 1 to 20. On your paper write beside the number corresponding to the test question the word "true" if the statement is true; the word "false" if the statement is false.

1. The discovery of gold in California was accidental.
2. Texas became a part of the United States by purchase from Mexico.
3. Polk was elected President because he favored the admission of Texas and the occupation of Oregon.
4. The Sisters of the Holy Names were the first Religious to labor in Oregon.
5. The United States wanted the land included in the Gadsden Purchase so that the projected railroad could be built entirely on United States territory.
6. Stephen Austin established a colony of American settlers in Texas.
7. The Ladies of the Sacred Heart opened the first free school west of the Mississippi River.
8. Some early American settlers declared an independent republic in California with the Bear Flag as its emblem just before General Kearny conquered the territory.
9. Before 1820 the people in Oregon were mostly gold seekers.
10. Before the "gold rush" California was inhabited mostly by Spaniards.
11. One cause of the Mexican War was President Polk's desire to obtain California.
12. Time has proved that the real wealth of California lies in her rich soil and mild climate.
13. England gave up her claim to Oregon in the Treaty of 1818.
14. The missionaries contributed to the cultural development of the West.
15. Father de Smet, the famous apostle of the West, kept peace between the Indians and the whites.
16. In the Treaty of 1846 the northern boundary line of Oregon was fixed at 54°40'.
17. The California missions were taken away from the Church by the government of Mexico after Mexico had declared her independence from Spain.
18. California was added to the United States as a result of a treaty with England.
19. In some regions of the West and the Southwest the Cross preceded the Flag.
20. The idea that the United States was bound to expand to its natural boundaries was known as "Manifest Destiny."

A Test of Time

Connect an event of importance with each of the following dates.

1818   1836   1845   1846   1848

Arrange the following in the order in which they occurred.

1. Annexation of Texas
2. Oregon Boundary settled
3. Gadsden Purchase
4. Mexican Cession
5. Father de Smet goes to the Flathead Indians

Mary's Scapular

HISTORY. On July 16, 1251, the Blessed Virgin appeared in England to St. Simon Stock, General of the Carmelites, and presented to him a scapular, in order that by it "the holy Carmelite Order might be known and protected from the evils which assailed it." Our Lady added: "This is the privilege granted to you and to all Carmelites; no one dying with this scapular on, will suffer everlasting fire." The privilege of wearing the scapular was extended by Popes to other religious and to lay people. The devotion spread quickly throughout the world. In place of th e scapular, a scapular medal may be worn. This is a medal with a figure of Our Lord showing His Sacred Heart on one side and Our Lady on the other (Decree of Holy Office, December 16, 1910).

THE DEVOTION. Priests who have the power can enroll you in the Scapular Confraternity of Mount Carmel. Thus, you can wear the Scapular and benefit by the privileges attached to it.

Prayer

O QUEEN who art the beauty of Carmel, pray for us.

An indulgence of 300 days (see "The Raccolta," the official book of indulgenced prayers, page 307).

MARY'S GIFTS OF DEVOTION. The Scapular is one of seven great devotions given to us through Mary. The other great devotions are the Hail Mary, the Rosary, the Miraculous Medal, the First Saturday Devotion, the Little Office of the Blessed Virgin Mary, and the Angelus. Through these devotions you appeal to Mary for the graces which, as Mother of God, she obtains to help you save your soul.

Courtesy of Rev. J. B. Carol, O. F. M.

UNIT THREE

SLAVERY—A BLOT ON AMERICAN HISTORY

CHAPTER I—GOD'S HUMAN IMAGES IN CHAINS

The Beginning of Slavery
The Slave Trade

CHAPTER II—SLAVERY, NORTH AND SOUTH— RESULT OF GEOGRAPHICAL DIFFERENCES

Slavery in the North and the South
Effects of Geographical Differences on the
North and the South
Conflicting Viewpoints about Slavery in the West

CHAPTER III—SLAVERY AND THE BALANCE OF POWER

Attempts to Solve the Slavery Question
Abolition Movement
The Missouri Compromise
Compromise of 1850
Events Which Aroused Public Opinion
Fugitive Slave Law
Kansas-Nebraska Act
Dred Scot Decision
John Brown's Raid

CHAPTER IV—WAR BETWEEN THE STATES—A CHALLENGE TO UNITY

Events Which Led to the Outbreak of the Civil War
Demands of the North and the South
Secession
Events during the Civil War
Results of the Civil War

UNIT THREE

SLAVERY—A BLOT ON AMERICAN HISTORY

THE UNITED STATES now stretched "from sea to shining sea." Annexation, victory, purchase, all added vast stretches of land to the original thirteen colonies. From the Atlantic to the Pacific, from Canada to the Gulf of Mexico, the Star-Spangled Banner floated proudly upon the breezes. It had taken courage, faith, determination, and hard labor to bring the Flag and the Cross to this vast wilderness.

But rapid growth of the United States brought with it a weakness. Divisions among the sections remained and in some respects grew worse. The North, the South, and the West had different ways of living and varied interests. At times these interests clashed. The Union was in danger because of the sharp differences between the North and the South on slavery.

In the early days there were slaves in all the colonies. Most people thought that slavery was not right. They hoped that some day it could be discontinued. The Revolutionary War, with its accent on liberty, provided the occasion for ending slavery in the Northern states. The fact that it had not proven profitable made it easier. Soon immigration was supplying labor for the factories and there was no thought of reviving slavery.

As time went on, the feeling of the North towards slavery became more intense. This led the South to become angry and to defend slavery. Disputes arose. These were frequently settled by compromise or half-and-half measures. But the feeling between the North and South grew more bitter.

In their desire to become wealthy and powerful, both the North and the South forgot that all men are brothers. They forgot that the Negro as well as the white man is created to the image and likeness of God, that both were redeemed by the Blood of Christ, and that both are destined for heaven.

CHAPTER I

GOD'S HUMAN IMAGES IN CHAINS

Points to keep in mind. In earlier chapters we saw the United States add territory after territory until she stretched from the Atlantic to the Pacific. We learned how vast wildernesses were explored, settled, and developed. We also saw how varied ways of living in the North, in the South, and in the West brought about different interests.

One of these interests on which the North and the South could not agree was slavery. Often they had heated disputes over it. This led to serious misunderstandings.

In the next few chapters we shall learn about these disputes and misunderstandings. In this chapter we shall study (1) An Evil Ship Darkens Our Shores; (2) Negroes Become Chattels.

1. An Evil Ship Darkens Our Shores

The original home of the North American Negro was thousands of miles away from the English colonies. It was on the coast of West Africa. Here, African culture, though primitive, was of a fairly advanced type. Home life was well organized. Much respect was shown to older persons. There was also a great deal of ancestor worship. Basket weaving, wood carving, iron working, and pottery were highly developed. The work of the early African artisans showed skill and beauty. Even though the Negro in this part of Africa did not know the true God, religion did play an important part in his daily life.

Slavery begins in our country. One day in 1619 a Dutch ship brought twenty Negroes from Africa to Jamestown, Virginia. These Negroes were sold as slaves. This was the beginning of slavery in the United States.

But it was not the beginning of slavery in the world. The Israelites were held in bondage by the Egyptians. In Greece, democracy was the privilege of the few, while the majority were often slaves. All the splendor that was Rome's was made possible because of slave labor.

Although slavery dates back to ancient times, it is too bad that it had to be introduced into this Land of Our Lady. More than that, it is too bad that slavery still exists in the twentieth century. It exists today in the countries behind the Iron Curtain. There is much economic slavery throughout the world, as well as this political type. There is only one thing that is strong enough to drive this evil completely from our world, and that is Christianity —we must live as Christians.

The slave population in America grew and grew. The tobacco crop, which required much hard labor, was the first to make slavery profitable in the South. In Virginia the people found the Negro well suited to this work, so they were glad to have many Negroes. Soon the production of tobacco became profitable in Maryland. Here, too, the Negro slave was in great demand. Later, some of the slaves were sold to the rice planters in South Carolina. Thus slavery gradually spread from colony to colony.

2. Negroes Become Chattels

Bartered and chained. Every year large numbers of Negroes were dragged from their homes in Africa and sold as slaves. Soon there was a flourishing traffic in slaves. During the seventeenth and eighteenth centuries, slave-trading vessels loaded with rum sailed from New England to the coast of West Africa. Here, Negroes, herded in huge pens, were waiting to be sold. Many native chiefs traded off members of their own tribe and the captives they had taken in the neighboring villages. These chiefs did not

Advertisement of a slave dealer

A slave auction in a Southern city

think of the welfare of their own people. They thought only of the rum which they would get in exchange.

Triangular trade — Negroes for rum and molasses. These Negroes were packed into ships and taken to the West Indies. A real triangular trade was carried on. The rum distilled in New England was bartered for Negroes in Africa. These slaves were exchanged for sugar and molasses in the West Indies. Then these products were brought back to New England. Trace this route on your map.

The trip from Africa to the West Indies was known as the Middle Passage because it lay between the voyage from New England to Africa and the voyage from the West Indies to New England. It took six to ten weeks to cross the ocean. Cut off from light and fresh air, the Negroes suffered intensely. During the trip many of them died from heat and from lack of water and proper food.

A slave auction. When the ships arrived at the West Indies, some of the slaves were traded for molasses. The others were taken to the English colonies in America. The molasses was distilled into rum in New England. This was used to buy more slaves. Each Negro taken to the colonies was sold to the person who paid the highest price. Planters bought slaves as they would buy a horse or a piece of land.

A slave auction was a most disgusting affair. The Negroes to be sold were examined and displayed in much the same way as a horse or a cow. The Negro slave now became a chattel, that is, the "property" of his master. He could be used or abused, bought or sold just like a horse, a plow, a piece of land, or any other piece of property.

Word study

original	ancestral	triangular trade
culture	bartered	Middle Passage
primitive	chattel	herded

A Test Exercise

Check the correct ending of each of the following statements.

1. Slavery was introduced into the American colonies in
 . . .a. 1492 . . .b. 1619
 . . .c. 1787 . . .d. 1737
 . . .e. 1609
2. The North and the South could not agree on
 . . .a. the West Indies
 . . .b. the price of molasses
 . . .c. slavery
 . . .d. trade
 . . .e. manufacturing
3. The original home of the Negro slaves in North America was in
 . . .a. Africa
 . . .b. West Indies
 . . .c. New England
 . . .d. Europe
 . . .e. India
4. Slavery in the world started in
 . . .a. colonial times
 . . .b. ancient times
 . . .c. modern times
 . . .d. medieval times
 . . .e. time of Christ
5. The first crop to make slavery profitable in the South was
 . . .a. cotton
 . . .b. indigo
 . . .c. tobacco
 . . .d. corn
 . . .e. sugar cane
6. The only thing strong enough to

drive slavery from the world is
 . . .a. good jobs for all
 . . .b. Christianity lived
 . . .c. good homes for all
 . . .d. sufficient money
 . . .e. kindness
7. The trip from Africa to the West Indies was known as the
 . . .a. Middle Passage
 . . .b. triangular trade
 . . .c. slave trade
 . . .d. straight route
 . . .e. narrow passage
8. African native chiefs often sold members of their own tribe as slaves in exchange for
 . . .a. money . . .c. molasses
 . . .b. rum . . .d. silks
 . . .e. cotton
9. The molasses obtained in the West Indies was used to
 . . .a. buy slaves
 . . .b. make rum
 . . .c. eat on bread
 . . .d. bribe England
 . . .e. win favor of governor
10. In the early colonial days there were some slaves in
 . . .a. one colony
 . . .b. some colonies
 . . .c. all colonies
 . . .d. a few colonies
 . . .e. several colonies

CHAPTER II

SLAVERY, NORTH AND SOUTH—RESULT OF GEOGRAPHICAL DIFFERENCES

A glance ahead. At one time slavery was on the decline in the North and in the South. People in both regions began to do some deep thinking. They thought how all "men are made to God's image and likeness." This helped them to realize that it was wrong to buy and sell human beings like cattle and to keep them in slavery. They eagerly looked forward to the time when slavery would disappear.

But their entire attitude changed when money again entered the picture. The cotton gin, a machine which quickly separated the cotton seed from the fiber, was invented in 1793. This made the growing of cotton very profitable. Large landowners now saw that they could gain much wealth if they used all their land to grow cotton. Soon large cotton plantations became common in the South. Since white persons could not endure the long hours of work in the hot sun, Negro slaves were used for this work. As a result, slavery took such deep root in the South that every movement to free the slaves was opposed. The South was convinced that it could not exist without the aid of slave labor. A breach was fast developing between the North and the South over the slavery question.

In this chapter we shall study: (1) Slavery Declined in the North and Increased in the South; (2) Effects of Geographical Differences on the North and the South; and (3) Conflicting Viewpoints about Slavery in the West.

1. Slavery Declined in the North and Increased in the South

Slavery was found in all the colonies before the Revolutionary War. In the North the Negroes were used chiefly as house servants, while in the South they were used as field hands in the cultivation of tobacco, indigo, rice, and cotton.

Slavery declined. After the adoption of the Declaration of Independence, the spirit of freedom abroad in the colonies, and the fact that France and England had freed their slaves, led the North to free most of the slaves. The South too soon found that slavery was no longer so profitable as it had been. Great Britain had been the largest market for the tobacco, rice, and indigo of the South. After the Revolutionary War, British merchants shifted their trade to other colonies which remained loyal to the King of England. As a consequence, the price of these products dropped.

Cotton, another crop of the South, could not be raised on a large scale with profit because it took too long to separate the seeds from the fiber.

Slavery increases in the South. Some of the Southern colonists were willing to free their slaves, but they knew that the thousands of Negro slaves in the South were not trained to support themselves, nor were they ready for such sudden liberty. Gradual emancipation or freeing of the slaves seemed to be the only solution to this serious problem.

Before emancipation could be accomplished, the entire picture changed. With the invention of the cotton gin by Eli Whtney in 1793 cotton could be processed more quickly. The spinning jenny and the power loom which had been invented previously could now be worked to capacity. The growing of cotton became highly profitable, and the South held on to the system of slavery.

It was this system which helped cause the Civil War.

2. Effects of Geographical Differences on the North and the South

As time went on it became clear that life in the North was becoming

Slaves operating a cotton gin

vastly different from that in the South. The North and the South were two entirely different regions. They differed in soil, in climate, and in industries.

Life in the North. In the North, especially in New England, the soil was rocky and not fit for large-scale farming. The climate was too cold for staple crops, such as tobacco, rice, and cotton. As a result the farms were small and people soon changed to other ways of making a living.

Because of the many streams and the excellent harbors, fishing, shipbuilding, and commerce became important. Factories sprang up throughout the North, from the Atlantic to the Mississippi. Although agriculture was still the chief occupation in the states which lay between the Ohio River and the Great Lakes, nevertheless manufacturing was fast becoming important. The water power in the East, the large deposits of coal and iron in the Middle States, the natural gas and oil in the states around the Great Lakes, and improved transportation, all tended to make the North an industrial region. For agriculture, fishing, shipbuilding, commerce, mining, and manufacturing, slave labor was not needed.

Life in the South. The geography of the South favored slavery. The climate was warm and the growing season was long enough to produce various kinds of crops. Timber was plentiful and there were many streams to provide cheap transportation. The soil was rich, the rainfall was well suited for growing cotton. The plantations were large, and therefore cheap labor was needed. After the invention of the cotton gin, and after improvements were made in weaving and spinning, there was a great demand for cotton. The planters felt they could not grow so much cotton without the help of Negroes. As the demands for cotton increased, the Southern planters began to look upon cotton growing and slavery as a source of prosperity.

Soon plantations spread all over the South. Each large plantation was like a little world in itself, covering thousands of acres of land. Cotton was grown on most of this land. The raising of cotton required a large number of slaves whose life was usually very hard.

Life of the slaves. Under a kind master the lot of the slaves was fairly good. They had their own cabins and plenty of wholesome food. In sickness they were often cared for by the mistress of the house. They were usually sure that they would be taken care of in their old age.

Some of the Negroes were used as house servants. Such slaves served as maids, butlers, and cooks. A few were taught to be carpenters, blacksmiths, or masons. Such slaves were often hired to the neighbors. Others were used as field hands. During the busy season men, women, children worked in the fields from sunrise to sunset. During this time the old women cared for the babies so that their mothers

Cotton is still picked by hand—truly a backbreaking work

could work in the fields. Do we have similar conditions today—women working in shops, factories, and offices while others care for their children?

Every group of about ten slaves had an overseer. It was the duty of the overseer to make sure that the Negroes did their work well. When the slaves were treated cruelly, it was usually by the overseer and not by the master. The slaves were the "property" of the master, and it was to his benefit to treat his slaves well.

The Negroes who had kind masters might be better off than the poor white factory workers in the North. The slaves worked all day in the open air and in the evening they relaxed and spent their time around their cabins, resting, singing folk songs and spirituals, and telling stories. The poorly-paid white factory workers in the North often spent twelve to fourteen hours in dingy factories and passed their evenings in cellars or crowded tenement houses where there was little, if any, fresh air.

The curse of slavery. The cruel and heart-rending thing about slavery was that when a kind master died the slaves were often sold along with his other property. The mothers, the fathers, and the children were frequently sold to different persons. Often they never met

93

Slaves greeting the master and mistress on Christmas Day

again in this world. Another curse of slavery was that of a cruel master, for in his hands the slaves had a frightful existence.

Poor whites. Most of the people in the South were not large plantation owners. Many southern slave holders had only one to four slaves and only a few acres of land. Side-by-side they worked in the fields with their slaves trying to earn a living. These were the white people that the slaves of wealthy planters referred to as "poor white trash."

3. Conflicting Viewpoints About Slavery in the West

When the Louisiana Territory was settled and new land was ac-

quired through the annexation of Texas and the Mexican Cession, there was a great deal of trouble between the North and the South.

Many in the North thought slavery was wicked. The South bitterly resented and opposed this viewpoint. Even though the people in the North did not approve of slavery, most of them never intended to force the South to free its slaves. They were convinced that it was a problem for the people of the South to solve. However, there was one place in which both were interested. That was the new territories in the West.

Settlers from the North were anxious to keep the West free. People from the South wanted to bring their slaves with them into the new lands. Every time a new territory was opened or a new territory asked to be admitted as a state, there was a dispute over the question of slavery, as you will see in Chapter Three. It seemed that this question could not be settled. It kept coming up again and again. Each time the dispute became more and more heated. Day by day the feeling between the North and the South became more bitter.

As we shall see later, this bitterness was finally to come to a head in the awful days of the Civil War.

Many men tried to prevent this war from breaking out, but other forces were too strong. We shall read about some of these facts in the next chapter.

Word study

decline
attitude
viewpoint

fiber
breach
resented

staple crop
dispute
justify

How well have you read?

1. Discuss the statement: "The North gave the slaves their freedom at an early date because Northerners had no need of them, not because they thought slavery was wrong."

2. On what grounds did the South try to justify slavery?

3. Find and discuss phrases in the Declaration of Independence that the Northerners quoted to show that slavery should not be permitted.

4. How did the Southerners defend their position that slavery was not morally wrong?

Test your memory

On a separate paper, write the correct word that fills the blanks in the statements below.

1. After the adoption of the Declaration of Independence the . . . . freed most of its slaves.

2. In the . . . . . . the Negroes were used chiefly as house servants.

3. Eli Whitney invented the cotton gin in . . . . .

4. The . . . . . . of the South favored slave labor.

5. The man whose business it was to see that the slaves did their work was called an . . . .

6. The demand for slave labor increased after the invention of the . . . .

7. Slavery grew rapidly in the South because slaves provided . . . . . labor for the plantations.

8. The North and the South were both interested in the new territories in the . . . . .

9-10. The climate in the North was too cold for the raising of tobacco, ... and . . . .

95

CHAPTER III

SLAVERY AND THE BALANCE OF POWER

Storm clouds gather. The rift between the North and the South widened day by day. At first the arguments for and against slavery were moderate. But as time went on, public opinion in both the North and the South was aroused through a chain of events, some of which came about through a lack of justice and charity.

In the attempt to settle the slavery question, slavery was often hotly debated in Congress. Great speeches were made both for and against slavery by men like Webster, Clay, and Calhoun. Many of those who attempted to solve the problem were sincere in their efforts and worked only for what they thought to be the common welfare.

We shall study: (1) Attempts to Solve the Slavery Question; and (2) Public Opinion Is Aroused.

1. Attempts to Solve the Slavery Question

The early anti-slavery leaders, that is, those who were against slavery, advocated gradual reform. One of the first of these leaders was Benjamin Lundy, a Quaker. In 1821 he started a newspaper, *The Genius of Universal Emancipation*, in which he tried to influence people against slavery.

The abolition movement. A few years later the abolitionists, or persons who wanted to do away with slavery, decided that slavery should be abolished immediately. This led them to acts of violence. The result was that much bitterness spread throughout the North.

One of the most violent of the abolitionists was William Lloyd Garrison. In 1831 he founded *The Liberator*, a paper that was used to attack slavery. In it he published many articles demanding that the slaves be freed at once. He declared that he would not excuse anyone who continued to make slaves of human beings. At first, people would not listen to him. They thought him too radical. But Garrison continued to write. He stated that he would not give in, that he would be heard.

Feeling became so intense that on several occasions Garrison and other abolitionists were nearly lynched or killed by mobs. The printing presses they used were destroyed, and an abolitionist editor in Illinois was killed. But the abo-

William Lloyd Garrison

litionists continued their crusade. They won new converts to their cause. Among these new converts were poets like Whittier and Lowell, and novelists like Harriet Beecher Stowe, who wrote against slavery. The extreme abolitionist point of view was opposed by most people in the North and in the South.

Slavery and the Northwest Ordinance. The first worthwhile legislation in the campaign against slavery in our country was the Ordinance of 1787. This Ordinance excluded slavery from the land north of the Ohio River, between the Mississippi River and the thirteen original states.

Missouri—slave or free state. In 1818 only one state, Louisiana, had been formed from the Louisiana Territory. No law about slavery in this vast stretch of land had ever been made. The French who settled there owned slaves, and Louisiana came into the Union as a slave state.

The problem of slavery became prominent in 1817, when Missouri requested to be admitted to the Union as a slave state. At that time there were eleven slave states and eleven non-slave or free states in the Union. The North opposed the admission of Missouri because it would upset the balance of slave and free states. If Missouri were admitted as a slave state there would be twelve slave states and only eleven free states. Since every state was allowed two Senators, the admission of Missouri would give the slave states more votes than the free states.

Slavery in the Constitution. What was to be done? Should the new territories be blighted by slavery? The Constitution recognized the slave system as legal. From your study of history you remember the Constitutional Convention. You recall how the delegates disagreed over slavery, and how finally the question was settled by means of compromise. The two compromises, dealing with slavery, in the Constitution are:

1. Congress could not stop the slave trade for twenty years, that is, not before 1808.
2. Five slaves should be counted as three free men in determining the number of representatives in the House of Representatives.

The question to be settled now was whether or not Congress had the right to permit or prohibit slavery in the territories. For two long years Congress debated this question.

The Missouri Compromise. In 1820 there came an opportunity to solve the problem. Maine, which had belonged to Massachusetts, petitioned to be admitted to the Union. Henry Clay decided that here was a free state to balance a slave state. He drew up a compromise bill. When two persons or two nations settle a quarrel by agreeing to give up part of what each one wants, we say such an agreement is a compromise. Henry Clay's compromise bill had these three points:

1. Maine should be admitted as a free state.
2. Missouri should be admitted as a slave state.

3. Slavery should be forever prohibited in any other state formed out of the Louisiana Territory north of the line of 36° 30′ north latitude.

The last point extended the Mason-Dixon Line. In BEARERS OF FREEDOM you read about the boundary dispute between Pennsylvania and Maryland. If you recall, the territory given to William Penn overlapped part of the region given to Lord Baltimore. After many disputes the boundary was fixed by two English surveyors, Mason and Dixon. This line came to be known as the Mason-Dixon Line. Later it was extended down the Ohio River to the Mississippi River to form the boundary between slave states and free states.

The compromise which admitted Missouri as a slave state and Maine as a free state extended the Mason-

THE MISSOURI COMPROMISE

Dixon line to cut the Louisiana Territory in two. This agreement, which is called the Missouri Compromise, became a law in 1820. Everyone thought that the slavery question was settled. But it was not settled; it was only put off for thirty years.

The slavery question makes itself felt. After the Mexican War in 1848 more territory was added to the United States, and the old question of slavery came up once more.

This time it was the turn of the South to get excited about the balance of power between free and slave states. Gold was discovered in California. The population grew so fast that soon there were enough people to form a state. California asked to be admitted as a free state. The Missouri Compromise could not be used to settle the question for it had been made only for the Louisiana Territory.

The quarrel continued for months. Congress could not find a way of settling the question so as to satisfy both the North and the South. How could the Union be saved?

The Wilmot Proviso. Various plans were offered. As early as 1846, David Wilmot, a representative from Pennsylvania, introduced into Congress a bill which forbade slavery in any territory which the Union might acquire from Mexico. This bill, known as the Wilmot Proviso, was passed in the House of Representatives but was rejected by the Senate. Although it had been defeated, the Wilmot

Brown Brothers
David Wilmot

Proviso aroused much discussion.
Demands of the North. Congress was faced with a difficult problem. The Northerners demanded that:

1. California be admitted as a free state,
2. slavery be prohibited in the territory gained from Mexico,
3. slavery be abolished in the District of Columbia,
4. the state of Texas be reduced in size,
5. every Negro who was accused of being a runaway be given a trial by jury.

Demands of the South. The Southerners insisted that slavery be permitted in California and that the 36° 30′ line be extended. This would cut California in two, making it half free and half slave. The people would not agree to this. The South also demanded that:

99

1. slavery should be allowed in the Territory of New Mexico,
2. slavery be continued in the District of Columbia,
3. Texas should retain her boundaries,
4. a law be passed requiring the return of runaway slaves without a trial.

Furthermore, South Carolina threatened to secede, or leave the Union, unless these problems were settled to the satisfaction of the South.

Three great leaders. What was to be done to save the Union? Congress itself was so divided on the question that it looked as if peace could not be maintained.

As you have already learned, the three outstanding men in Congress were Webster, Clay, and Calhoun. At this time they were still active.

John C. Calhoun

Calhoun continued to speak for the South, Webster for the North and the Union, and Clay for the West and compromise.

A great peacemaker. Henry Clay, now a venerable old man of seventy-three, but still a peacemaker, once again came to the rescue. He was a Kentuckian and a slave holder, but he cared more for the Union than for anything else. With his great power of oratory he pleaded for compromise.

The Compromise of 1850. The first and fourth points of Clay's compromise bill were planned to please the North, while the second and fifth were expected to satisfy the South. Here are his proposals:

1. Admit California as a free state.
2. Organize the rest of the land taken from Mexico into two territories, Utah and New Mexico. Permit the people in these territories to decide for themselves whether they should be slave or free states.
3. Pay Texas $10,000,000 for giving up its claim to a part of New Mexico.
4. Prohibit the slave trade, but not slavery in the District of Columbia.
5. Pass a new law that would prevent Northerners from helping runaway slaves to escape to Canada.

A staunch Southerner. John C. Calhoun, now old and feeble, practically dying of consumption, wrote a powerful speech opposing the bill. On the day of the speech he feebly entered the Senate chamber to make his last appeal. He was too weak, however, to speak and sat silent and attentive while a friend read for him his speech which clearly expressed the point of view of the South regarding the Union. In this speech he pointed out the threatening dangers:

"Senators, it can no longer be disguised that the Union is in danger . . . the danger arises from the discontent of the Southern States, and the belief that they cannot remain as things now are . . . with honor and safety, in the Union."

Calhoun believed that Congress should divide the western territories equally between the North and the South. He also believed that the Union could not last if the interests of the Southern states were not considered and therefore ended his speech with these words:

"If you who represent the stronger portion, the North, are not willing to settle on these principles, say so, and let us separate in peace."

A firm supporter of the Union. Three days later, Webster, also old and ill, took up Calhoun's challenge. He pleaded earnestly for the bill because he thought it would strengthen the Union. His love of the Union and his desire to see peace between the North and the South proved stronger than his hatred of slavery. He urged the preservation of the Union:

"I wish to speak today not as a Massachusetts man, not as a Northern man but as an American. I speak today for the pres-

Brown Brothers

Daniel Webster

ervation of the Union. . . . I hear with distress the word secession! Why, sirs, our ancestors— our fathers and grandfathers — would reproach us, and our children and grandchildren would cry out 'Shame!' To break up this government . . . to astonish Europe with an act of folly! No, sir! There will be no secession. Gentlemen are not serious when they talk of secession."

War is avoided. In spite of Calhoun's opposition, Clay won the day. The Compromise of 1850, sometimes called "The Omnibus Bill" because it carried so many measures, was finally adopted after months of debating. Once again secession was postponed.

In the meantime, the North was growing at a much faster pace than the South.

Capture of a fugitive slave

2. Public Opinion Is Aroused

The Compromise of 1850 was hailed as the final settlement of the slavery trouble. For a few years this seemed to be true. But the interests of the two sections of our country were so different that even the Compromise of 1850 could not satisfy both sides. Less than four years after it had been passed, the whole question of slavery in the territories was reopened.

The Fugitive Slave Law. Even before this, many Southerners grumbled because slavery was restricted in the Mexican Territory. In the North feeling still ran high. The Fugitive Slave Law, passed as a result of the Compromise of 1850, required federal officers to help in the capture of runaway slaves. It did more; it made it a crime to refuse to assist in the capture of such a slave if asked to do so. Under the new law any white man who helped a runaway slave to escape was to be punished. This law proved to be very unpopular. Sometimes the slaves were treated cruelly. They would run away. These runaway slaves were called fugitives. They tried to get to the Northern states, or if possible to Canada. Some of them succeeded, but others were caught. Generally, runaway slaves who were caught were punished.

An unjust law. The Fugitive Slave Law was unjust because sometimes Negroes, who had been free for years, were claimed by slave own-

102

ers. They could do nothing to defend themselves. Another injustice of the law was that a fugitive slave was not permitted a trial by jury, nor was he allowed to have witnesses. What does the Bill of Rights say about a trial by jury?

Personal Liberty Laws. Many people in the North disliked the Fugitive Slave Law. The feeling against this law was so strong that the Northern states passed Personal Liberty Laws. These laws forbade anyone to assist in the return of runaway slaves. They also gave slaves the right of trial by jury. The Personal Liberty Laws made it almost impossible to enforce the Fugitive Slave Law.

The Underground Railroad. In the Northern states even prominent citizens helped to devise another means of making the Fugitive Slave Law practically worthless. They organized the "Underground Railroad" to assist slaves to escape. The "railroad" consisted of a chain of private homes from the border of the slave states to Canada. Each home was called a "station." Certain families in each area acted as "conductors." The runaway slaves were conducted from station to station. During the day they were fed, clothed, and kept in hiding. At night the fugitives were passed on to the next station with remarkable success. A slave was never sure of his freedom until he reached Canada.

A placard warning colored people against kidnapping

Bettmann Archive

Harriet Beecher Stowe

Brown Brothers

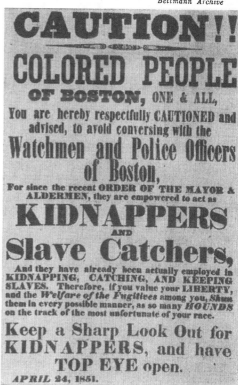

Fugitive slaves are received at a "Station" of the Underground Railroad

"Uncle Tom's Cabin." At this time *Uncle Tom's Cabin*, a story about a runaway slave, was written by Harriet Beecher Stowe, of New England. Its publication in 1852 fanned the anti-slavery sentiment to white heat. This dramatic story presented the most hideous side of slavery. Mrs. Stowe, who had been in charge of one of the "stations" of the Underground Railway, merely wrote about slavery as she had heard it described by runaway slaves. Although the cruel acts she described in this novel sometimes took place, they were not common.

The Kansas-Nebraska Act. The strongest feeling of indignation in the North arose over a bill that Congress passed in 1854. There was a vast stretch of the Louisiana Purchase Land, called Nebraska, which was still a territory. So many people had entered this fertile region by 1853 that it was necessary to have a government.

President Pierce appointed a committee to plan a government for Nebraska. Stephen A. Douglas, who was chairman of this committee, proposed that this region should be divided into two territories: Kansas to the south and Nebraska to the north. He suggested that the people should be allowed to decide for themselves whether they would permit slavery. He called this principle of letting the people decide for themselves "Popular Sovereignty." Find the 36° 30' line on the map. Since Kansas and Nebraska are north of the 36° 30' line why should slavery become a subject for discussion at this time?

Squatter Sovereignty. In the Compromise of 1850, the principle of "Popular Sovereignty" was known as "Squatter Sovereignty." This term was adopted because people who settled on unclaimed lands were called squatters, and the Compromise Bill, which gave them the power to decide the slavery question for themselves, made them supreme or sovereign in this matter.

The Kansas-Nebraska Act was passed in spite of loud protests from the North. This Act

1. divided the rest of the Louisiana Purchase lands into two territories—Kansas and Nebraska,
2. repealed the Missouri Compromise by permitting the people of Kansas and Nebraska to decide whether their state should be free or slave,
3. established the principle of "Squatter Sovereignty."

The race for Kansas. Everyone expected that slavery would be permitted in the southern territory, Kansas, and that Nebraska would become free. Things did not turn out as peaceably as Douglas had expected. The Kansas-Nebraska Act had repealed the Missouri Compromise. This angered the North. Consequently, groups of Northerners started "The Emigrant Aid Society" for the purpose of settling Kansas with anti-slavery groups.

Settlers from the North poured into Kansas. They were determined

THE KANSAS-NEBRASKA ACT

FREE

SLAVE

TO BE DECIDED BY VOTERS

Ruffians going to Kansas to vote. Does this scene give you any idea why it was called "Bleeding Kansas"?

to make it a free state. But the South would not be outdone. Southerners also settled in Kansas. When the day came for Kansas to decide whether it would be slave or free, there were actually more anti-slavery than pro-slavery settlers in the region. Before the sun was high above the horizon, bands of pro-slavery men from Missouri poured into the territory to vote. When the votes were counted, there were more votes cast for slavery than there were inhabitants.

"Bleeding Kansas." The anti-slavery men refused to abide by this vote. Two governments were set up. Riots followed, and there was actual warfare between the two groups.

The situation grew so bad that President Pierce had to send in the United States troops to restore order. A new governor was appointed. A constitution which favored slavery was drawn up, but the voters rejected it. Kansas was finally admitted to the Union in 1861 as a free state. Many people had given up their lives in the struggle between freedom and slavery in Kansas so that the territory earned itself the title "bleeding Kansas."

The immediate result of the Kansas-Nebraska Act was the establishment of the new Republican party which pledged itself to oppose the extension of slavery in the territories.

The Dred Scott Decision. During the wrangling and fighting over Kansas, the Supreme Court handed down a decision which opened all the territory of the United States to slavery. Dred Scott was a Negro slave who belonged to a citizen in Missouri. In 1834, his master took him to the free territory in Minnesota. After several years he was brought back to Missouri, where he claimed that he had become a free man by living in a free territory. His master claimed that he was still a slave.

Urged by abolitionists, Scott sued for his freedom in the courts of Missouri. His plea was denied on the ground that he had no right to sue in the court because he was not a citizen.

In 1857 his case was taken to the Supreme Court. The court decided that Dred Scott was still a slave. As such he was not a citizen of the United States, and therefore, he had no right to bring a case to court.

Roger B. Taney, a Catholic, who was Chief Justice at the time, said that since the Constitution looked upon slaves as "property," and since it guaranteed property rights, the following decisions were the only ones possible:

1. A slave could not become free by being taken into free territory, as slaves were considered "property" and Congress had no right to deprive a citizen of his property.

2. Congress could not prohibit a citizen from taking slave "property" into any territory of the United States any more than it could forbid a citizen to take a horse into any territory.

Dred Scott

Chief Justice Taney

Results of the decision. This decision was not the personal opinion of Chief Justice Taney. It was an explanation of the Constitution. As Chief Justice, it was Taney's duty to explain the Constitution. He did that and only that. Personally, Taney seems to have opposed slavery. In a letter dated August 19, 1857, Taney discussed the relations between the Negroes and whites. He added that over thirty years ago he had freed all but two of his slaves. As these two were too old to provide for themselves, he kept them and supported them as long as they lived.

According to Chief Justice Taney's decision Dred Scott was still a slave, the Missouri Compromise was unconstitutional, and all territories of the United States were open to slavery. This was a powerful blow to the anti-slavery forces in the North. The Dred Scott Decision made the Northerners more determined than ever before to do all in their power to abolish slavery.

John Brown's fanatical raid. John Brown, a violent hater of slavery and an extremist, believed that he was commissioned by God to free the slaves. His plan was to secure guns, to free some slaves, and to start an uprising in the South. On the night of October 16, 1859, he and a small party of followers raided the United States Arsenal

The Marines storming the place where John Brown took refuge at Harper's Ferry

at Harper's Ferry, Virginia, in order to obtain arms. But the United States Marines, under Robert E. Lee, upset Brown's plans. They captured Brown, who was tried in the Virginia courts, found guilty of treason and murder, and hanged.

This effort to bring about an uprising terrified the people of the South. They feared that the slaves would make war upon their masters. Although many Northerners considered John Brown a madman, the abolitionists sympathized with him and regarded him as a martyr to a glorious cause. The Southerners regarded John Brown not only as a troublesome madman, but as a proof that the North and South could find no way of living and working together peacefully. Secession seemed to many the only way to settle the slavery question.

Word study

balance of power	staunch	Squatter Sovereignty
rift	preservation	property rights
sincere	fugitive	unconstitutional
anti-slavery	prominent	compromise
abolitionist	"conductor"	secede
lynched	"station"	

How well have you read?

1. Did Taney place the Constitution above the Bill of Rights or the Bill of Rights above the Constitution?
2. Discuss the conflict between the Kansas-Nebraska Act and the Missouri Compromise.
3. Discuss the right and wrong use of propaganda.
4. Discuss the attitude of Webster, Clay, and Calhoun on the Compromise of 1850.

How many do you know?

On the line before each number in Column One write the letter found before the phrase in Column Two which best matches it.

Column One	Column Two
...1. Compromise	a. excluded slavery from the Northwest Territory
...2. Dred Scott Decision	b. is an agreement between two parties to settle a quarrel by each giving up a part of what he wants
...3. Ordinance of 1787	c. was extended to cut the Louisiana Territory in two
...4. Kansas-Nebraska Act	d. was passed in 1820
	e. fought to preserve the Union
...5. Missouri Compromise	f. established the principle of "Squatter Sovereignty"
...6. Mason-Dixon line	g. declared slaves personal "property"

CHAPTER IV

WAR BETWEEN THE STATES—A CHALLENGE TO UNITY

Storm clouds break. We have seen how rapid expansion in the West brought prosperity to the North and to the South, but to the nation as a whole it brought serious problems.

With prosperity came selfishness. Both the North and the South became so engrossed in their own interests that they forgot the virtues of justice and charity. Each section feared that the other would gain more power in Congress and thereby control the policies of the goverment. Eagle-eyed, each watched that the balance of free and slave states was maintained.

Balance of power was maintained until about 1859. California, Minnesota, and Oregon joined the Union as free states and the North gained greater power in the Senate. The South felt that the situation was hopeless.

The South had already suffered from the abolition movement, John Brown's raid, Squatter Sovereignty, and *Uncle Tom's Cabin*. Therefore, when the break in the balance of power came, many in the South believed that separation from the Union was the only solution to the problem.

These people in the South believed that a state had the right to secede, that is, to leave the Union and to form a separate government if it felt that its rights were not respected.

Lincoln had already been nominated for President. Earlier, in speeches he had given before large groups of people, he had spoken about the evils of slavery and he had urged his audiences to prevent the spread of slavery into new territories.

The people of the South had heard of these talks. They became angry and warned the country that if Lincoln were elected President they would secede. Lincoln was elected and the South seceded.

Four years of bloody warfare followed. Brother fought against brother, friend against friend, neighbor against neighbor. It seemed as if the progress of almost a century would be undone.

In this chapter we shall consider: (1) Events and Conditions Which Led to the Outbreak of the Civil War; (2) Events During the Civil War; (3) Results of the Civil War.

1. The Events and Conditions Which Led to the Outbreak of the Civil War

The quarrel over slavery was not the only issue which was forcing the North and the South farther and farther apart. These two sections of our country, as you have already seen, held different views about protective tariffs, States' Rights, and the interpretation of the Constitution.

But the real cause of the conflict between the North and the South was deeper than any of these problems. The economic and social system of the South was different from that of the North. This difference in ways of living was the source of all the misunderstanding between the two sections.

Life in the North centered around industry, commerce, and diversified agriculture which rested on free labor. In the agricultural South, life was based on the plantation system, which employed slave labor to produce cotton, tobacco, sugar, and indigo. This situation led to interests and needs in one section that were directly opposed to those of the other.

THE NORTH
  wanted a high protective tariff
  had no use for slaves
  did not believe in States' Rights

THE SOUTH
  did not want a high protective tariff
  believed in the necessity of slaves
  believed in States' Rights

Formation of the Republican Party. At this time, a cause of increased uneasiness in the South was the rise of a new political party. Before the Compromise of 1850, the Free Soil party was formed to fight the spread of slavery into the territories.

In 1854, shortly after the Kansas-Nebraska Act was passed, Free Soilers, anti-slavery Whigs, Know-Nothings, and moderate abolitionists decided to unite all anti-slavery groups into a single political party. Several conventions of anti-slavery sympathizers were held. The result of these conventions was the formation of the new Republican Party. Its chief purpose was to keep slavery from spreading to the territories.

From that time until the present, the Democratic and Republican parties have been the two leading political groups in our country.

Lincoln-Douglas debates. In 1858 a series of famous debates on the troublesome question of slavery was held in Illinois between the Republican and Democratic candidates for the office of Senator. One debater in this unusual political campaign was Stephen A. Douglas, Democratic candidate. The other was Abraham Lincoln, the Republican candidate. The two traveled the length and breadth of the state of Illinois and often appeared on the same platform to challenge and refute each other.

In his opening speech in this campaign, Lincoln made clear his view on slavery. He said:

"A house divided against itself cannot stand. I believe that this government cannot exist permanently half slave and half free. I do not expect the Union to be dissolved; I do not expect the house to fall, but I do expect it will cease to be divided. It will become all one thing or all the other."

Later, at a debate held at Quincy, Illinois, Lincoln stated that slavery was a moral, social, and political wrong. Douglas in his reply, said in part:

"If each state will only agree to mind its own business and let its neighbors alone . . . this republic can exist forever divided into free and slave states, as our fathers made it and the people of each state have decided."

Douglas and Lincoln were very different characters. Lincoln was tall, awkward, homely in appearance, carelessly dressed, and practically unknown to the nation. Douglas was short, stout, well-dressed, pleasing in appearance, and very popular.

Lincoln spoke simply and forcefully. He appealed to the intelligence of his hearers. But above all he appealed to their moral sense and religious convictions. Although he was slow in speech his clear strong arguments made a great impression. His language and ideas were clearly formed by the Bible. Douglas spoke cleverly. He appealed to the feelings of the people.

A Lincoln-Douglas Debate

Brown Brothers

Public interest in the debates.
Whenever a debate was announced there was great excitement. People came from miles around to applaud "Honest Abe" and to cheer the "Little Giant," as Douglas was called. Each debate was made a local semi-holiday. The gatherings were enlivened by the playing of brass bands and the carrying of placards with slogans, such as "Abe, the Giant Killer," "Free Territories and Free Men," "The Little Giant Chawing Up Old Abe."

In these debates Lincoln had the advantage over Douglas. Lincoln knew where he stood on the slavery question. He did not believe in slavery. Furthermore, he had to please only one group, the Republican party. This was easy because the party also was opposed to slavery.

Douglas, on the other hand, had favored two ideas which contradicted each other. He agreed with the idea of Squatter Sovereignty, which permitted the people of a territory to forbid slavery. This was popular in the North. At the same time he upheld the Dred Scott Decision, which denied Congress the right to prohibit slavery in the territories. This was popular in the South. Furthermore, he had to please all the Democrats, those in the North who disliked slavery and those in the South who favored it.
Freeport Doctrine. At Freeport, Illinois, Lincoln forced Douglas to make a difficult decision. Douglas had to choose between Squatter Sovereignty and the Dred Scott De-

Brown Brothers
Stephen A. Douglas

cision. Lincoln very pointedly asked Douglas how he could favor both. Douglas had to decide quickly and did so in favor of Squatter Sovereignty. Cleverly he found a way out of the dilemma by saying, "Slavery cannot exist a day or an hour anywhere unless it is supported by local police regulations." This decision probably won for him the election to the Senate, but it greatly displeased the South. A man who did not favor the Dred Scott Decision could not hope to gain the support of the South.

True, Lincoln lost the election to the Senate, but the debates made him known throughout the nation. His speeches were printed in the leading newspapers of the country. These speeches convinced Northerners that Abraham Lincoln was the man the country needed. On one occasion he said, "Slavery is the spirit that says '*You* work and toil and earn bread, and *I'll* eat it.'" Later, he ended a speech in New York with the following appeal: "Let us stand by our duty fearlessly. Let us have faith that right makes might, and in that faith let us, to the end, dare to do our duty as we understand it."

The election of 1860. The election of 1860 was an exciting one. The Democratic party was hopelessly split into two parts. The Northern Democrats nominated Stephen A. Douglas, who still stood for Squatter Sovereignty. The Southern Democrats, who held that Congress did not have the right to keep slavery out of the territories, chose John C. Breckinridge as their candidate.

The Republican party nominated Lincoln as candidate for President.

John C. Breckinridge

Brown Brothers

He pledged to keep slavery from spreading into the new territories and to preserve the Union.

The campaign was extremely important. The Southerners realized that the Republican party had an excellent chance to win because of the split in the Democratic party. In one of his debates with Douglas, Lincoln had said that the country could not continue half slave and half free. This convinced the South that he meant to abolish slavery.

Lincoln in his campaign speeches had repeatedly denied that he wanted to abolish slavery, but the people of the South remained fearful. Many leading Southerners declared that they would leave the Union if Lincoln were elected President. No one in the North took this threat seriously.

Secession. Lincoln was elected. Immediately the people of the North asked themselves, "Will the slave states really carry out their threat to secede?" The answer to this question was not long in coming. Before Lincoln took the oath of office, South Carolina declared itself "a free and independent nation." Within a short time Florida, Georgia, Alabama, Mississippi, Louisiana, and Texas followed the action of South Carolina and left the Union.

The Confederate States. Delegates from the seceding states met at Montgomery, Alabama, on February 4, 1861, to organize a government for the new nation, which was to be called the Confederate States of America. Jefferson Davis was

Inauguration of Davis

Jefferson Davis

elected President and Alexander Stephens Vice-President. A constitution much like that of the United States was drawn up. This new Constitution declared that protective tariffs could not be levied. It also provided for the protection of slavery and the right of Secession. A new flag, the stars and bars, was adopted, and Montgomery was made the capital of the Confederacy.

States' Rights. Did the states have the right to secede? This was the big question in the mind of everyone. From the early days of the Union many persons looked upon the Constitution as *an agreement between the states*. They believed that any state had a right at any time to leave the Union. Those who supported this theory felt that they would be *traitors to their state* if they did not secede.

On the other hand, others believed that the Union was above the states. They held that the Constitution was a system of government for the people of *one nation*, and that no state had a right to secede. Those who supported this idea felt that anyone who seceded was a *traitor to the nation*.

President Buchanan, who was still in office, did not believe that the states had a right to secede. He said that he had no authority, however, to keep them from seceding, if they wished to do so. Lincoln, although determined to save the Union, could do nothing about it until after his inauguration on March fourth.

Meanwhile, the seceded states

President Buchanan

Lincoln's Inaugural parade

began to act as an independent nation. They seized forts, supplies, and shipyards belonging to the United States. This was treason, but President Buchanan, who was still in office, could do nothing about it, short of war.

Senator Crittenden of Kentucky made a final attempt to save the Union by compromise. He suggested that the Constitution be amended to provide for the extension of the Missouri Compromise line to the Pacific. He also wanted the government to pay the slave owners in full for their escaped slaves. This last effort to preserve the Union failed. A war between the states could not be prevented.

Lincoln's inauguration. With the North and the South on the verge of war, Lincoln became the first Republican President of the United States. On this occasion all Washington seemed tense and uneasy. Some feared that Lincoln would be assassinated. Winfield Scott, who was General-in-chief of the Army, was determined that this would not happen. He took every possible precaution. As the President-elect rode from Willard Hotel to the Capitol he was well guarded. At every corner were mounted orderlies. Soldiers were stationed at intervals along Pennsylvania Avenue. On the housetops were groups of riflemen. All the wings of the Capitol were heavily guarded. Even the very platform from which Lincoln was to deliver his inaugural address hid from view fifty or sixty armed soldiers. Fortunately, however, no attempt was made on the President's life.

One incident on this occasion

gave promise of better days. As Lincoln rose to give his inaugural address, he could find no place to lay his high silk hat. Douglas quickly came to the rescue of his old rival and took the hat which Lincoln held helplessly in his hand. That morning Douglas had said that he was going to make the people understand that he intended to stand behind Lincoln in his attempt to save the Union. This little act of courtesy was proof that Douglas meant what he said.

At noon on March 4, 1861, Lincoln took the oath of office before the unfinished capitol. He, like all other Presidents of the United States, solemnly swore to "preserve, protect, and defend" the Union.

No one realized better than Lincoln the grave duty that was his. In his inaugural address he said that:

1. The states had no right to secede.

2. It was his duty to preserve the Union at any cost.

3. He had no intention of interfering with slavery in the states where it existed.

4. He was opposed to the spread of slavery into the territories.

Lincoln begged the South to consider the whole subject carefully. He pleaded:

"My countrymen, one and all, think calmly and well upon this whole subject. Nothing valuable can be lost by taking time. . . . Intelligence, patriotism, Christianity, and a firm reliance on Him who has never yet forsaken this favored land are still competent to adjust in the best way all our present difficulties."

President Lincoln declared that the laws of the Union would be faithfully enforced in all the states. At the same time he assured the people of the South that there would be no bloodshed unless it was forced upon the government. He said:

"The government will not assail *you*. You can have no conflict without being yourselves the aggressors. *You* have no oath registered in heaven to destroy the government, while *I* shall have the most solemn one to 'preserve, protect, and defend it.' "

This was the last attempt to save the Union. The tragedy was that it failed.

Lincoln's advisers. Immediately after his inauguration Lincoln chose his Cabinet, among whom were some of the ablest statesmen of the country. Some of these were his political enemies. Some were Democrats. Seward and Chase, who had been his rivals for the Republican nomination, he made Secretary of State and Secretary of the Treasury.

2. Events During the Civil War

Shortly before Lincoln became President certain acts of war were committed against the Union.

As soon as a state seceded, it organized its own army and took over all national forts, arsenals, and

Lincoln and his Cabinet

navy yards within its borders. There had been no bloodshed, as in nearly every case the officers in charge sympathized wholeheartedly with the South and willingly surrendered to the Confederate soldiers.

Attack upon Fort Sumter. There was, however, one important exception. Major Robert Anderson, who was the commander at Fort Sumter, refused to surrender the fort to South Carolina. He sent word of his decision to Washington. President Buchanan sent supplies and reinforcements by means of an unarmed ship flying the American flag. As the ship was about to enter the harbor it was fired upon by Confederate forces and forced to turn back without landing its supplies.

Surrender of Fort Sumter. Shortly after Lincoln took office, he received word from Major Anderson that he could not hold out much longer without reinforcements and supplies. Lincoln, against the advice of his Cabinet, prepared to send supplies to Fort Sumter even though it might mean war. Before the supplies arrived, South Carolina again called upon Major Anderson to surrender. The demand was refused. At dawn on April 12, 1861, Confederates fired the first shot of the Civil War. Two days later, with the fort in ruins, his men exhausted, and his supplies gone, Major Anderson was forced to surrender. The Civil War had begun.

Northern reaction. The firing on the flag at Fort Sumter tended to unite the people of the North. Many of Lincoln's bitterest enemies hastened to support him. Douglas, Pierce, and Buchanan, who had been sympathetic towards the South, declared their undivided allegiance to the Union.

President Lincoln's call for seventy-five thousand volunteers to defend the American flag was enthusiastically received. More than ninety thousand men responded immediately.

The Union or the Confederacy? President Lincoln's call to arms forced the remaining Southern states to choose between the opposing sides. Virginia, North Carolina, Tennessee, and Arkansas joined the Confederacy. Maryland, Delaware, Kentucky, and Missouri finally decided to remain in the Union. The mountaineers of the western part of Virginia refused to secede. They set up the new state of West Virginia, which was admitted into the Union in 1863.

Union at any cost. Lincoln made it clear that the great question of the hour was no longer slavery. The North went to war to save the

Bombardment of Fort Sumter. The fort is almost in ruins, but the U. S. flag still flies bravely

Brown Brothers

Union; the South to defend the right of the states to secede and form a new nation.

"Capital" the goal. Shortly after the war began, the Confederacy moved its capital from Montgomery to Richmond, Virginia. The plan of the North was to capture Richmond, Virginia, the capital of the Confederacy, while the South wanted to take Washington, D. C. It was thought that the capture of either capital would bring the war to a speedy close and decide the issue. Therefore, "On to Washington" became the cry of the South, while "On to Richmond" resounded throughout the North. From a strict military standpoint, neither Richmond or Washington was very important. The effort made to capture them served only one purpose—it prolonged the war.

Strength of the North and the South. When the war began the South seemed to be no match for the North. Twenty-two states remained faithful to the Union, while the Confederacy had only eleven. In population, in government, in resources, and in wealth the North had a tremendous advantage. Its government was well esablished, while that of the South was in its infancy. The North owned practically all the warships and most of the merchant ships. It was able to produce almost everything it needed. It far surpassed the South in wealth, in the number of railroads, shipyards, and factories. It was able to control the sea, to obtain overseas supplies, to borrow money, to equip its Army, and to move its soldiers and supplies easily and quickly.

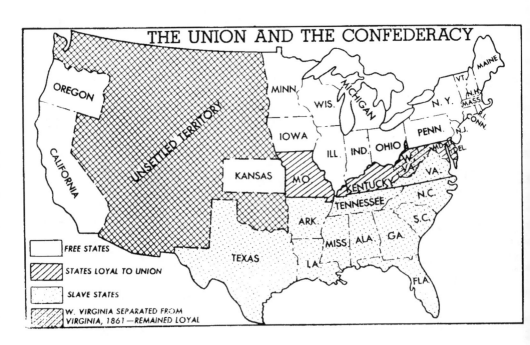

THE UNION AND THE CONFEDERACY

FREE STATES

STATES LOYAL TO UNION

SLAVE STATES

W. VIRGINIA SEPARATED FROM VIRGINIA, 1861—REMAINED LOYAL

Brown Brothers

The Confederate Capitol at Richmond

The South, on the other hand, had few of these advantages. It had to import most of its manufactured goods. It had no warships. It had few railroads, few factories, few shipyards, and little ready cash. Furthermore, it had little skilled labor.

Advantages of the South. The South did, however, have some advantages. The slaves tilled the fields and raised food for the Army. The Confederate soldiers were accustomed to outdoor life and had been trained in the use of firearms in early childhood. They were close to their base of supplies. They were fighting on familiar ground and in friendly territory. They knew the swamps, the thickets, and the mountain barriers.

Besides these advantages, there were short rivers which provided many a trap for the Northern soldiers. They were fighting in enemy territory and far from their base of supplies.

Many of the officers of the regular Army were Southerners. When their respective states seceded, they immediately offered their services to the Confederacy. A great number of these Southern leaders had experienced actual warfare during the Mexican War. This loss of officers forced the North to find new commanders, often only after costly experiments.

Robert E. Lee on his favorite horse, "Traveler"

Robert E. Lee. One of the officers of the regular Army, who joined the Confederacy, was Robert E. Lee. He was a true patriot, and loyal supporter of the Union. He was deeply devoted to his country and did not believe in slavery. Shortly after South Carolina seceded, Francis P. Blair, in the name of President Lincoln, offered Lee command of the United States Army. It was on this occasion that Lee remarked that he was devoted to the Union, that he would do everything in his power to save it, and that if he owned all the slaves in the South, he would give them up to save the Union.

Lee had a difficult choice to make. He had to choose either the Union or the Confederacy. If he chose the Union he would be obliged to take up arms against his relatives, his neighbors, and his friends. Like most Southerners, Lee felt that his first duty was to his native state, Virginia. He was a man who always put duty before everything else; therefore, only after much thought, did Robert E. Lee come to a final decision to reject Blair's offer.

Immediately following his resignation from the United States Army, Lee hastened to explain his action to his sister. He wrote: "With all my devotion to the Union and the feeling of loyalty and duty of an American citizen, I have not been able to make up my mind to raise my hand against my relatives, my children, my home. I have therefore resigned my commission in the Army, and save in defense of my native state, . . . I hope I may never be called on to draw my sword."

Later, when Virginia did secede Lee was called upon to become Commander-in-Chief of the military and naval forces of Virginia. On this occasion, *The Richmond Enquirer* printed the following:

A more heroic Christian, noble soldier and gentleman could not be found . . . no man is superior in all that constitutes the soldier and the gentleman — no man more worthy to head our forces and lead our army. There is no one who would command more of the confidence of the people of Virginia than this distinguished officer, and no one under whom the volunteers and militia would more gladly rally. His reputation, his acknowledged ability, his chivalric character, his probity, honor, and — may we add to his eternal praise — his Christian life and conduct make his very name a "tower of strength.". . .

In a very short time Lee was raised to the rank of General in the Confederate Army.

The Battle of Bull Run. Although

The Federal troops retreat at Bull Run

Brown Brothers

the North held most of the advantages, the war began with early victories for the South. The men who had volunteered for three months' service in the Union Army did not realize the need for long military training. They were anxious to attack the Confederate Army. Against General Winfield Scott's advice, President Lincoln yielded to the cry of "On to Richmond." General McDowell with an army of thirty thousand men was ordered to advance against the South.

The two armies met for the first time near a small stream called Bull Run, in Virginia. At first it looked as if the North would win. Shortly after the battle began, some of the Southern soldiers became confused and started to retreat. As they ran up the slope an officer, seeing that General Jackson and his men stood there calmly awaiting the onset, cried out in encouragement to his retreating troops, "There is Jackson standing like a stone wall." Ever after the General was known as "Stonewall" Jackson.

When things seemed hopeless to the Confederates, Albert Sydney Johnson's troops appeared on the scene. At the sight of reinforcements, the Southern soldiers rallied and completely overcame the Union forces. The soldiers of both sides had fought bravely. But the South had had better generals. Thus, the battle was won by the South, much to the surprise of the North.

Northern reaction to the Battle of Bull Run. This defeat was good for the North. It broke down the over-

confidence of the Union soldiers and showed them that the war was not to be won so easily.

After a few days the soldiers recovered from the effects of the shock. They were fired with anger, enthusiasm, and determination to defeat the Confederacy. Lincoln called for more volunteers. A large army was organized under the command of General George B. McClellan. During the first two years both sides fought bravely. Battles were won and lost. Several of the victories of the West were won by the Yankees (Northern soldiers), but the Confederates won most of the battles in the East.

The four-point plan of the North. The four-point plan of the North to defeat the Confederacy was:

1. to starve the Confederacy by a rigid blockade of Southern ports,
2. to invade Virginia and capture Richmond, the Confederate capital,
3. to cut the Confederacy in two by getting control of the Mississippi River and its branches,
4. to split the eastern section of the Confederacy by sending a destroying army across it and by getting control of the railroads between the mountains and the Mississippi River.

The Northern blockade. Soon after war was declared, Lincoln ordered a blockade of all Southern ports. Immediately, the Navy set to work to prepare for this gigantic task. Ships were built, bought, or reconditioned. In a few months all was in readiness. Warships were placed all along the Southern coast, a distance of some three thousand miles. Little by little the blockade became effective.

Cotton, the crop from which Southerners derived their income, could no longer be sold to European countries. Arms, manufactured goods, medicines, and other supplies could not be imported. The South was slowly being starved.

"Merrimac" and "Monitor." At the end of the first year of warfare, the South made a desperate effort to defeat the federal Navy. There was a partly destroyed federal warship at Norfolk, Virginia, called the *Merrimac*. The Confederates raised this ship and cut her down almost to water level. They covered her sides with heavy sheet iron and renamed her the *Virginia*. Then they sent her out to destroy the federal ships lying in the harbor.

For one day the *Merrimac* had everything her own way. She sank two ships, the *Cumberland* and the *Congress*, and then made her way towards the *Minnesota* and the *St. Lawrence*. However, since night was fast coming on, she turned and steamed slowly back to her berth. All felt certain that there was little chance to save the *Minnesota* and the *St. Lawrence*.

During the night, however, a queer-looking vessel came upon the scene. It was the ironclad *Monitor*

A blockade-runner being chased by a Federal sloop

125

The *Monitor* meets the *Merrimac*. Can you see why the *Monitor* was called "a cheesebox on a raft"?

of the Union. All that could be seen of this ship was a round box called a turret sitting atop a hull that was almost even with the water. Inside the turret were two eleven-inch guns. The turret was made to revolve, or turn around, so that the guns could be fired in any direction without changing the position of the ship. Many who saw this strange-looking ship called her "a cheesebox on a raft." The *Monitor* anchored alongside the *Minnesota* where she could not be seen by the Confederates.

Early the next morning the *Merrimac* made her way for the *Minnesota*. The *Monitor* steamed straight for her. The crew of the *Merrimac* did not know what to make of the odd little vessel. All morning the two ships battled, but neither was able to destroy the other. Finally, the *Merrimac*, her crew weary and exhausted, turned back. She was a sorry looking sight. Her iron beak was twisted, some of her armor-plate was damaged, her smokestack and steam pipes were riddled, and her anchor and flag staff were shot away.

Neither the *Merrimac* nor the *Monitor* could claim a victory, but the South realized that there was little hope of defeating the federal Navy. The clash of the *Merrimac* and the *Monitor* proved to the world that the day of wooden warships had passed.

Foreign relations during the war. At the beginning of the Civil War most of the European nations declared themselves neutral. Lincoln had, however, one big worry. England and France were very sympathetic towards the Confederacy. France had even encouraged the South to purchase war vessels built in French shipyards.

To keep the good will of these nations, President Lincoln sent personal representatives to Europe. One of these representatives was Archbishop John Hughes of New York. The task of the Archbishop was to explain the cause of the North and to urge the French government not to recognize the Confederacy. We do not know definitely how successful Archbishop Hughes' efforts were, but in a letter written to Secretary Seward, he did say, "A Roman gentleman told me a few days ago that the Southern Catholics who happen to be here hold me responsible for having prevented England and France from coming to the aid and support of their cause. My answer was, 'I hope the accusation is true'."

Bishop Lynch of Charleston, South Carolina, was sent by the Confederacy on a similar mission. He visited Ireland and Rome in the interests of the South.

The "Trent" affair. In spite of the work of Archbishop Hughes and others, an incident occurred during the blockade which almost caused war with Great Britain. Mason and Slidell, two representatives of the Confederate government, set out for England. They embarked on the *Trent,* a British mail steamer. A Union vessel, captained by Charles Wilkes, overtook the *Trent* and ordered her to stop. Captain Wilkes then seized Mason and Slidell and made them prisoners.

When the capture was reported, all England became highly indignant. The British government demanded the immediate release of the prisoners and began to make preparations for war. Lincoln and the Northern leaders realized the danger. They released the prisoners and explained to the British government that Wilkes had acted without any order from the United States government.

The "Alabama" claims. The next year another difficulty arose. England continued to show sympathy for the South because she heavily depended on it for cotton. President Davis ordered some warships from an English shipbuilding firm. Our ambassador to Great Britain protested vigorously. In spite of these protests the British government allowed the vessels to put to sea.

The most troublesome of these English-built ships was the *Alabama.* For almost two years she roamed the seas. She sank or captured scores of Union merchant ships and caused damages amounting to millions of dollars.

Finally, near the end of 1864, the *Alabama* was overtaken by the

Mason, the Confederate representative, is taken from the *Trent*.

Union warship, *Kearsarge*. A furious battle followed. After an hour of fighting, the *Alabama* was so badly damaged by the heavy guns of the *Kearsarge* that she sank.

After the war the United States Government claimed that Great Britain should pay the damages caused by the *Alabama* and other vessels built in English ports. War could have followed but the United States and Great Britain had found a better way to settle disputes.

In 1871 a court of arbitration met at Geneva, Switzerland. The court declared that Great Britain had violated the laws of neutrality and should pay the United States $75,000,000. England paid the full amount and another war was avoided. Arbitration, or this peaceful way of settling quarrels between nations, was a definite victory in favor of peace.

Women in the war. During the Civil War brave women of America rendered devoted service to friend and foe alike. In the North a woman planned and organized a Sanitary Commission to aid in preventing disease from wiping out the Army. The members of this Commission helped in the care of the sick and wounded. They also collected money, medicines, food, clothing, and comforts for the soldiers.

Clara Barton, who later founded the American Red Cross, and Doro-

Clara Barton

Dorothea Dix

thea Dix, who was famous for her work in behalf of the insane, gained their first experiences on the battlefield during the Civil War. In both armies women not only served as nurses, but some also acted as scouts and even as spies.

The women in the North and in the South took up the work of the men. In the North they replaced the men in factory and in field. In the South, the women, left alone with the slaves, managed the farms and plantations. They sacrificed every comfort to keep the soldiers supplied with food and clothing.

The patience, courage, and self-sacrifice of the women at home during the war made Lincoln exclaim: "If all that has been said by orators and poets since the creation of the world were applied to the women in America, it would not do them justice for their conduct during this war."

Angels of mercy. When the war broke out there was no organized system of nursing and care for the wounded. To fill this need, hundreds of Sisters, representing eleven different Communities, exchanged the work of the classroom and the hospital for the care of the sick, wounded, and dying of both armies.

The Ursulines of Texas and the Sisters of Our Lady of Mt. Carmel in New Orleans transformed their convents into hospitals. In these as well as in many other hospitals the Federal and Confederate soldiers found relief, consolation, and often peace of soul. Only the Sisters of Charity from Emmitsburg, however, were allowed to serve on the firing line. Their deeds of valor and heroism could not be surpassed by those of the bravest of men.

Often the Sisters had to teach men how to die. Many a soldier was led to make his peace with God. Some were baptized. Others found comfort in the words of sympathy, encouragement, and cheer of these valiant women.

These faithful Sisters were untiring in their service of the sick and dying. Many a non-Catholic learned to admire and respect the Sisters for their noble, unselfish work. Many a soldier during and after the war was won to the Catholic Church because of the example of the modest, self-sacrificing, and heroic lives of these women.

General Benjamin Butler, after observing their work of mercy and devotion on the battlefield said of them:

> Sisters to all mankind, they know no nation, no kindred, neither war nor peace. Their all-pervading charity is like the boundless love of Him who died for us all, whose servants they are, and whose pure teachings their love illustrates.

On the monument which was erected in Washington, D. C., to the memory and honor of the Sisters on the battlefield, we find these words:

Scene in a Civil War Hospital in New York

130

Lincoln reads the draft of the Emancipation Proclamation

THEY COMFORTED THE DYING. NURSED THE WOUNDED. CARRIED HOPE TO THE IMPRISONED. GAVE IN HIS NAME A DRINK TO THE THIRSTY.

Lincoln's Emancipation Proclamation. In the fall of 1862 Lincoln took another step which helped prevent England or France from supporting the Confederacy.

At the beginning of the war neither the North nor the South made slavery the chief issue. As time went on, however, it became clear that the slaves were a great help to the South in carrying on the war. They raised food and cotton, dug trenches, and did many other kinds of work which in the North had to be done by the soldiers. Therefore, in September, 1862, Lincoln warned the people of the South that if they did not return to the Union by January 1, 1863, he would on that date declare all their slaves free. The South paid no attention to the warning.

On January 1, 1863, President Lincoln issued his famous Emancipation Proclamation which declared that all slaves in the *seceded* states were free.

The Emancipation Proclamation was a war measure. It attempted to gain more support for the North and to prevent England from joining with the Confederacy, for many people in England were against slavery. Although not a single state returned to the Union, the Proclamation did gain for the Northern cause the sympathy and support of men everywhere. Even the abolitionists, who cared little about fighting to keep the slave states in the Union, now supported the North wholeheartedly.

War in the West. The attempt of the North to gain control of the Mississippi started early in 1862. The Confederacy had built Fort Henry and Fort Donelson twelve miles apart on the Tennessee and Cumberland Rivers. It had also strongly fortified the Mississippi at many points.

Northern troops under Ulysses S. Grant cooperated with the river gunboats in the capture of these forts. Victories were won in quick succession. Fort Henry and Fort Donelson with all their ammunition and their fourteen thousand men fell.

The next battle was fought at Shiloh, in southern Tennessee. There Grant and his army met the Confederates under Albert Sydney Johnston, one of the ablest generals

THE CIVIL WAR

of the South. It was one of the bloodiest battles. Many were killed or wounded. Towards the close of the first day Johnston's leg was shot off by a cannon ball. Although in great pain, he ordered the doctors to care first for the wounded soldiers near him. He refused aid so long that he finally bled to death.

Only the arrival of reinforcements saved Grant's army from destruction. The next day the battle resulted in a Northern victory. Grant then moved his army southward. The Southern army lost hope of holding the upper Mississippi and abandoned it as far south as Vicksburg. This made it easier for Grant and his men to take Corinth. Through this victory the North gained control of the railway junction connecting the important cities of the South.

While Grant was advancing on Corinth, Admiral David G. Farragut, with a large fleet of the Union Navy, attacked New Orleans. In spite of stubborn opposition he succeeded in entering the mouth of the Mississippi. With shot and shell raining upon them, Farragut's ships ran past the forts on either side of the river. Although the Confederates fought desperately, Farragut took New Orleans on April 26, 1862. The Union then controlled the whole Mississippi with the exception of a short stretch of two hundred miles between Port Hudson and Vicksburg.

The taking of Vicksburg. In order to get control of the entire Mississippi River it was necessary to seize Vicksburg. On a steep bluff overlooking the Mississippi, Vicksburg, the "Gibraltar of the West," was protected by mountains and swamps.

Grant, aided by Sherman, laid siege to Vicksburg. The Union fleet came up the river and together the fleet and the Army besieged the city from both land and water. The Confederates held out until Vicksburg was almost blown to pieces. On July 4, 1863, it became plain that the city could hold out no longer. A white flag was raised. Since this meant surrender, firing stopped immediately. It was a great victory for the Union. The Southerners had put up a heroic resistance, but Grant's attack was so well planned that it was impossible to send help to the defenders of Vicksburg.

As soon as the Confederate commander at Port Hudson learned of the fall of Vicksburg, he too surrendered. The second part of the four-point plan of the Union had been accomplished. The North had gained complete control of the Mississippi, and the Confederacy had been cut in two.

After the victory at Vicksburg, Grant came to the aid of the Union forces under General Rosecrans and General Thomas. Both armies fought hard and well, but the Confederates were defeated. As a result Chattanooga, an important railroad junction, came under the control of the North. By the end of 1863 nearly all of Tennessee had been won by the Union forces.

War in the East. While Grant was

winning battles in the West, McClellan with a large, well-trained army was advancing on Richmond. The Union generals in the East, however, were no match for Generals Robert E. Lee and "Stonewall" Jackson. Battle after battle was lost. Nevertheless, Lincoln would not give up the fight for Richmond. He next sent General Joseph Hooker against the Confederate capital. Lee did not wait for the Union forces to reach Richmond, but advanced to meet them. The two armies clashed at Chancellorsville. A decisive battle followed, which resulted in the worst defeat that the Union forces had ever suffered.

The South also suffered a heavy blow in the death of "Stonewall" Jackson. In the midst of the battle Jackson was mistaken for a Union general and killed by his own men. In the death of "Stonewall", Lee suffered a loss that could never be repaired.

Draft riots. Towards the close of the year 1862, many people became dissatisfied with Lincoln and his administration. The cost of living was high. The Northern generals did not seem to be a match for the Southern generals. It looked as if the North could never overcome the South. Lee was planning another invasion of the North. As the end of the war was nowhere in

Draft riots in New York. What was the cause of these riots?

Pickett's men charging the Union troops at Gettysburg

sight, few men enlisted in the Army and the number of deserters increased.

Attempts were made to draft new recruits into the Army. In several states many men protested against being drafted. In July, 1863, the draft riots in New York City resulted in the loss of many lives and the destruction of about one and a half million dollars worth of property.

Many leaders urged the people to obey the laws. Once again Archbishop Hughes was called upon. At the time the Archbishop was too sick to go to the people. When Governor Seymour of New York asked him to use his influence with the people, he had notices posted throughout the city inviting the people to come to him. Vast crowds responded to his call. In spite of his illness he came out on the balcony of his home. For over an hour he reasoned with them and begged them to obey the laws and keep peace. They heeded his wishes. From that time on there were no more draft riots in the city of New York.

The Battle of Gettysburg. Encouraged by his victory at Chancellorsville, Lee decided to invade the North a second time. He had already attempted such an invasion, but was turned back after the Battle of Antietam in 1862. In June,

1863, he led his Army across the Potomac into Pennsylvania. A large force of Union soldiers under General Meade was sent to check Lee's advance. On July 1, 1863, the Union and Confederate forces met near the little town of Gettysburg. The struggle lasted for three days. Time after time, Lee tried to break through the Northern lines, but all his attempts failed. On the second day, General Meade sent Meagher's Irish Brigade to capture Little Round Top, an important hill. Then followed an inspiring scene. Before ascending the hill the entire Irish Brigade knelt, and with bowed heads received general absolution from their Chaplain, Father William Corby, C.S.C. After a well-fought battle they secured Little Round Top.

On the third day, General Lee ordered General Longstreet's division to storm a ridge held by the Federals. Spearheaded by General Pickett's brigade, the Confederates made a heroic charge. But they were met by a resistance equally heroic. Through shot and shell they went up the steep ascent. Large gaps were torn in their ranks. Still, on they went. After a battle of two hours they reached the top and endeavored to plant their flag there. But a handful remained! Some of these died in the hand-to-hand encounter which followed. Others

Lincoln delivers the famous "Gettysburg Address"

were driven back. Finally, Lee realized that the battle was lost and ordered a general retreat.

Gettysburg dedicated. A part of this battlefield was made a national cemetery. Here lie the soldiers of both the Blue and the Gray who gave their lives in that great battle. At the dedication of this cemetery on November 19, 1863, President Lincoln addressed the assembled people. Lincoln spoke for about three minutes. But he touched the hearts of the American people by the greatness of his thinking. His address, though brief, was so heartfelt and sincere that it will live on for all time as one of the greatest speeches in our language.

FOURSCORE AND SEVEN YEARS AGO our fathers brought forth on this continent a new nation, conceived in liberty, and dedicated to the proposition that all men are created equal.

Now we are engaged in a great civil war, testing whether that nation, or any nation so conceived and so dedicated, can long endure. We are met on a great battlefield of that war. We have come to dedicate a portion of that field as a final resting-place for those who here gave their lives that that nation might live. It is altogether fitting and proper that we should do this.

But, in a larger sense, we cannot dedicate — we cannot consecrate — we cannot hallow — this ground. The brave men, living and dead, who struggled here, have consecrated it far above our poor power to add or detract. The world will little note nor long remember what we say here, but it can never forget what they did here. It is for us, the living, rather, to be dedicated here to the unfinished work which they who fought here have thus far so nobly advanced. It is rather for us to be here dedicated to the great task remaining before us — that from these honored dead we take increased devotion to that cause for which they gave the last full measure of devotion; that we here highly resolve that these dead shall not have died in vain; that this nation, under God, shall have a new birth of freedom; and that government of the people, by the people, for the people, shall not perish from the earth.

Grant's plan to win. Early in the year 1864, Lincoln, whose term of office was drawing to an end, made every effort to bring the war to a close. To do this he needed a strong commander-in-chief of the Army. The only Northern general who had a series of important victories to his credit was Ulysses S. Grant. He also had the necessary skill and courage. Accordingly, Lincoln made Grant commander-in-chief of all the Union forces.

General Grant had a plan to bring the war to a speedy close. He intended to march on Richmond from the north. Another Federal army was to attack Richmond from

Virginia. At the same time Sherman was to move his army from Chattanooga to Atlanta. Starting at Atlanta, he was to march through Georgia to the ocean and make it impossible for Lee to get supplies from Georgia.

Sherman's march to the sea. On September 3, 1864, Sherman captured Atlanta. Its manufacturing plants were burned. Supplies and machinery were destroyed. Then he started his march of three hundred sixty miles from Atlanta to the sea. Rails were torn up, bridges were blown up, buildings were burned, great stores of cotton awaiting shipment were destroyed. Everything that could serve the troops, such as horses, mules, and supplies were taken. Sherman's destroying army pushed on, leaving nothing but waste and destruction in its wake. Shortly before Christmas, Savannah was forced to surrender, and the march across Georgia was completed.

A path of destruction sixty miles wide stretched across Georgia. This act of Sherman's army broke the backbone of the Confederacy. Then, with his purpose achieved, Sherman moved northward to join Grant, who was near Richmond.

Grant marches on Richmond. In the meantime, Grant had begun his campaign to capture Richmond. His route lay through a thickly

Marching through Georgia. Sherman's men leave destruction in their path.

138

wooded region. Here the Confederate army put up a strong resistance. The losses in the Union army were so heavy that people thought that Grant had little regard for human life. But he knew that war meant sacrifice, and he was determined to continue to fight to end the war.

The Confederates wondered about this General. He was so unlike those who had gone before him. Nothing discouraged him. He never gave up. No matter how many times he was repulsed, he kept on attacking.

During the spring and summer of 1864, Grant met Lee in three battles, but could not defeat him. Finally, Grant swung his army around and attacked Richmond from the South.

Sheridan's ride. At the same time that Sherman was marching from Atlanta to the sea, and Grant was marching on Richmond, another campaign of destruction was taking place.

The Shenandoah Valley was one of the chief sources of supplies for Lee's army. In the fall of 1864, Sheridan drove out the Confederates and laid waste the rich farms of this beautiful valley. He destroyed supplies and everything else that might help the enemy. Sheridan, after defeating his enemy, started for Washington.

Somehow the Confederate general, Jubal Early, learned that Sheridan was absent. Early attacked and completely routed the Union soliders.

General Grant

When Sheridan heard the firing, he returned with speed. On the way he met his retreating soldiers. By a glance of his eye and the words, "Turn, boys, turn. We're going back," he led them to victory.

Lincoln's reelection. In the meantime, Lincoln was reelected by an overwhelming majority for a second term of office. The nation did not think it wise to turn the management of the war over to a new President. As Lincoln put it, they decided "not to swap horses while crossing the river."

The closing words of Lincoln's second inaugural address show his great generosity and charity:

"With malice toward none; with charity for all; with firmness in the right, as God gives us to see the right, let us strive on to finish the work we are in; to bind

Surrender at Appomattox

up the nation's wounds; to care for him who shall have borne the battle, and for his widow, and his orphan — to do all which may achieve and cherish a just and lasting peace among ourselves, and with nations."

Richmond falls. In the spring of 1865, Grant was still fighting his way to Richmond. At last, on April 3, 1865, Petersburg, the last stronghold, fell. Later that same day the Union forces marched into Richmond.

Lee evacuated the city and began a retreat. As the retreat continued, he saw no hope of aid from any source. He realized that further struggle was useless. "There is nothing left me to do but to go and see General Grant," he said, "and I would rather die a thousand deaths." Soon a white flag

was raised above the Southern ranks, and the fighting ceased.

The surrender of Lee. On April 9, 1865, Lee met Grant at a plantation mansion in a little town called Appomatox Court House, in Virginia, to arrange the terms of surrender.

The two officers presented a marked contrast in appearance. Ulysses S. Grant, short with slightly stooped shoulders, was dressed in the uniform of a private with the straps of a lieutenant-general. His blouse was unbuttoned, his trousers were tucked into his mud-splashed boots, and he carried no sword. Robert E. Lee, tall and dignified, wore a new full-dress uniform of Confederate gray. His coat was buttoned to the throat and his handsome sword hung at his side.

Grant was generous in victory; Lee heroic in defeat. After meeting Lee, Grant "felt like anything rather than rejoicing at the downfall of a foe who had fought so long and so valiantly."

The generosity and kindheartedness of Grant impressed Lee. Everything was done to soften the humiliation of the defeat. General Grant did not boast of his victory. When the Union soldiers heard of the surrender, they commenced firing salutes along the line to celebrate. Grant ordered these stopped, saying, "The war is over; the rebels are our countrymen."

Terms of surrender. The terms of surrender were very generous. Grant refused to take Lee's sword and allowed the Confederate officers to keep their side arms. Confederate officers and men were allowed to return home after giving their word that they would remain loyal to the Union. They were permitted to take with them their horses and personal property.

No prisoners were taken. The Union soldiers shared their rations with the half-starved Southern veterans. General Lee signed the terms of surrender and thanked Grant for his consideration.

Lee shook hands with Grant and mounted his horse. As the great commander rode away, the Federal officers, led by Grant, raised their hats and stood bareheaded until Lee disappeared from sight.

Sadly, Lee rode back to his soldiers. Officers and men gathered around their beloved leader. Many a weather-beaten face was wet with tears. Some tried to take Lee's hand. Then, with tears in his eyes and a choked voice, Lee said, "We have fought through the war together. I have done the best I could for you. My heart is too full to say more."

3. Results of the Civil War

The war was over and the United States was once more a single, undivided nation. The Union was saved, the questions of Secession and States' Rights were settled, and slavery was abolished.

Thirteenth Amendment. Lincoln's Emancipation Proclamation was merely a war measure. It did not free a single slave in the states that remained loyal. Therefore, shortly before the war ended, Congress passed the Thirteenth Amendment

to the Constitution. It was adopted in December, 1865. The Thirteenth Amendment assured the slaves of freedom with the words

Neither slavery nor involuntary servitude, except as a punishment for crime whereof the party shall have been duly convicted, shall exist within the United States or in any place subject to their jurisdiction. Congress shall have power to enforce this article by appropriate legislation.

The cost of the war. The cost of the war was great. Besides taking the lives of over a half-million men, our government had spent millions of dollars. In the South, where the fighting took place, the property loss was tremendous.

These sacrifices set free the slave and preserved the Union. They settled for all time the question of secession.

The assassination of Lincoln. During the latter part of the war Lincoln made plans for reuniting the war-torn nation. He did not intend to punish the South any further than the hardships of war had already punished it. His idea was to bring back the seceded states into the Union as quickly as possible. He made that clear in his second inaugural address.

But the great President was not to carry out his wise and noble plan. The joy of the nation was soon turned to mourning. Just five days after the close of the war there came a tragic event. Lincoln, while sitting in a box at Ford's Theater, was shot by John Wilkes-Booth, a

John Wilkes Booth assassinates Lincoln at Ford's Theatre

half-crazed actor. The wounded leader was carried unconscious to a private home across the street, and medical aid was summoned. The President lived through the night, although he never regained consciousness. Early the next morning, surrounded by relatives and friends, he went to meet his God.

Swiftly the news spread throughout the country and the entire nation was plunged in grief. No other man could have been so sorely missed. By intuition, Lincoln seemed to know what people wanted and how they felt. He had a patience and a sense of honor that enabled him to bear slights, sorrows, and wrongs that would have crushed another man. General Grant truly said of him, "In his death the nation lost its greatest hero; in his death the South lost its most true friend." And seldom in history did a nation face a crisis under the leadership of so religious a man. God was an ever-present reality and he never took a decisive step without prayer. It was because he reverenced the law of God that he faced the storm of civil strife unafraid. Can you believe that with heroes such as he our country has been non-religious?

Word study

nominated	protective tariff
issue	inaugurate
conflict	concealed

142

territories	reliance	blockade	federal
secession	reinforcements	sympathetic	legislation
Constitution	allegiance	arbitration	assassination
traitor	proclamation	fourscore	
emancipation	determination		

Something to think about

1. Discuss reasons why the Northern Blockade was such a deadly weapon.
2. Compare the characters of Lee and Grant. Which was the nobler of the two? How did he show his nobility?
3. Discuss ways and instances in which the North and the South forgot the virtues of justice and charity.
4. Discuss the part played by Catholics during the Civil War, women during the war, Sisters during the war.

Test your sense of time

Arrange the events in each column below in the order in which they took place by numbering them 1, 2, 3, 4, and 5.

...Lincoln inaugurated
...Kansas-Nebraska Act
...Secession of Southern States
...Lincoln-Douglas debates
...Lincoln elected President

...Battle of Gettysburg
...Emancipation Proclamation
...Surrender of Lee
...Battle of Bull Run
...Surrender of Fort Sumter

REVIEW OF UNIT THREE

Minimum essentials

1. All men regardless of color, nationality, or creed are brothers.
2. All men, Negro as well as white, were created by God, were redeemed by the Blood of Christ, and are destined for heaven.
3. God wants all men to be and continue free — free from slavery to men or to sin — free under His reign of love.
4. Slavery violates Christ's teaching of charity and justice to all.
5. Negro slavery in what is today the United States began in Virginia in 1619.
6. Triangular trade referred to the voyage from New England to Africa, the West Indies, and back to New England, for the purpose of exchanging Negroes for rum or molasses.
7. The North, the South, and the West had different ways of living and varied interests.
8. Slave labor was not needed in the industrial and commercial regions of the North.
9. The geography of the South favored slavery.
10. The compromises in the Constitution, the Ordinance of 1787, the Missouri Compromise, the

Wilmot Proviso, and the Compromise of 1850 were attempts to settle the differences between the North and the South in regard to slavery.

11. Public opinion on slavery was aroused through the passage of the Fugitive Slave Law and the Kansas-Nebraska Act, the publication of *Uncle Tom's Cabin,* the Dred Scott Decision, Squatter Sovereignty, and John Brown's raid.

12. Know and understand the meaning of and reason for each quotation given in this Unit.

13. Know and understand the points of the compromises given in this Unit.

14. Be able to define and explain these terms:

slave auction
Emancipation Proclamation
geographical differences
Fugitive Slave Law
Personal Liberty Laws
Underground Railroad
Squatter Sovereignty
States' Rights
Nullification
Secession
Dred Scott Decision
Union
compromise
chattel
Freeport Doctrine
Trent Affair
Alabama Claims
Thirteenth Amendment
abolitionist
Kansas-Nebraska Act

Activities

1. Continue the illustrated time-line begun in Unit One.

2. Prepare and present a panel discussion or a dramatization to show the attitude of the North and of the South towards slavery. Mention your opinion about the attitude of each.

3. Make a series of slides showing the high points of slavery and the Civil War. As each is thrown on the screen, one pupil should be prepared to explain it to the class. Be sure to include the following:

    a. the dignity of the Negro as a human being

    b. the rights and duties of the Negro

    c. the reasons for the viewpoint of slavery held by the North and the South

    d. the injustice and uncharitableness of some of the events which aroused public opinion

    e. the attempts made to solve the slavery question

    f. the reasons for the attitude of the North and the South towards protective tariff and nullification

    g. the results of the Civil War

End the discussion on how you can keep God's law "to love your neighbor as yourself." Did all the slave owners, slave traders, and other persons love the slave as themselves?

4. Hold an open forum on the question "Is there any slavery in the United States today?"

5. Select one or more of the following leaders of the Civil War period for study and report: Robert E. Lee, Ulysses S. Grant. "Stone-

wall" Jackson, David G. Farragut, Philip Sheridan.

6. Make a list of slavery songs and Civil War songs. Learn some of them.

7. Prepare a floor talk upon one of these topics:

    a. The influence of the geography of the South upon the Civil War.

    b. The emancipation of the slaves.

    c. The work of the Navy in the Civil War.

    d. The work of the Catholic Sisters during the war.

8. Make a map on which you indicate important places mentioned in the Unit.

MASTERY TEST

I. Identification Test

Behind the "1" below each quotation write the name of the person who spoke or wrote those words. For this purpose use the names listed in Column I below. A name may be used several times.

Behind the "2" below each quotation write the occasion on which the words were spoken or the name of the person or group of whom they were spoken. Use the items listed in Column II for this purpose. An item may be used more than once.

Column I

1. ". . . that this nation, under God, shall have a new birth of freedom, and that government of the people, by the people, for the people, shall not perish from the earth."

    1. . . . .

    2. . . . .

2. ". . . felt like anything rather than rejoicing at the downfall of a foe who had fought so long and so valiantly."

    1. . . . .

    2. . . . .

3. "A house divided against itself cannot stand."

    1. . . . .

    2. . . . .

4. "A more heroic Christian, noble soldier and gentleman could not

Column II

be found . . . His reputation, his acknowledged ability, his chivalric character . . . and — may we add to his eternal praise — his Christian life and conduct make his very name a 'tower of strength'. . ."

    1. . . . .

    2. . . . .

5. "Slavery is the spirit that says 'You work and toil and earn bread, and I'll eat it.'"

    1. . . . .

    2. . . . .

6. "Slavery cannot exist a day or hour anywhere unless it is supported by local police regulations."

    1. . . . .

    2. . . . .

7. Ordered the firing of salutes stopped, saying, "The war is over; the rebels are our countrymen."

    1. . . . .

    2. . . . .

8. "Let us have faith that right makes right, and in that faith, let us, to the end, dare to do our duty as we understand it."

    1. . . . .

    2. . . . .

9. "If you who represent the stronger portion, the North, are not willing to settle on these principles, say so, and let us separate in peace."

    1. . . . .

    2. . . . .

10. "Nothing valuable can be lost by taking time. . . . Intelligence, patriotism, Christianity, and a firm reliance on Him who has never yet forsaken this favored land are still competent to adjust in the best way all our present difficulties."

    1. . . . .

    2. . . . .

11. "Sisters to all mankind, they know no nation, no kindred, neither war nor peace. Their all-pervading charity is like the boundless love of Him who died for us all . . ."

    1. . . . .

    2. . . . .

12. "With malice toward none; with charity for all; with firmness in the right, as God gives us to see the right, let us strive on to finish the work we are in; to bind up the nation's wounds; . . ."

    1. . . . .

    2. . . . .

13. "We have fought through the war together. I have done the best I could for you. My heart is too full to say more."

    1. . . . .

    2. . . . .

14. "In his death the nation lost its greatest hero; in his death the South lost its most true friend."

    1. . . . .

    2. . . . .

15. "If all that has been said by orators or poets since the creation of the world were applied to the women of America, it would not do them justice for their conduct during this war."

    1. . . . .

    2. . . . .

Column I	*Column II*
Lincoln	Lincoln-Douglas Debates
Grant	First Inaugural Address
Douglas	Second Inaugural Address
Calhoun	Assassination of Lincoln
Lee	Surrender of Lee at Appomatox
General Benjamin Butler	News of the Surrender of Lee
	Speech in New York
	Speech to the Senate
	Farewell words to his men at close of the War

II. Matching Test

On the line before each group of words in Column I write the letter found before the name in Column II which best matches it.

Column I

. . . 1. was a Confederate general who did not believe in slavery but thought that his first duty was to his native state, Virginia.

. . . 2. was a Catholic who was Chief Justice at the time of the Dred Scott Decision.

. . . 3. was a staunch Southerner who believed in States' Rights.

. . . 4. was the Catholic chaplain of the Irish Brigade.

. . . 5. broke the backbone of the Confederacy through his march from Atlanta to the sea.

. . . 6. was the author of the Kansas-Nebraska Act.

. . . 7. was the Catholic clergyman who was sent to Europe by President Lincoln to explain the cause of the North.

. . . 8. was a Northern general who showed himself a generous victor.

. . . 9. was a Northerner whose love for the Union was stronger than his hatred of slavery.

. . .10. was a violent abolitionist.

. . .11. was a Catholic who was commander of the Union Navy at the taking of New Orleans.

. . .12. was a general who led a campaign of destruction through the Shenandoah Valley and thus cut off Lee's source of supply.

. . .13. wrote *Uncle Tom's Cabin*.

. . .15. was a Southerner who cared more for the Union than anything else.

Column II

a. John C. Calhoun

b. Roger B. Taney

c. Henry Clay

d. Robert E. Lee

e. Ulysses S. Grant

f. Harriet B. Stowe

g. Philip Sheridan

h. Archbishop John C. Hughes

i. David G. Farragut
j. Rev. Wm. Corby, C.S.C.

k. Wm. Lloyd Garrison
l. Stephen A. Douglas

m. Daniel Webster

n. William T. Sherman
o. Joseph E. Johnston

p. "Stonewall" Jackson

III. Essay Test

1. Explain: If the Civil War was not fought to free the slave, then why did Lincoln issue the Emancipation Proclamation?

2. Prove that the Emancipation Proclamation did not do away with slavery.

Mary's First Saturday Devotion

HISTORY. The custom of setting apart every Saturday of the year as a day of special devotion to Mary is very old. The Church has dedicated Saturday to our Blessed Lady in order to urge us to honor the memory of her grief on the day following the death of her divine Son. The faithful showed their devotion to Mary on this day in various ways, by attendance at Mass, by reception of Holy Communion, by fast and abstinence, and since the time of St. Dominic, by praying the Rosary.

After the First Fridays were dedicated to the Sacred Heart of Jesus, the faithful began to dedicate the First Saturdays to Mary's Immaculate Heart. Then, at Fatima, Our Lady asked that this devotion be practiced in order to obtain world peace.

THE DEVOTION. At Fatima the blessed Virgin asked that the following devotion be practiced on the first Saturday of five consecutive months: 1) Confession and Communion, 2) Recitation of five decades of the Rosary, 3) Meditation for fifteen minutes on the mysteries of the Rosary, 4) The intention of making reparation to the Immaculate Heart of Mary.

Prayer

MARY taught the children at Fatima the following prayer to be recited when praying the Rosary:

O my Jesus, pardon us!
Save us from the fires of hell!
Lead all souls to heaven,
Grant help especially to those
Who most stand in need of it!

From *The Rosary: Its History and Meaning,* Willam-Kaiser, Benziger Brothers, Inc., New York, 1953, page 158.

DEVOTIONAL GIFTS OF MARY. The First Saturday Devotion is one of seven great devotions given to us through Mary. The other great devotions are the Hail Mary, the Rosary, the Miraculous Medal, the Scapular, the Little Office of the Blessed Virgin Mary, and the Angelus. Through these devotions you appeal to Mary for the graces which, as Mother of God, she obtains to help you save your soul.

Courtesy of Rev. J. B. Carol, O. F. M.

UNIT FOUR

BINDING UP THE NATION'S WOUNDS

UNIT FOUR

BINDING UP THE NATION'S WOUNDS

THE UNITED STATES had safely passed through a terrible crisis. The nation was again at peace! That is, it was at peace so far as actual battles were concerned, but it took a long time before the North and the South heeded the advice of Lee: *"Do not hate, but make your sons Americans. Remember that we form one country now,"* and those memorable words of Lincoln's second inaugural address: *"With malice toward none, with charity for all . . . let us strive . . . to bind up the nation's wounds."*

Lincoln had no thought of punishing the South. He felt that the ravages of war had been enough punishment. He wanted to bring the seceded states back into the Union as soon as possible. He hoped to see the wounds caused by the war quickly healed and forgotten.

But Lincoln was not to carry out his wise and noble plan. Just six weeks after he spoke the memorable words of his second inaugural

address, an assassin's bullet ended his life. The tragic death of Lincoln, the only man who might have peaceably brought together the two sections of our country, left the future of the South in the hands of hostile men in Congress.

Lincoln had planned to treat the South generously. Others were determined to punish the South for the long and bloody war. Perhaps if Lincoln had lived, the pages of United States history would not have been stained by the "Crime of Reconstruction." As slavery is a blot on American history, so too is the Period of Reconstruction a stain on the pages of the history of our country. For nothing could have been worse than the unjust method used by a radical Congress.

The victory of the North established the fact that the Union is indivisible. It freed the Negroes, and settled forever the question of secession. But it brought forth a host of new difficulties.

CHAPTER I

THE CRIME OF RECONSTRUCTION

Reconstruction — charitable or revengeful? At the close of the Civil War, the nation faced a difficult period. When the fighting ceased, many people in the North and in the South thought that the trouble was over and that the country could go on as though nothing had happened. But they soon found out that it was not as simple as that. No earthquake or tornado could have damaged the South more than the Civil War had done.

The nation faced the task of rebuilding the South, of reuniting the two sections, and of fitting the millions of freed Negroes into national life. The years during which Americans were trying to solve these problems is known in history as the *Period of Reconstruction*. During this period the South learned many valuable lessons. It learned to develop its natural resources and to depend upon itself for the future.

In this Chapter we shall learn about the shameful manner in which the South was treated during the years of Reconstruction. To understand better this period of our history, we shall study (1) The Generous Plan of Lincoln; (2) The Plan of Johnson; (3) The Plan of Congress and the Way It Was Put into Effect; and (4) The New South.

1. The Generous Plan of Lincoln

Washington founded the Union; Lincoln saved it. Throughout the dark days of the War, Lincoln went ahead with courage, patience, kindness, and wisdom. He was confident of victory. The Union must be saved at any cost. He would not let the precious heritage of American freedom be lost. At the close of the war, he was ready to attack the problems of Reconstruction with the same energy, prudence, and generosity that he had displayed during the war.

Lincoln's attitude towards the defeated South was one of kindness. He was anxious to make it very easy for the Southern States to regain their rights. Lincoln held that the seceding states had never been out of the Union, but had been in rebellion. If they were rebels, then the President had the power to pardon them. Lincoln, therefore, proceeded to carry out his plans in 1863. With the exception of a few high ranking Confederate leaders, he offered pardon to all who would take an oath of allegiance to the United States and who would agree to obey the laws against slavery. Furthermore, he said that as soon as ten per cent of the qualified voters of any seceding state would do these two things, that state could reorganize its government and send representatives to Congress. At the close of the war, Louisiana, Arkansas, and Tennessee had accepted this offer, and their governments were recognized by President Lincoln.

Had Lincoln lived, the problem of bringing the rebellious states back to the Union would most likely have been settled quickly and peacefully. But Lincoln did not live to carry through his generous plan of Reconstruction. The next few years proved that General J. E. Johnston was right when he said that *"Lincoln was the best friend the South had."*

2. The Plan of Johnson

A few hours after Lincoln's death, the heavy duties of President fell upon Andrew Johnson, the former Vice President. Johnson was a good and well-intentioned man, but, unfortunately for the South, he did not possess the confidence of the people nor of Congress.

Andrew Johnson was born in the mountains of Tennessee, and had the mountaineer's hatred of slavery. As a Southerner, he was not inclined to be severe with the South.

His plan for bringing the Southern states back to the Union was

Brown Brothers

Andrew Johnson

similar to that of Lincoln. He appointed a governor for each state. Like Lincoln, he required a convention to be called which would repeal the ordinance of secession and ratify the Thirteenth Amendment. This convention was obliged also to repudiate the Confederate war debt. For eight months after Lincoln's death Johnson pushed forward the *reconstructing* or rebuilding of the Southern states. By December of 1865, the seceded states, with the exception of Texas, had agreed to the "Presidential Plan," as the plan of Johnson was called, and had chosen representatives to Congress. But Congress, when it met in December, refused to accept Johnson's plan.

3. The "Harsh Plan" of Congress

Many Congressmen felt bitter to-

153

wards the South. They believed that the white people of the South should be severely punished for having brought on the war. Congress, on the whole, insisted that the rebellious states had forfeited their rights as states when they seceded. It claimed that the seceded states must be admitted as new states. Furthermore, Congress declared that since the Constitution gives the power of admitting new states to Congress and not to the President, Congress had the right to lay down the conditions under which the seceded states should be taken back. This same Congress also felt that the freed Negroes would not be given their rights under Johnson's plan. Besides, Northern factory owners did not want the farm states of the South to join with the West in Congress and repeal high tariffs and other measures favoring business.

Black Codes of the South. Congress likewise resented the "Black Codes" of the South. These were laws which the Southern states had passed to handle the problem of sudden emancipation. In some states, these laws practically reenslaved the freedman. One of these was the Vagrancy Law which provided for the arrest of any Negro caught not working or wandering about without a home. If the Negro could not pay the fine imposed, and a white man paid it, the Negro was obliged to work for the white man. Other states passed an Apprentice Law which provided that orphaned and abandoned Negro children were

to work until they became of age for anyone who was willing to support them. Still other laws forbade Negroes to own land, to act as witnesses in court, to assemble in political meetings, and to carry arms. These "Black Codes," which the Southern whites considered essential for their own protection, convinced the Northern leaders that harsh measures must be taken to keep the South from dealing unfairly with the Negro.

The South made another mistake which gave Congress a reason for rejecting Johnson's plan. The newly organized governments of the South sent to Congress men who had taken an active part in the rebellion. It was natural for the South to turn to its most prominent men. This move, however, gave Congress another reason to believe that the South was still rebellious. Consequently, when Congress met in December, the Southern senators and representatives were refused admittance.

The refusal of Congress to admit the Southern representatives angered Johnson. Furthermore, he resented the blocking of his plan of Reconstruction. Johnson meant well but he did not have Lincoln's ability to manage men. A bitter quarrel followed between the President and Congress. In the end, Congress had its own way. Johnson's plan was discarded, and the cruel plan of Congress went into effect.

After rejecting the plan of Johnson, Congress appointed a commit-

A school for young Freedmen

Bettmann Archive

tee to study conditions in the South. While this investigation was taking place, Congress proceeded to pass some laws for the protection of the Negro.

Freedmen's Bureau Act. In spite of Johnson's opposition, Congress passed the *Freedmen's Bureau Act.* This act established a relief agency known as the Freedmen's Bureau. Through this organization, the United States government provided food, clothing, and advice to poor Negroes and divided unused or confiscated land among them. It was hoped that in this manner the Negro would settle down and become an independent farmer. The plan, although good, failed because it produced the harmful results which brought about the passage of the Vagrancy Laws by the South.

Civil Rights Act. This act gave the Negro all the rights of a citizen except the right to vote. It enabled him to purchase and sell land, to make contracts, to move from place to place, and to have the same protection of the law as a white man.

Both the Freedman's Bureau Act and the Civil Rights Act were vetoed by President Johnson. Congress, nevertheless, passed them again by the necessary two-thirds majority, and they became laws without the President's signature.

The Fourteenth Amendment. As the feeling between the President and Congress became bitter, Congress grew more and more determined to have its own way. Up to this time, when the number of representatives to Congress was determined, a slave was counted as three-fifths of a man. The freeing of the slaves made possible a much larger number of Southern representatives. Since the Negro did not have the right to vote, the Southern whites had more power in Congress. With this in mind, Congress, in 1866, passed the Fourteenth Amendment to the Constitution. By the terms of this Amendment:

(1) The Negro became a full-fledged citizen entitled to protection of the law.

(2) A state, when determining its number of representatives to Congress, could not count the Negroes in its population unless it allowed them the right to vote.

(3) All former government officials who had taken sides against the Union were forbidden to hold office until pardoned by Congress.

(4) The war debt of the Confederacy and all claims for freed slaves were declared void and non-payable.

The chief purpose of this Amendment was to protect the freedmen and punish the white leaders of the South. Point three caused much bitterness in the South, because it disqualified practically all Southern leaders from holding office.

Tennessee alone approved the Fourteenth Amendment and was admitted at once to the Union. All the other Southern states felt that the terms were too harsh.

The Reconstruction Act. In March, 1867, Congress passed the Reconstruction Act. Under this act, the ten states that refused to accept the Fourteenth Amendment were divided into five military districts. Over each district was placed a military governor. The government of these states had been previously recognized by Johnson. Now these governments were declared illegal; consequently, conventions were to be held to organize new state governments. In these conventions Negroes were allowed to vote and to hold office. Southern whites who had fought against the Union were refused the right to vote. When finished, the new state constitutions were to be submitted to Congress for approval.

Admittance to the Union was refused to each of the ten states until Congress had approved its new constitution and the new state government had accepted the Fourteenth Amendment. Despite the harshness of this plan, seven states were admitted to the Union by 1868. The three states: Mississippi, Texas, and Virginia remained under military rule nearly three years longer.

Impeachment of Johnson. President Johnson felt that the Reconstruction Act and the Amendments were unfair to the white people of the South. He also thought that they gave too much freedom to the Negro. He therefore did everything in his power to prevent Congress from carrying out such revengeful measures. Each time Johnson vetoed a bill, the breach between the President and Congress widened. Finally, annoyed at Johnson's constant opposition, Congress passed a series of bills over his veto. Some of these greatly reduced the power of the President. For instance, one, the Tenure of Office Act, forbade the President to remove a member of his Cabinet without the approval of the Senate.

President Johnson refused to recognize the law as constitutional and proceeded to remove Edwin Stanton, his Secretary of War, who was constantly working against him. Immediately the radicals in the House of Representatives, who had been looking for a way to remove the President, passed a motion to impeach him for "high crimes and misdemeanors." To impeach an officer is to charge him with official misconduct.

Johnson was tried before the Senate which was presided over by Chief Justice Chase. The trial did not prove any misconduct on the part of Johnson. Furthermore, the Tenure of Office Act did not apply to Stanton, because he had been appointed by Lincoln. The trial showed that Johnson, though sometimes tactless, was honest and faithful to his convictions and to his duty. To convict a President, it is

The impeachment of Andrew Johnson

necessary to have two-thirds of the Senate vote him guilty. The radicals were defeated by one vote. Johnson remained in office and the nation was saved the disgrace of removing an honest President because he was disliked by Congress.

"Carpetbag" government. Conditions in the South were wretched. Many of the South's leading citizens were not allowed to vote or hold office and, furthermore, the Fifteenth Amendment which was passed in 1869 insured the Negro the right to vote. It provided that no citizen should be deprived of his right to vote "on account of race, color, or previous condition of servitude." State governments, consequently, fell into the hands of ex-slaves who had no experience in governing themselves and far less in governing others.

These illiterate Negroes became the easy tools of selfish white men who wanted to get control of the Southern state governments. These dishonest white politicians were called "Carpetbaggers" and "Scalawags."

The "Carpetbaggers" were Northerners who saw a chance to get rich quickly. They were called "Carpetbaggers" because they brought all they owned in a carpet-bag valise. These evil men from the North were joined by unscrupulous white men from the South, called "Scalawags," or "scamps," because they were regarded as traitors to the Southern whites. The "Scalawags" swore, sometimes falsely, that they had never fought against

A cartoon about the Carpetbaggers

the Union and thus had the right to vote and to hold office. These white rascals from the North and the South, through the vote of illiterate Negroes, soon got control of the local and state governments.

These Southern state governments, controlled by the votes of freedmen who were influenced by "Carpetbaggers" and "Scalawags," almost ruined the South. The office holders for the most part were uneducated Negroes led by corrupt white politicians. Most of these office holders could neither read nor write, much less govern wisely. The expenses of the government rose enormously. Huge sums of money were spent foolishly. Outrageously heavy taxes were laid upon the Southern landowners, who had already been impoverished by the war. Public funds were misappropriated and public property was stolen. Money was recklessly voted for improvements that were not needed and that were never made. The state treasuries were plundered on all sides. Most of the plunder found its way into the pockets of the "Carpetbaggers" and the "Scalawags." The South suffered for years from this kind of evil doing, and thousands of Southern people were ruined.

The Ku Klux Klan. The rule of the "Carpetbaggers" and "Scalawags" filled the South with hatred. Finally, the white men of the South, driven to sheer desperation, could endure it no longer. To defend themselves against such a government and to protect their interests, they organized secret societies. The most important of these was the Ku Klux Klan. The purpose of the Klan was to intimidate the Negro, and to keep him from the polls so that the white people could get control of the government. In order to do this, the members of the Klan played upon the superstitious fears of the Negro. At night the members of the Klan, garbed in long white sheets and hideous masks, prowled around the cabins of the blacks. With ghostly voices they warned the Negroes to refrain from voting. The terrified Negroes listened in fear and trembling to the warnings and took great care to obey them. "Carpetbaggers" and "Scalawags" were instructed to leave the South. If the warning had no effect, they were flogged and sometimes even hanged.

Before long, lawless men, protected by the disguise and secrecy of the Klan, did many cruel things to gratify their own personal hatred and brutal passions.

This Ku Klux Klan is not the same as the anti-Catholic, anti-Jewish, and anti-Negro organization of the same name which was very active during the years following World War I. But the seeds of the later Klan were certainly present in Reconstruction times.

The Force Acts. After a few years Congress passed Force Acts to disband the Klan and to maintain the power of the Republican party in the South. In 1870, President Grant, who succeeded Johnson in 1869, readily signed these Acts. The Force Acts empowered the President to send troops to the South to

Ku Klux Klansmen

Brown Brothers

159

enforce the Amendments and to stamp out the Ku Klux Klan.

Southern whites gain control. Although soldiers tried to break up the Klan the midnight visits continued. Negroes soon became afraid to use their power and "Carpetbaggers" and "Scalawags" were driven from office. Gradually, the Southern white people again gained control of local and state governments.

Those who had been mere boys during the war had now grown to manhood. Since they had not fought against the Union they were permitted to vote and to hold office. During Grant's administration, in 1872, Congress passed the Amnesty Act. Through this Act the right to vote was restored to all but a few ex-Confederates.

President Hayes succeeded Grant in 1877. One of his first official acts was to withdraw the troops from the South. Thus twelve years after the close of the Civil War, the Federal troops were withdrawn from the last of the Southern states and the disgraceful period of Reconstruction came to an end. This was part of the compromise arranged in Congress over the disputed election of 1876. Hayes, a Republican, was allowed to take office without a struggle in return for allowing the South to handle her own affairs. This understanding lasted until the "Fair Deal" of President Truman.

President Hayes and his Cabinet

When the white people of the South finally gained control of the government, they took measures to get around the Fifteenth Amendment and thus prevent the Negro from voting. They passed laws which permitted only those to vote who

(1) were able to read and to explain a clause of the Constitution.
(2) owned a certain amount of property or could pay a poll tax.
(3) had voted in 1860, or whose father or grandfather had done so.

These qualifications barred practically all Negroes. Few could read, very few owned property or could pay a poll tax, and the "Grandfather Clause," as the last qualification was called, automatically eliminated all former slaves. The Grandfather Clause was inserted to keep these rules from shutting out poor or ignorant whites. The Grandfather Clause was declared unconstitutional in 1916.

"Jim Crow" laws. Southern leaders further restricted the rights of the Negroes by passing "Jim Crow" laws. These laws provided for separation of colored and white people in schools, streetcars, trains, theaters, hotels, and restaurants.

Negro leaders resent these laws, for they do not want their people to be treated as inferior. They reasonably ask for full rights as citizens and free men. Unfortunately, they have not yet succeeded.

The "Solid South." The Southern people found it hard to forgive the North for the sufferings they had endured. They never quite forgot the misrule of the "Carpetbag" governments. Since they regarded the Republican party as the cause of all this misfortune, they became strong supporters of the Democratic party. In election after election, the Southern states voted solidly for the Democratic candidate. That is why people speak of the "Solid South."

4. The New South

In spite of these adverse conditions and events, a new South, greater and far more prosperous than it had ever been in the days of slavery, gradually came forth from the Civil War and Reconstruction. The slave had been freed. It was almost impossible for the planters to continue in the old way; therefore, many large plantations were divided into small farms. Some of these were worked for wages, while others were rented on the share system. Under this system the Negro tenant received food, tools, and mules from the owner. In return the tenant gave the owner one-half to two-thirds of the crop. This kept him very poor, but it was better than slavery. Many poorer white people were now able to purchase small farms. Cotton remained the chief crop. Large quantities of tobacco, sugar, and rice continued to be raised. On the other hand, new crops put in their appearance. Grains, fruits, and vegetables suited to the Southern climate were produced.

Free labor. Free labor was employed. Modern machinery and methods replaced the wasteful management of the plantations, and the agricultural South became in time more productive than ever. Although additional crops were grown, the production of cotton increased threefold. This proved that cotton could be raised without the aid of slaves.

With the coming of free labor, new industries sprang up in the South. Northern capitalists invested large sums of money in the building of factories. Cotton manufacturing was especially profitable because of the many streams and the nearness of raw material. Lumber camps were developed. Mining also became an important industry because of the large deposits of coal and iron ore.

As industry developed and shipping facilities were improved, modern cities and large manufacturing centers grew up in the South. Gradually the Southern states, which had been so ruined by the war, began to make their way back to prosperity; and the Southern people, in spite of the injustices of the Reconstruction Period, were once again loyal supporters of the Union.

Negro education in the South. The development of the South after the period of Reconstruction was not limited to business alone. Schools were built to educate the Negro. At first these were provided by Northerners, but after a while, the Southern states made educational provisions for the colored people. In the North, the Negroes were permitted to attend the same schools

Booker T. Washington

as white children. In the South, they were cared for in separate schools. Higher schools for the Negroes, like Hampton Institute in Virginia, Howard University in Washington, D. C., Tuskeegee Normal and Industrial Institute in Alabama, Fiske University in Tennessee, and Xavier College in Louisiana have helped many Negroes to become intelligent citizens and leaders of their race.

In the work of educating the Negro, members of the race itself have played an important part. The most outstanding of these was Booker T. Washington who spent his life endeavoring to uplift his people. Born in slavery a few years before the Civil War, he experienced the evils of Reconstruction. He was educated at Hampton Institute and was a member of its faculty for a number of years.

He believed that the Negro should be made self-supporting. He claimed that while the Negro is receiving his education, he should also be trained for work in one of the various trades or occupations. Such practical education would fit him to make better use of the land and to become a leader in his own community. In 1881, he founded Tuskeegee Institute in Alabama in which members of his race could receive such an education. He started without building or equipment, but provided all of this with the aid of his students. His success at Tuskeegee won him national fame among American educators.

Word study

reconstruction	impeached	Black Codes
radical congress	unscrupulous	Grandfather Clause
Carpetbagger	Ku Klux Klan	Amendment
Scalawag	amnesty	Jim Crow law

How well have you read?

1. Explain how the "Solid South" is a natural result of Reconstruction Period.
2. Contrast Lincoln's Plan of Reconstruction with that of Congress. Which was more Christian? Why?
3. Do you think reconstruction should ever be based on revenge and punishment? Give reasons for your answer.
4. Discuss the causes of the origin of the Ku Klux Klan.
5. Do you think it was wise to give the vote to the freed Negroes immediately after the Civil War? Why?
6. Discuss the provisions of the Fourteenth and Fifteenth Amendments.
7. What is meant by the "New South?"

What will your score be?

Copy the terms and names in Column One on your paper. Behind each name on your paper write the letter found before the phrase in Column Two which best matches it.

Column I	*Column II*
...1. Grandfather Clause	a. gave the Negro his freedom.
	b. caused federal troops to be withdrawn from the South.
...2. Fourteenth Amendment	c. called for the arrest of any Negro not working, or wandering about without a home.
...3. Fifteenth Amendment	
	d. deprived the Negro of his right to vote.
...4. Thirteenth Amendment	e. made the Negro a citizen.
	f. gave the Negro the right to vote.
...5. Tenure of Office Act	g. forbade the President to remove a member of his Cabinet without consent of Senate.
...6. Vagrancy Law	

163

CHAPTER II

THE CHURCH AND THE NEGRO IN THE UNITED STATES

What has the Church done for the Negro? In the last Unit we saw that during the days of slavery the lot of the Negro slave depended on his master. Under the law, the Negro was looked upon as "property." He was not free. He was always under the control of someone else. He had little or no hope of rising in the world. He could be punished, sold, or killed. He was regarded as not much more than an animal.

The Church has always been the defender of the weak and downtrodden. In her eyes the Negro is a human being composed of body and soul, possessing mind and free will. He is a child of God and an heir of heaven.

True to her belief that all men are essentially equal in the eyes of God, the Church sees no difference between the white man and the colored man. She knows that one race is not by nature superior to another, because all human beings are descendants of Adam. Consequently, she insists that the Negro should be treated as a brother in Christ and should be given the same basic rights as other men. He should be allowed to earn his living under conditions that will enable him and his family to lead a decent, respectable life.

It is the purpose of this chapter to discuss the work of the Church for the Negro: (1) before the Civil War and (2) after the Civil War.

1. Before the Civil War

The Catholic Church in America has had the care and instruction of the Negro at heart since early colonial days. From the very beginning she saw the injustices of slavery and tried to change them. She tried to protect the slave and to help him win his God-given rights as a human being.

The Church and emancipation. From her centuries of experience, the Church realized that the Negro slave in America was not ready for sudden and complete emancipation or freedom. She weighed both sides of the question. She considered the happiness and security of the Negro and the rights of the Southerner under the Constitution. She thought that gradual emancipation would be fairer and safer for both. **Education of the Negro.** In her wisdom, the Church realized that the best way to advance the Negro and bring him to Christ was to begin with the education of the children. She tried to establish schools and to staff them with Catholic teachers.

Oblate Sisters of Providence. In 1829 the first colored Sisterhood in the United States was founded. Father Joubert, a priest of Baltimore, asked four young colored women to help him instruct the Negro children. These women were anxious to consecrate their lives to God in order to do more good for the colored people. With the approval of the Church, they founded the Oblate Sisters of Providence.

That same year they opened St. Frances School in Baltimore for colored children. This school is known today as St. Frances Academy. For over one hundred twenty years these Sisters have helped thousands of colored children to become better Catholics and citizens.

Sisters of the Holy Family. Another congregation of colored Sisters was founded in New Orleans as a result of an accident.

Miss Alicot, a young white French lady, came to New Orleans to visit her sister. As she was getting off the boat the gangplank slipped and she was plunged into the Mississippi River. She was saved from drowning by a Negro who risked his own life to save hers. Miss Alicot was so grateful that she promised to devote her whole fortune to the welfare of the Negro race.

In 1842 Divine Providence gave her an opportunity to fulfill that promise. She became acquainted with two colored women who wanted to become Sisters in order to work for the betterment of their race. Miss Alicot helped these two women to found the second colored Sisterhood in the United States, the Sisters of the Holy Family.

These sisters taught the colored children their catechism and prepared them for Confession and First Holy Communion. Today they have over twenty schools for training the Negro. They also conduct homes for the aged.

Bishop John England. One of the best friends of the Negro during the days of slavery was Bishop John England of Charleston, South Carolina. The Negroes, both free and slave, were his first care. He loved them and did all he could for their welfare. He taught them and founded schools for them. On Sun-

Bishop England

165

day mornings he would say Mass for the colored slaves. Every Sunday evening the cathedral was reserved for the colored of his flock. Here he instructed them. If, as sometimes happened, he could not preach two sermons, he would disappoint the white people but never his colored congregation.

Bishop England was opposed to slavery, but he did not believe in immediate freeing of the slaves. He thought that hasty action in this matter would do more harm than good to society and to property. There were others, too, who felt the same way. One of these was Bishop Hendricks of Philadelphia, Pennsylvania.

2. After the Civil War

Plenary Councils. "Father of Provincial Councils" is a title often given to Bishop England. He saw the good that could be done if all the bishops of the United States could assemble to discuss the problems of the Church in America. He tried to make this idea come true. Often he suggested it to his archbishop, but nothing could be done at the time. It was not until October, 1829, when the First Provincial Council met, that he had the happiness of seeing his plan carried out. The First Plenary Council of all the bishops of the United States was held at Baltimore in 1852, ten years after the Bishop's death.

The Cathedral of the Assumption, meeting place of the Second Plenary Council of Baltimore

In 1866 a Second Plenary Council was held in Baltimore. That was just one year after the close of the Civil War. During this Council the bishops spent a great deal of time discussing the problems of the freed Negroes. At the close of their discussion they begged for priests from all parts of the country to work among the Negroes. They even sent to Europe for young priests.

Missionaries from Europe. In answer to the call of the Council, the Josephite Fathers came to America in 1871. This society was founded in 1866 at Mill Hill, London, to train priests for the Negro missions. Since their coming to America, these priests have devoted themselves entirely to work among the Negro people.

The Josephite Fathers were not the only ones to accept the invitation of the bishops. Three other groups came from Europe. The Fathers of the Holy Ghost sent priests to Kentucky. The Benedictine Fathers arrived in Charleston, South Carolina, a few years later. In 1881 the Franciscan Sisters came from Mill Hill, London, to work among the Negroes. The Church has been very active in securing missionaries who devoted themselves to the education and conversion of the Negroes in America.

Sisters of the Blessed Sacrament. In addition to the European missionaries, Miss Katherine Drexel of Philadelphia, Pennsylvania, founded the Sisters of the Blessed Sacrament in America. In an audi-ence with Pope Leo XIII Katherine begged the Pope to send missionaries to the poor neglected Indians and Negroes of North America. People Leo XIII looked at Katherine and whispered, "My child, why not become a missionary yourself?" That was enough for Katherine. In 1891 she took the Holy Father at his word and devoted herself and all her wealth to the Indian and Negro missions. Today, in every region of the United States where Negroes are located you will find the Sisters of the Blessed Sacrament laboring among them.

All belong to the Mystical Body. The Church does not distinguish between freeman and slave, between white and black. She ministers to all alike. She brings the same sacraments to both. She looks upon each human being as a member of the great family whose Father is God and whose Redeemer is Christ, the Son of God. And she expects all to help her in her work. She invites the Negro, as well as members of all other races, to the priesthood and the religious life.

In 1888 Father Augustus Tolton, a former slave, was ordained in Rome. He was the first Negro priest in the United States. In our own century Father Stephen Theobald was ordained. Father Theobald was the first colored diocesan priest to be ordained in the United States. He received Holy Orders at St. Paul, Minnesota, in 1910. Many more have been ordained since.

St. Augustine Seminary. The

Fathers of the Divine Word who conduct seminaries for the training of priests for the poor dioceses of the South and the West opened St. Augustine Seminary in Bay St. Louis, Mississippi, in 1920 to train colored priests for the South. Through this seminary, much is being done for the betterment of the Negro.

Do you know of any Negro saints or martyrs?

Through missionaries, churches, schools, hospitals, orphanages, and social workers, the Church has done much for the Negro. But there is still much to be done. In our country alone, there are thirteen million Negroes. Of these only about three hundred thousand are Catholic.

Before and after the Civil War many persons were concerned about the stand of the Catholic Church in regard to Negro slavery and to emancipation. Certain Protestant sects had split on the slavery question. Not all Catholics thought the same about slavery, nevertheless, the Catholic Church was able to uphold her teachings and to remain a united group. Her bishops and priests generally saw the injustices in the system of slavery and tried to change them. They baptized the slaves and gave them the Sacraments — thus showing they were brothers in Christ. Although American Catholic bishops and priests looked upon Negro slavery as wrong, many of them feared that sudden emancipation, or the freeing of the slave, might do more harm than good.

The Second Provincial Council of Baltimore had appealed to priests in Europe and America to work among the Negroes of the South. The call, however, was practically unanswered, for few priests in Europe ever heard of the appeal, and the religious Orders in America had no members to spare for the work. It was not until some time after the war that any considerable missionary work was conducted among the Negroes of the South. We are still suffering because of our failure to convert the Negro.

How well have you read?

1. Why are there so few Negro Catholics in the United States?

2. Discuss the opportunities you have to bring Christ to the Negro through prayer, good example, spreading Catholic literature, and other means.

3. Discuss some ways in which Catholics keep Negroes from becoming Catholics.

4. Discuss the rights and duties of the Negro.

5. Find what other orders besides those mentioned here labor among the Negroes.

CHAPTER III

OUR LAST FRONTIER DISAPPEARS

Looking backward and forward. In Unit Two we saw how a vast army of pioneers moved steadily westward until they reached the Pacific. But contrary to what we would naturally expect, the Pacific coast land was not the last frontier. In the settlements of the pioneers from the Atlantic to the Pacific there was one gap.

About 1840 the eastern edge of the Great Plains was reached. Here for the first time the pioneers met a vast stretch of treeless grassland with few streams and sparse rainfall. As the plains were so different from the forested regions to which the pioneers were accustomed, they passed over some fifteen hundred miles of prairie land and settled the Pacific coastlands.

The Indians of these plains were rather peaceful until 1861. In that year, thousands of miners in their search for gold invaded the hunting grounds of the Indians. After the Civil War, the cowboys and the farmers found other uses for the high plains of the West. The advance of the white settlers, together with the dissatisfaction of the Indians with their treatment by the government, led to trouble.

This chapter will tell about (1) Our Last Frontier; (2) Last Stand of the Indians; and (3) Father de Smet Aids the Indians and the Government.

1. Our Last Frontier

After the exploration of the Louisiana Purchase, the first range of states west of the Mississippi was quickly settled because the geography and the climate were similar on both sides of the river.

Not long after, the Pacific coast became well populated. News of the fertile country of Oregon led stouthearted pioneers across plains and mountains to this region. The discovery of gold, likewise, caused an endless stream of fortune seekers to pour into California. But for a long time the vast region between Missouri and California had been passed over. It was called the "Great American Desert" because it was thought to be a region of barren mountains and dry plains. Nothing grew there except sagebrush, buffalo grass, and cactus. The winds which blew east from the Pacific Ocean dropped their moisture on the western slopes of the high Rocky Mountains. Consequently, when they reached the plains on the eastern side they were so dry that little rain fell. The settlement of such a region seemed impossible. The westward moving pioneers, therefore, passed through this country as quickly as possible on their way to Oregon and California. For some years, therefore, this region remained the home of the buffalo and the Indian.

Two events, however, at the beginning of the Civil War encouraged the development of this region —our last frontier.

The Homestead Act. The first of these was the Homestead Act. All the land of the high plains was public land. It was property of the government. At first the United States sold public land to pioneers at a very low price. But even this low price kept poor people from settling the West.

In 1862, Congress passed the Homestead Act which granted free land to settlers. Anyone over twenty-one years of age could have 160 acres of public land free, if he would cultivate the land and live on it for five years. At the end of that time he became the owner without further cost. Such a piece of land was called a homestead. The Homestead Act opened to quick settlement millions of acres of land that might have lain idle for many years. It was a fair act, because it opened public lands to rich and poor alike.

Railways encouraged development. A dream come true was the second event that helped to people the high plains. Shortly after the Homestead Act was passed, the first continental railroad was begun. Before the Civil War men had thought seriously of linking the East with the West. But at first Congress was opposed to such a project. It considered it a wild venture. In 1862, however, Congress voted money and grants of land to two companies that offered to construct the proposed railroad.

Work commenced during the Civil War. The Union Pacific began at Omaha and pushed westward. The Central Pacific started at Sacramento, California, and worked eastward. Over seventeen hundred miles of track had to be laid over plains, deserts, and mountains. The task was tremendous. Both companies had to build through uninhabited regions. Snowstorms, scorching sun, and hostile Indians were encountered. Food and material had to be brought hundreds of miles. Fortunately, thousands of buffaloes roamed the plains. In order to keep the men supplied with fresh meat the railroad companies hired men to kill the buffaloes. The Indians of the plains watched with hostile eyes the building of the railroad and the killing of the buffalo. To them, it meant the loss of their hunting grounds and eventually starvation. To prevent this, the Indians fought desperately to drive the workmen away. The builders had to be always on guard. At times the men worked with armed troops

Laying track on a railroad in the West

guarding them. At other times, they kept rifles near at hand.

No matter what obstacles were encountered, the railroad building went steadily onward. Mile by mile the two railroads crept closer together. At length the enormous task was accomplished. On May 10, 1869, the two groups met at Ogden, Utah.

The last spike. A crowd had gathered to see the last spike driven in. The last wooden tie was made of laurel wood from California. The rails were fastened to it with spikes of gold from California, silver from Nevada, and iron from Arizona. The sound of the blows which drove in the golden spike had hardly died away when two engines approached from opposite directions. As the two engines touched, the men standing on their cowcatchers shook hands amid the cheers of the crowd.

The work was finished. At last the East and the West were united by steel rails. Telegraph wires flashed the news all over the country. In a few more years there were five railroads crossing the United States to the Pacific, while branch lines led from them to the North and to the South.

The pushing back of the frontier was still far from complete. The early pioneers faced many hardships and dangers before the West was completely settled.

The development of our last

Ready to drive the golden spike at Promontory, Utah, May 10, 1869.
Why is this event important?

frontier was the work of three groups of people: miners, ranchers, and farmers, with the help of their families of course.

Miners open up the mountain country. It was the miners who first led the way to the settlement of the last frontier. When the gold in California gave out, some of the disappointed miners began to wonder if gold might not be found elsewhere in the region. Soon the fur hunters and trappers who first explored these mountains were replaced by the miners. With pick and shovel, they combed the mountains and streams in search of the precious metal.

Gold found in other states. In 1858 gold was found near Pike's Peak in Colorado. As soon as the news leaked out another gold rush was on. Again thousands of fortune seekers hurried to the scene. Denver sprang up overnight. Much of the gold in this region was embedded deeply in the rocks. Expensive machinery was needed to get it out. Many, therefore, who went to Colorado were disappointed and returned East. Some stayed to work the mines and others settled down to farming in the fertile valleys. In this way mining led to the beginning of settlement in Colorado.

The next year, another rich discovery was made in the western part of what is today the state of

172

Nevada. A few years later great deposits of silver were found in the same region. This silver deposit, which is the richest in the world, is known as the Comstock Lode. When word of the discovery spread, thousands swarmed to the place. Within a year it had become a settlement of ten thousand people.

While the Civil War was being waged in the East, gold was discovered in Idaho and Montana. Again thousands of prospectors hastened to the scene. Men, searching eagerly for gold, worked their way northward through the mountain passes and along the river valleys. As a result of their search, gold was found in Wyoming in 1868 and in the Black Hills of Dakota in 1874.

Mining towns. Mining camps sprang up throughout the Rocky Mountain region. Some of these vanished almost as quickly as they appeared. Others grew into villages which in time became large and prosperous cities. Though the miners who inhabited these boom towns were not a very promising or stable population, they did prepare the way for the ranchmen and the farmers.

Ranchers develop the western plains. While the miners made their way into almost every gulch and valley of the mountains in search of gold, cattlemen helped

Cross section of the Comstock Mine in Nevada

Bettmann Archive

A ranch home in the early West

to develop the western plains.

Cattle raising in the United States began in Texas and California. When the buffalo still roamed the western plains, great herds of half-wild cattle grazed over the Texas country. They had such long horns that they were called Texas longhorns. These animals were descendants of cattle which had come from Europe.

Three hundred years before, when the Spaniards settled Mexico, they brought with them cattle and horses. These multiplied rapidly and soon there were immense herds of cattle on the plains of Texas. When American settlers moved into Texas they obtained large grants of land from the Mexican government and started cattle grazing. But for a time, cattle had little value because there was no market for them.

Cattle business grows. After the railroad was built the cattle business began to thrive. In the East and Middle West there was a growing demand for fresh meat. Secondly, during the building of the railroad, the buffalo was killed off. Now cattle could be driven northward over the plains to railroad points called "Cow Towns" in Kansas and Nebraska. The long drive across Indian country was full of danger. But the thought of a market with good prices led the

174

hardy cattlemen to undergo the risk.

During the drive northward, the cattle grazed on the grass of the prairie. At the end of their long journey they were usually fatter than when they started. This taught cattlemen that the pasturage of the northern plains was even better than that in Texas. Ranchers then began to drive their cattle north to fatten them. As the buffalo disappeared, the high plains from Canada to Mexico became a cattle range.

The ranches had no fences, and the cattle roamed freely over the open range. Twice each year, in the spring and fall, the cattle were rounded up for branding. At these round-ups, the cowboys separated the cattle of each ranch from those of the other ranches. It was easy to tell who owned a calf because it always followed its mother, who had already been branded.

The cowboy. Without the cowboy, the open ranches would have been impossible. He was a striking figure with his broad-rimmed felt hat, his heavy shirt and neckerchief, and his trousers tucked into his high-heeled pointed-toe boots.

Every part of the cowboy's outfit had a purpose. The high-heeled boots kept him from slipping from the stirrup. His chaps, or two broad, full-length trouser legs made of heavy calf-skin, which covered only his lower leg and thigh, were worn for protection against cactus,

175

A cowboy

separated the cattle and branded the calves. To do this, they had to be daring horsemen and skillful in throwing the lasso. The lasso was a long rope with a loop at one end. The cowboy had to throw it so that the loop landed around the neck of the animal or caught it around the feet.

After the round-up the long drive north began. Guiding the cattle and keeping them together was hard work. While on the trail, the cowboy's greatest fear was a stampede. The slightest noise at night could frighten the cattle. The whole herd, panting and bellowing, might start running and scatter far and wide. Then the cowboys on their tough, wiry little ponies would have to dash for the head of the herd. Once at the head, they would do everything possible to turn the leaders and start the herd running in a circle. After a stampede or during a storm the cowboys often quieted the herd by singing. Do you know any cowboy songs?

With the invention of barbed wire, the open range came to an end and with it the colorful life of the cowboy.

The rancher's frontier lasted only about twenty years, but it helped to develop the western plains and prepare the way for the settlers.

Farmers settle the high plains. The railroad which made possible the cattle business also helped to bring an end to the open cattle range. After the first continental railroad was completed, thousands of families took up claims under the Home-

thorns, and briers. The bright silk handkerchief loosely knotted around his neck could be pulled up over his mouth and nose and thus protect him against clouds of dust kicked up by the moving herds. His broad-rimmed hat answered many purposes. It shielded him from the rain and the sun. In the winter, it could be tied down so as to keep his ears warm. Gloves, of which he was very particular, a gun, a lasso, and a whip completed his costume. Each of these was so necessary to the work of the cowboy that he could not get along without them.

Life of the cowboy. The life of the cowboy was hard but very exciting. It was his job to keep the cattle from straying away and to protect them from Indians and wild animals. At the round-up, the cowboys stead Act. Unlike the miners and the ranchers, these pioneers came to stay and to raise crops. They put up barbed wire fences around their property to keep the cattle from eating the crops. Soon the prairie was dotted with homesteads surrounded by flourishing farms.

During the time of settling the public lands of the plains, many "land rushes" took place. These were just as exciting as the gold rushes of earlier days. As soon as a tract of public land had been surveyed and divided into sections, the government would announce the date on which it would be open for settlement. On the day appointed, and sometimes days ahead of time, thousands of people would gather at the border. Some were on foot. Others were in carriages, covered wagons, or on horseback. Restlessly they would await the signal which was given by the sound of a bugle or the firing of guns. Then would take place a wild dash to obtain the best land possible. What was once thought to be useless desert plains soon became thriving settlements.

Life of the homesteader. The pioneer farmer of the high plains had many difficulties to overcome. His home had to be made of sod because there were no trees to provide logs for his cabin. He was also confronted with the problem of getting sufficient water. There was enough water underground, but it

Mad dash of early settlers to stake out homestead claims

Brown Brothers

was too deep to be reached by the homemade well of the East. After drilling machinery was invented in 1870, the farmers' problem was partly solved. Then deep wells were drilled and the windmill was used to bring the water to the surface. The windmill was cheap and valuable. It pumped water as long as the wind blew. And the wind on the plains blew constantly.

The homesteaders had still other hardships to endure. In summer there was little protection from the scorching sun and the hot winds. Often there were droughts, cyclones, dust storms, and prairie fires. At other times, there were plagues of grasshoppers which ate everything green in the region. The winters were severe, and wolves and coyotes sometimes destroyed the livestock.

In spite of these difficulties, new farmers kept coming. More and more land was fenced in and the cattlemen were pushed farther and farther westward to the region just east of the Rocky Mountains. Here the plains were too rugged and dry for farming, but could be used profitably for cattle and sheep raising. With the settlement of the Great Plains, the American frontier ceased to exist.

2. The Last Stand of the Indians

The rapid settlement of the plains brought about a great deal of trouble with the Indians. The Western Indians were excellent horsemen. They wanted to roam freely over the plains and supply their needs from the wild herds of buffalo. As they found themselves being pushed farther and farther back, they became restless and angry.

Treaties with the government seemed to be useless. The white people settled where they pleased. It was always the Indian who had to move on. Then too, government agents sent to care for the Indians were not always honest. They cheated the redmen and treated them cruelly.

Indians face starvation. In addition to all this, the Indians saw the buffalo swiftly disappear until few were left. To the Plains Indian this spelt starvation and death. Enraged, he resisted every advance of the pioneer. One Indian attack followed another until the white men, never too friendly to the redmen, learned to hate and to fear the Indian. For years, merciless cruelty and injustices were practiced by both.

When the Civil War broke out, the Sioux Indians decided that the time was favorable to destroy the increasing white settlements of the plains. With the help of arms received from England, they slew nearly a thousand white people. They also destroyed almost two million dollars worth of property. Troops were sent to subdue them.

No matter what the Indians did, they found it impossible to stop the westward advance of the settlers. They were constantly being forced from lands which they had been told would be theirs forever. Finally, driven to desperation by the injustices and mistreatment of the white men, the Indians of the West decided to fight a war to the finish. Both the white men and they would die!

3. Father de Smet Aids the Indians and the Government

It was into this explosive scene that Father de Smet was drawn. Since his first contact with the Indians, almost three decades before, they had never wavered in their loyalty to him. They knew that he would never betray their cause. They fully trusted him. Twice before, at the request of the government, Father de Smet had by his influence put down an Indian revolt. But the peace had been broken, and every time it was the white man who was the offender.

Once again, in 1868, when every Indian tribe in the West was set on war, Father de Smet was sent as ambassador of peace to the Indians. With the rank of major he travelled West with five generals of the United States army.

At first the generals thought that war would be the only way to subdue the Indians. As they hurried west, Father de Smet, however, led them to agree upon peace terms to be offered to the Indians. They were to offer the Indians as their permanent hunting ground a huge reservation in Nebraska Territory extending from the Missouri to the Rocky Mountains. Father de Smet was chosen to negotiate with the Indians.

All realized that peace-making would have to be done little by

little. Each tribe would have to be approached separately before a grand council could be called. The first conference held at Omaha proved to be a success. After that Father de Smet sought out the discontented tribes. He asked the generals to stay behind and follow later. As a missionary, alone and unprotected, he went ahead to invite the hostile Indians to meet the generals at Fort Rice.

On the peace trail. Father de Smet was sixty-eight years old, yet in the midst of the heat of summer, he trudged across the burning plains from camp to camp without a thought of honor or of reward. He only wanted to stop the shedding of blood and to get some justice for his red-skinned children.

Having secured peace promises from the different tribes, he set out across the Bad Lands to find Sitting Bull, the most hostile of Indian chiefs. They all warned him that he was marching to a sure death. But assuring them that Our Blessed Mother Mary would protect him, Father de Smet went on with his search.

On June 18, 1868, Father de Smet came to the camp of Sitting Bull. He unfurled his banner, on one side of which was an image of the Blessed Virgin, on the other the name of Jesus. At the sight of the banner, Sitting Bull and his chiefs were filled with anger. Sensing the situation, Father de Smet assured them that it was not the flag of the United States but a sign of peace. Then the missioner received a warm

Sitting Bull

became common. This time Father de Smet was not there to make peace. He, the greatest friend of the Indians, had died on May 23, 1873.

In 1876 the government sent armies to find the Indian leaders, Crazy Horse and Sitting Bull, and force them to go to the reservation. One troop of two hundred and sixty soldiers under General Custer was trapped by a large body of Indians. In the bloody battle that followed, Custer and every one of his men were killed. This event was followed by other battles between government troops and the Indians. The soldiers in time overcame the Indians. Sitting Bull and some of his warriors escaped to Canada.

welcome from Sitting Bull and secured his promise to attend the council of peace at Fort Rice.

At the meeting at Fort Rice, fifty thousand Indians were represented. Their leaders listened attentively and willingly received the peace terms of a permanent final hunting ground. It was the fourth of July, 1868, when peace was made with the Indians. Father de Smet, happy in the thought that at last peace had been established between the Indian and the white man, travelled back to St. Louis. Now mission work among the Indians could flourish.

The Indians' last stand. Six years later the peace was broken. Gold was found in the Black Hills. Once again white men invaded Indian Territory. Sitting Bull was furious and encouraged his warriors to make a last stand. Fierce battles

Indians become citizens. When the Indian Wars came to an end in 1877, the Indians had been forced to live on large tracts of land called reservations. This policy was not too good. The Indians were used to a free life in the open country and did not like to be confined in this manner. In 1887, therefore, the Dawes Act was passed. This act permitted the reservations to be broken up and each Indian to be given a small farm and in time to become a citizen of the United States. Schools were established to train them to be good citizens.

By 1890 the Indian Wars had ceased, the open range was gone, the day of the Wild West was over, the plains were settled, and our last frontier had disappeared. Finally, in 1924 Congress passed a bill which made all Indians born in the United States citizens.

General Custer makes his last stand against the Indians

The Bureau of Catholic Indian Missions, together with many Jesuit, Benedictine, and Franciscan Missionaries are working to help the Indians. They do all they can to bring the Catholic faith to these people, along with schools, hospitals, and other means to assist them in better living.

Some Indian tribes are entirely Catholic, and about one-third of the Indians are now Catholic. Many others are still pagan.

There are over 200 priests engaged in Indian mission work, aided by over 700 Sisters, Brothers, lay teachers and catechists. This number, however, is very small in comparison with the work to be done.

The federal government has had charge of Indian affairs and has made some efforts to help the Indians. However, its influence for bettering Indian conditions has often been weak, and in some cases has even been unfavorable to the best interests of the Indians themselves.

The work of the Bureau of Catholic Indian Missions and the missionaries can be extended through the help of American Catholics. We should remember that the Indians are our brothers in Christ, and need our efforts for their welfare. Besides, the Indians have often been mistreated. By assisting the work of the Catholic missionaries we can help to remedy, at least in part, some of these injustices.

Terms to understand

prairie	Bad Lands	reservations
high plains	cowboy	"war to the finish"
homestead	round-up	decade
cattle range	brand the cattle	revolt
ranch	citizen	ambassador
continental railroad	stampede	negotiate
frontier	public lands	hostile
Comstock Lode	drought	peace council
		permanent

Points for discussion

1. Discuss with your classmates the importance of natural resources in the development of our last frontier.

2. Was the white man justified in his treatment of the Indian? Give reasons for your answer.

3. Discuss the helps and hindrances in the settling of the Great Plains.

4. Discuss how the Homestead Act and the transcontinental railroad speeded up the settlement of the West.

5. Discuss the greatness of the work of Father Pierre de Smet, S.J., for the Indians, his country, and his God.

6. Would you think that family life helped develop the West?

7. Were the Indians justified in becoming angry when the white men broke their word of honor? Is this a frequent cause of war?

How many of these do you know?

Copy the sentences, filling in the blanks.

1. The high plains between the first range of states west of the Mississippi River and the Rocky Mountains was known as the ....

2. The passage of the .... Act and the construction of the first .... encouraged the development of the plains.

3. The development of our last frontier was the work of three groups of people: the ...., the ...., and the ....

4. The richest silver mine in the world is the .... Lode. It is in the State of ....

5. Cattle raising in the United States began in .... and ....

6. The first cattle and horses were brought to Mexico by the ....

7. The cattle business thrived after the building of the ....

8. The open range came to an end with the invention of .... in 1873.

9. The only white man trusted by all the Indian tribes was ....

10. Most of the Indians of the United States had been moved to .... by 1877.

REVIEW OF UNIT FOUR
Minimum essentials

1. The period of Reconstruction was the time immediately following the Civil War. It was the period when the seceded states were gradually restored to their normal relations to the Union.

2. Lincoln looked upon the seceding states as states in rebellion. As rebels he had power to pardon them.

3. Congress thought that the seceding states had no rights because they were out of the Union. Congress claimed that it had the right to lay down the conditions under which they would be admitted as new states.

4. The three plans for reconstruction of the South were:
   a. Lincoln's Plan:
   Under Lincoln's Plan
   1. Pardon was granted to all (high ranking Confederate officers excluded) as soon as they
      a. took an oath of allegiance to the government of the United States.
      b. agreed to obey the laws that abolished slavery.
   2. The government of a seceded state was to be recognized as soon as 10% of the number of voters of 1860 had fulfilled the above conditions.
   b. Johnson's Plan:
   Often called the Presidential Plan, was similar to that of Lincoln.
   1. Appointed a governor for each seceded state.
   2. Required a convention to be called. This convention was obliged to
      a. repeal the Ordinance of Secession.
      b. ratify the Thirteenth Amendment.
      c. repudiate the Confederate war debt.
   3. Restored all former rights and privileges to any seceded state which complied with the above requirements.
   c. Congressional Plan:
   Placed each state under military control until it would
   1. call a convention which included Negroes.
   2. draw up a constitution which would give the Negroes the right to vote.
   3. ratify the Fourteenth Amendment.

5. Lincoln's plan for reconstructing the South was noble because it was generous, just, and charitable.

6. Reconstruction, as carried out by Congress, was unjust.

7. Lincoln was great because he was humble, fair, sympathetic, had faith in God and in man, and still was not afraid to face the problems of his office.

8. The Thirteenth Amendment freed the Negro.
   The Fourteenth Amendment made the Negro a citizen.
   The Fifteenth Amendment gave him the right to vote.

9. Carpetbaggers were northern politicians who invaded the South after the Civil War and gained power and wealth.

10. Scalawags were Southerners who worked hand-in-hand with the Carpetbaggers for their own benefit.
11. Measures which the North took to protect the Negro and to punish the South:
    Freedmen's Bureau
    Civil Rights Act
    Fourteenth Amendment
    Reconstruction Act
12. Means which the South used to regain control of the government and to prevent the Negro from using his right to vote:
    "Black Code" among which were the Vagrancy Law and the Apprentice Law
    Ku Klux Klan
    Laws which required voter to have the ability to read to own property or pay a poll tax
    Grandfather Clause
13. President Hayes withdrew the last troops from the South in 1877. Then the real work of reconstruction began, partially at the expense of the Negro.
14. New crops and the development of its natural resources brought prosperity to the South.
15. Under free labor the South produced more cotton than with slave labor.
16. Booker T. Washington, a Negro born in slavery, worked for the uplift of his race. He founded Tuskeegee Institute.
17. The Church did very little for the Negroes until some years after the Reconstruction Period because of the lack of priests and Sisters.
18. The Oblate Sisters of Providence and the Sisters of the Holy Family were two congregations of colored Sisters founded to work among the Negroes.
19. The Josephite Fathers came to America in 1871 to work among the Negroes.
20. The Sisters of the Blessed Sacrament, founded by Katherine Drexel in 1891, devoted themselves to work among the Indians and Negroes.
21. The settled region of our country on the edge of the wilderness was known as the frontier. From the settlement of our country until about 1890 the frontier was a shifting zone.
22. Our last frontier was a land almost a thousand miles wide, stretching from Canada to Mexico and from the first states just west of the Mississippi River to the Rocky Mountains.
23. The courage and perseverance of the pioneers overcame all difficulties and opened up the last frontier to settlement.
24. Two events which led to the settlement of the last frontier were:
    a. the passage of the Homestead Act
    b. the construction of the first transcontinental railroad.
25. The development of our last frontier was the work of the miners. the ranchers, and the farmers.
26. Trouble with the Plains Indians was brought about by
    a. the killing of the buffalo
    b. the settling of the plains
    c. the dishonesty and cruelty of some government agents
    d. the breaking of treaties by the white men
    e. the attempt to force the Indian to live on reservations.

27. All Indians in the United States were on reservations by 1877.

28. In this unit we see
   a. the goodness and wisdom of God in storing gold, silver, copper, and other minerals in the mountains for our use.
   b. how men in each region of our country make use of its natural resources.
   c. a spirit manifested by the Indians in their cooperation with Father de Smet.
   d. the influence of the justice and charity of Father de Smet

upon the Indians.
   e. how Father de Smet sacrificed himself for the civilization and salvation of the Indians without any hope of an earthly reward.
   f. the troubles which arise when men are unjust to one another.

29. Father de Smet in his work with the Indians taught us the true spirit of democracy which is based on Christ's command, "Love one another."

Things to do

1. Continue the illustrated time-line begun in Unit One.

2. Prepare and hold a panel discussion on How Just Was the Congressional Plan of Reconstruction? — or — The Hostility of the Indians towards the White Men during the Settlement of the West Was Justified.

3. Show by means of a series of drawings how a seceded state could get back into the Union after the Civil War under the plan of Lincoln and under the plan of Congress.

4. Make dioramas or stage sets portraying incidents of Reconstruction and of the last frontier, such as,
   a. Return of a Confederate soldier
   b. A scene under Carpetbag rule
   c. A Ku Klux Klan escapade
   d. A miner's camp
   e. A roundup
   f. A homestead on the plains
   g. An Indian reservation

5. Make an illustrated chart showing the differences between the

Thirteenth, Fourteenth, and Fifteenth Amendments.

6. Hold a round table discussion on the attitude of the white and colored races towards each other before the Civil War and after Reconstruction. Work out what you would consider a correct code of conduct for each.

7. Make a map showing the location of the various frontiers from 1790 to 1890.

8. Report on the work of the following:
   Father Pierre de Smet, S.J.
   Booker T. Washington
   Freedmen's Bureau
   Work of the Church for the Negro
   An Indian Agent

9. Learn and sing songs of the period, such as,
   The Little Old Sod Shanty
   Oh, Bury Me Not on the Lone Prairie
   or others which can be found in song books, such as, *The Golden Song Book* and *The American Songbag*, by Carl Sandburg.

Association test

Each of the following facts refer to a plan for the reconstruction of the South. Before each fact associated with Lincoln's plan put L. Indicate Johnson's plan with a J; those associated with the Congressional plan with a C.

1. Proposed to follow the plan already formed by Lincoln.
2. Refused to recognize the new government in the states which had seceded.
3. Demanded that all who had taken up arms against the Union take the pledge of loyalty.
4. Questioned the right of the President to restore the seceded states.
5. Refused to allow newly-elected Southern congressmen to be seated in Congress.
6. Planned a Freedmen's Bureau to act as an employment bureau for the free Negroes.
7. Was determined that Negroes have the same rights and privileges as white people.
8. Planned that the Negro who had been given his physical freedom now be given political rights and privileges.
9. Never admitted that the Southern states had left the Union.
10. Punished the states which seceded by suspending for a time certain rights.

Test on terms

On your paper write the numbers from 1 to 15. Behind each number write the term listed below that corresponds with the definition given.

1. Persons who took up land for homes
2. One who explores to find precious metals or minerals
3. Restoring the rights and privileges of the Union to the states which had seceded
4. A mark burned on the hide of an animal with a hot iron to show to whom it belongs
5. Persons who take up arms against the Union
6. Persons who give help to the enemy in time of war
7. The act of gathering all the cattle together
8. An obligation of loyalty which a person owes to his government and to its officers
9. A tract of land which was set aside for the use of the Indians
10. Laws which restricted the liberty of the Negroes
11. A railroad which crosses the country from ocean to ocean
12. An employment bureau for the newly-freed slaves
13. A law allowing settlers to take up free land for homes
14. The act of freeing the slaves
15. Charging a public official with a crime or with the misconduct of his office

allegiance	emancipation	homesteader
Reconstruction	brand	Black Codes
Homestead Act	traitors	reservation
continental	rebels	impeach
round-up	prospector	Freedmen's Bureau

Selection Test

Choose the ending which makes the statement correct.

1. Booker T. Washington was (an educator, a Northerner, a homesteader, a traitor, a general).

2. Political privileges were denied to the (Confederates, Yankees, "Scalawags," "Carpetbaggers," Northerners).

3. The State governments of the South had to be (reconstructed, copied, broadened, kept).

4. The settlement of the West was encouraged by (the friendliness of the Indians, the free land policy of the government, Congress, the Northerners, the Canadians).

5. The state government of the Confederate states was not recognized by (Congress, Southerners, Northerners, Westerners, Lee).

6. A great missionary and friend of the Indians of the West was (Father Isaac Jogues, Father de Smet, John McLoughlin, Father Demers, Bishop Blanchet).

7. Lincoln directed all his energy towards saving the (Union, slaves, Confederacy, North, South).

8. The task of reconstructing the South was (easy, difficult, fairly easy, good, well done).

9. The Northerners were the ("Carpetbaggers," "Scalawags," traitors, rebels, freedmen).

10. The Fifteenth Amendment (freed the slaves, gave the slaves a right to vote, made the Negro a citizen, withdrew troops from the South, deprived Negroes of the vote).

11. The first group of people to prepare the way for the settlement of the last frontier were the (ranchers, miners, settlers, hunters, adventurers).

12. The slaves were freed by (Lincoln, Washington, Lee, Johnson, Grant).

13. A congregation of Negro Sisters founded to work among the colored people is (the Sisters of the Holy Family, the Sisters of the Blessed Sacrament, the Ursuline Sisters, Notre Dame Sisters, Sisters of St. Joseph).

14. A confederacy is a (disunion, league of states, separation, dissension).

15. The Ku Klux Klan was organized to fight (the Constitution, Carpetbag rule, Lincoln, Grant).

Essay test

1. Contrast Lincoln's attitude towards the seceded states with that of Congress

2. Account for the influence that Father de Smet had with the Indians.

Mary's Little Office

HISTORY. The practice of saying the Little Office of the Blessed Virgin Mary arose about the middle of the eighth century at the Benedictine Monastery at Monte Cassino, in Italy. Soon it had spread throughout Europe. Many groups of religious recite it, and it is the official liturgical prayer of most religious orders of women. Lay people also say the Little Office.

THE DEVOTION. The Little Office of the Blessed Virgin Mary consists of seven sections called Hours. They are: Matins, Lauds, Prime, Tierce, Sext, None, Vespers, and Compline. The prayers in these Hours are taken from the Psalms, and other parts of the Bible. There are also hymns, canticles, verses and responses.

Since these prayers are brief, they are called the *Little* Office of the Blessed Virgin.

Separate books or pamphlets containing the Little Office in English enable lay people to join with the Church in honoring Our Lady, and through her, in giving praise to God.

Prayer

VOUCHSAFE that I may praise thee, O Sacred Virgin;
Give me strength against thine enemies.

An indulgence of 300 days, each time. The faithful who devoutly recite the Little Office of the Blessed Virgin Mary, even though bound thereto, may gain an indulgence of 500 days for each hour of the same Office; an indulgence of 10 years for the entire Office; plenary indulgence once a month for daily recitation of the entire Office, on the usual conditions (see "The Raccolta," the official book of indulgenced prayers, page 215).

DEVOTIONAL GIFTS OF MARY. The Little Office is one of seven great devotions given to us through Mary. The other great devotions are the Hail Mary, the Rosary, the Miraculous Medal, the Scapular, the First Saturday Devotion, and the Angelus. Through these devotions you appeal to Mary for the graces which, as Mother of God, she obtains to help you save your soul.

Courtesy of Rev. J. B. Carol, O. F. M.

UNIT FIVE

AMERICA—ONE FAMILY FORMED FROM MANY

UNIT FIVE

AMERICA — ONE FAMILY FORMED FROM MANY

WHEN OUR LAST FRONTIER had vanished, Americans had explored every valley, crossed every plain, and found every mountain pass from the Atlantic to the Pacific. The sons and daughters and grandchildren and great-grandchildren of those first brave immigrants of our country had spread over the entire land and prepared the way for later tides of immigrants from Europe.

An immigrant is a person who enters a country, not his own, to live there permanently. The United States is a land of immigrants. Except for the Indians, every man, woman, and child in this land of ours is either an immigrant or a descendant of immigrants.

The greatest resource of any nation is its people. America is fortunate in her people. For almost four hundred years, men and women from many parts of the world have come to the United States to live. Americans, drawn from many lands, are a capable, intelligent, industrious, and peace-loving people.

A steady stream of immigrants from the countries of northern and western Europe poured into the United States until about 1880. After that date, the number of immigrants not only increased but stemmed from a different source.

Conditions in northern Europe had grown better while those in southern and eastern Europe caused the persecuted, the poor, and the ignorant to flock to America, the land of opportunity. Large numbers came also from the Orient.

During most of the nineteenth century, America welcomed anyone who wished to come to her shores. Even though there had been outbreaks of ill-feeling towards the immigrant, like those of the Nativist and Know-Nothing movements, most Americans realized the value of the immigrant to the United States and all desirable aliens were admitted until about the twentieth century.

CHAPTER I

TAKING GOD'S PEOPLE IN

A glance ahead. Some three hundred years ago America was a vast wilderness. The untiring efforts of people from many countries have made it what it is today. That is what the motto on the official seal of the United States means. *E pluribus unum* or *Out of many, one* tells us that the people of many races and nations make up the population of the United States of America.

The very first immigrants to our country suffered many hardships and overcame many difficulties. They set up laws, formed governments, built homes, churches, and schools, and developed the resources of land and sea. These were the early colonists. Most of them were English, but even at that early date there were scattered groups from other nations living among them. There were Swedes, Germans, French Huguenots, Scotch-Irish, Irish, and a few Italians.

This chapter tells the story of (1) Immigration before 1880 and (2) Immigration after 1880. It also tells how these millions of people who differed in race, creed, and in nationality were one in their love of freedom and their loyalty to-wards the land of their adoption.

1. Immigration before 1880

The only native Americans are the Indians. But the real Americans, those who have cleared our forests, built our cities, developed our industries; in short, who have built America, are not the Indians. They are the millions of immigrants from every part of the world who, through their love of freedom courageously braved the perils of a dangerous voyage and faced the loneliness, the toil, the hardships, and the disappointment of pioneering in a new land to purchase this freedom.

The early immigrants were men of courage and determination. They were energetic and dependent. Without these traits, they would not have sought new homes amid such perils and hardships. Such men had ideals and were determined, if need be, to die for them.

The "old" immigrants. The driving forces which brought the nineteenth-century immigrants to America were not very different from those which impelled the seventeenth-century colonists. A few looked for adventure, but the

Immigrant life below decks on the way to America

great majority sought freedom. Some came to escape starvation; they wanted to find work and improve their condition in life. Others wanted to be free to worship God according to their own beliefs. Still others did not like the government under which they lived; they wanted to get away from the tyranny of selfish rulers and their endless wars.

Most of the immigrants who established the colonies from which our nation sprang and those who organized our government were from the British Isles. For almost a hundred years, people who came to live in our country were chiefly from northern and western Europe.

On the whole they created no real problems, for these immigrants were much like those who first settled here. It was easy to fit them into the population. They became Americans very readily.

. During the Revolutionary War and shortly after, few immigrants came to the United States. There was, however, a steady rise in the number of immigrants between the War of 1812 and the Civil War.

Immigrants from the British Isles. The early settlers in what is today the United States were mainly from England. At the time of the Revolutionary War about ninety per cent of our population was made up of immigrants from England, Scot-

193

land, and Wales. People from these nations continued to come to our country during most of the nineteenth century. Conditions in these countries were crowded and opportunities for work were unfavorable. To better their condition and to be free from religious and political persecution, many came to America.

The Irish, discontented under English rule, found a way to the New World even during colonial times. It was not, however, until the middle of the nineteenth century that immigrants from Ireland came in large numbers.

Irish Immigrants. Around 1840 severe potato famines in Ireland caused many men, women, and children to die of hunger and cold. As conditions grew worse, thousands of Irish people swarmed to the United States seeking relief from starvation and from religious and political persecution.

Most of the Irish immigrants were unskilled workers. They were too poor to buy farms or to open shops. The majority of them found their way into factories or secured jobs constructing railroads, canals, or highways. As a rule, they settled in or near the large cities along the Atlantic coast.

Because the large number of Irish immigrants who landed in New York were Catholic, Archbishop John Hughes felt responsi-

These Irish immigrants have just landed in old New York

ble for them. He noticed that many of them on landing were bewildered. They did not know where to go or what to do. He also learned that many of them were penniless because dishonest officials had taken their money and baggage. To aid these immigrants, Archbishop Hughes organized the Irish Emigrant Society. It was the duty of the agents of the Society to protect and aid the immigrants. Later this Society established the Emigrant Industrial Savings Bank. This bank, which is today one of the outstanding banks in our country, was not only to care for the immigrant's savings, but it was to provide in various ways for his welfare and to help him find employment. Its work was somewhat like that of an advisory board or a guidance clinic.

Tenement life. The Irish Emigrant Society, however, did not help to better the lives of the Irish who lived in the crowded tenement sections of our large cities. There was poverty, misery, and squalor in these slum districts, but the poor Irish people had no other choice. They simply had to make the best of a miserable situation. The majority of them were extremely poor. They had left Ireland because there, too, they had suffered hunger and want. When they arrived here, many of them remained close to the port so that they might be sure to find work.

Despite their wretched condition, they were not easily lured by the free lands of the West. First, they did not have the money necessary

Brown Brothers
The Emigrant Savings Bank

to travel, and secondly, most of them were not farmers. However, having strong Catholic faith, they preferred to remain in the cities near a Catholic church where they could practice their religion.

Between 1848 and 1850, however, Bishop Matthias Loras of Dubuque, Iowa, and Bishop Joseph Cretin of St. Paul, Minnesota, did succeed in helping a large number of these Irish immigrants to settle in Iowa and Minnesota. Furthermore, thousands of them who were employed in constructing railroads and canals eventually settled down and took up farming along the routes which they had helped to develop.

Those who remained in the cities as well as those who went West, soon took a strong interest in politics and government. By the end of

195

the nineteenth century, many of them had entered politics, a field for which they were well suited.

Immigrants from Germany and Scandinavia. In 1848 the German people failed in their attempt to rid themselves of tyrannical rule and to set up a free government. The leaders of the revolution had to flee the country. Many other Germans, realizing that they could not enjoy liberty ·at home, fled to the United States. Between 1840 and 1860 almost a million Germans emigrated to the United States in search of political freedom.

Besides this, the crop failures in southern Germany and the cheap land policy of the United States led thousands of Germans to this country, especially to the northern part of the Mississippi valley.

A large number of the German immigrants were skilled workmen. These found employment in the factories of Eastern states. Others settled in the Midwest and took up farming. Some preferred cities and settled in large numbers in Chicago, Cincinnati, Cleveland, St. Louis, Milwaukee, and other large centers.

Wherever these German immigrants settled, they were a credit to the region. They were thrifty, law abiding, and were trained to be good citizens. Moreover, the Catholics were a credit to the Church for they brought to their new commu-

An old-time German Band. These men are playing in Yorkville, the German section of New York

Brown Brothers

nities deep Catholic faith. They respected and practiced their religion and were always ready to make sacrifices for it.

Scandinavian immigrants. Few people came from the Scandinavian countries of Norway, Sweden, and Denmark before the Civil War. After the passage of the Homestead Act, in 1862, many Swedes and Norwegians left their small, rocky holdings in Scandinavia, to find large fertile farms on our western prairies. A large number of immigrants from Scandinavia arrived in America between 1870 and 1890. The majority of these became wheat farmers in Minnesota, Wisconsin, and the Dakotas. Some became active in the lumber industry of the Northwest. After 1890, most of the government land had been taken and the number of immigrants from these countries gradually declined.

The immigrants from England, Ireland, Scotland, Wales, Germany, and Scandinavia were very much like the early colonists and first immigrants who came to "the land of the free." They quickly adopted the language and customs of their new land and became loyal American citizens.

Native Americanism. As the immigrants grew in numbers, especially the Irish and the Germans, and their churches and schools multiplied, friction was naturally unavoidable.

In BEARERS OF FREEDOM we learned that in the seventeenth century the Puritans tried to purify the Church of England. They wanted to do away with all the ceremonies and devotions that looked like remnants of the days when England was Catholic. When they were not permitted to carry out their plans, they settled in New England and established a church according to their ideas. They believed they had been chosen by God to prevent the spread of the Catholic religion in America. Their reason for coming to America was a hatred of everything Catholic.

As immigrants began coming to the United States in large numbers, there was genuine alarm among the people of the Eastern states. New England had been a Puritan stronghold. New immigrants, especially Irish Catholics, were becoming very prominent in industry, in politics, and in other positions. Their willingness to accept a low wage made it impossible for native Americans to compete with them. Furthermore, the fact that they were Catholics stirred up old Protestant bigotry.

The Native Americans, most of whom were descendants of the Puritans, felt that it was all right for the immigrants to live here, but they did not think they should be allowed to vote or to have anything to do with politics or government.

Riots and bigotry. The jealousy and ill-feeling of these Native Americans towards the immigrants soon led to violence and bloodshed. Writers and preachers attacked the Catholic Church. In 1834 a mob attacked the Ursuline Convent at Charlestown, Massachusetts, in the middle of the night. The nuns and their pupils were forced to leave, and the convent was burned to the ground. During the following days, Catholic churches in other places were set on fire. On these occasions, the fire companies simply looked on and did nothing to help. Irish indignation was aroused, and a few Protestant churches were set on fire in retaliation.

The panic of 1837 helped to increase these bitter feelings. The unemployed blamed all their troubles on the immigrants.

In 1844, riots which lasted three days occurred in Philadelphia. Whole rows of immigrant homes went up in flames. The seminary was set on fire, convents were pillaged, and at least two Catholic churches were burned to the ground. Finally, after thirteen persons had been killed and about fifty wounded, the militia stopped the rioting. In St. Louis and other cities where Irish immigrants were numerous, riots also occurred.

In New York, Archbishop Hughes warded off the mob by warning them that the Catholics would defend their churches and their property.

The Know-Nothings. From this prejudice grew a national party to keep the immigrants in their place. It was a secret organization known as the Star-Spangled Banner party.

A "Nativist" mob, having set fire to a Catholic church, is dispersed by the militia

Its members were pledged to vote only for what they called native Americans. They also tried to raise the period of naturalization to twenty-one years, but they failed to do so. The party was dubbed the "Know-Nothings" because its members, when asked about the purpose or plans of the party, always answered, "I don't know."

The Know-Nothings succeeded in electing a number of candidates to office, especially in 1854, but they could never become a major party because the bulk of Americans rejected such prejudice. When the Civil War came, the party died out and foreigners were more than welcome in the Army and Navy. The large number of immigrants that fought for the Union during the War between the states was a striking answer to the Nativists who had questioned the loyalty of these citizens to the land of their adoption.

The German immigrants as a rule were not attacked by the Nativists and the Know-Nothings. On a few occasions they did come into violent conflict with the Puritans of the West over the joyful manner in which they celebrated Sunday. These conflicts, however, were mild compared to those suffered by the Irish immigrants.

The fact that the Germans as a whole settled more in the West than in the large Eastern cities helped to ward off conflicts. Then too, the Irish in the East antagonized the Nativists by considering themselves full-fledged Americans from the day they landed. On this score the German immigrants gave little cause for complaint. Usually the Germans did not consider themselves entitled immediately to all the privileges of American citizenship.

The Catholic Central Verein of America. The founding of the Catholic Central Verein of America, in 1855, to safeguard German Catholics against the attacks of the Nativists was another means to prevent trouble. Today this organization is firmly established in many states. It is doing much to promote social justice and to foster a strong Catholic faith among its members. It keeps them well-informed through its magazine the *Social Justice Review*. It fosters the establishment of cooperatives and credit unions. Furthermore, it insists that its members, if at all possible, send their children to parochial schools. At all times it encourages the members to be loyal citizens of the United States and faithful children of holy Mother Church.

Groundless fears. The fears of the Nativists and the Know-Nothings that the Catholics were going to conquer and take over the United States were groundless. Although these movements caused riots and persecutions, they did not accomplish much. The immigrants kept right on coming to our land. So much interest in the Catholic faith was aroused that converts entered the Church.

In the end the persecutions helped to strengthen the faith and unity of the immigrants.

2. Immigration after 1880

After 1880 there was a definite change in the national groups that immigrated. Although people from northern and western Europe continued to come to the United States, those from southern and eastern Europe began coming in large numbers. A few persons from some of these countries had settled in Colonial America before the Revolutionary War. At that early date, the Italians and the Polish, though few in number, played an important part in the War for Independence. The flood of immigrants, however, increased until in the early part of the twentieth century it totaled nearly a million a year.

The "new" immigrants. Almost all the free government land had been exhausted by 1880, but railroad building and various industries were developing so rapidly that there was a shortage of labor. It soon became necessary to attract laborers from other countries. For this purpose, many American firms sent agents to countries where the labor supply was plentiful. They told the people about the wonderful opportunities to be had in the United States.

At this time, living conditions in southern and eastern Europe were wretched. These countries were overpopulated. Consequently, there were many more people than jobs. Because they lacked steady employment, their standards of living were at times very low. The people in these countries were, nevertheless, thrifty and hard working.

When they learned that they could get steady work at good wages, they eagerly accepted the proposals of the agents from American firms. People from Russia, Poland, Austria-Hungary, the Balkans, and especially from Italy flocked to the United States in large numbers.

These "new" immigrants from southern and eastern Europe were strong and hardy. Generally, they were unskilled laborers. Many of them found jobs in construction and irrigation projects. Others found their way into mining and lumber camps.

Another group of people that sought admission to the United States at this time were the Jews who lived in eastern and southern Europe. Because they were often persecuted for their religion they came to our country in large numbers. Some of them became tradesmen and shopkeepers while others became active in the clothing industry.

After the discovery of gold in 1849, immigrants from the Orient found their way here. Between 1860 and 1870 thousands of Chinese were brought to the United States to work on the Central Pacific Railroad. The Japanese did not come in large numbers until after 1890. Most of the immigrants from the Orient settled in and around California.

The "new" immigrants presented a problem. The people from southern and eastern Europe faced the same hardships that the "old" immigrants conquered. Most of them

Chinese immigrants working on the construction of a railroad in the West

were poor and illiterate. They were used to hardships and accustomed to low standards of living. They were satisfied to work for low wages. This caused low wage levels in the areas in which they settled.

Like the Irish of the earlier days, these "new" immigrants did not scatter through the country. Most of them stayed in the East and in the industrial centers. Here they lived in groups or colonies. Soon many large cities had a "Little Italy," a "Little Russia," a "Little Hungary," a "Chinatown," or other such foreign colonies.

There was, however, a reason for this massing of people of the same nationality in the slum areas of large cities. The majority of them were poor and could not travel far. Their language, customs, and background were different from those of Americans and the "old" immigrants. It was easier for them to live together in groups with those of their own nationality where they could speak their native language and live according to their customs. Like the Irish and many of the Germans of earlier tides of immigration, most of these "new" immigrants were Catholics. They preferred to stay in those localities where they were sure to find Catholic churches.

National parishes. This desire to be near a Catholic church fre-

These children are playing on a fire escape of a crowded tenement

quently led to the establishment of parishes for the various national groups. In the early days when large numbers of Catholics from the different countries of Europe flocked to our shores, national parishes were a wise thing. Here, these strangers in a strange land felt right at home. They were guided by priests of their own nationality, heard the Faith explained to them in their own language, and attended services which were the same as those in the land of their childhood.

It was never the intention of the Church to establish permanent national colonies in the United States. She merely wanted to prevent the faith of her children from suffering shipwreck and to help her people adjust themselves to the land of their adoption. As long as the United States was a missionary country, national parishes were not only a good thing but they were a necessity. Today, the United States is no longer a missionary country; therefore, Church law provides that there should be no further establishment of national parishes without the consent of the Holy See.

Colonization projects. The Church realized that the immigrants from each country had many characteristics and much cultural heritage to share with the people in the United

States. She therefore tried to preserve much that was good in each nationality while at the same time she endeavored to Americanize these children from various lands.

No one realized better than Bishop John Lancaster Spalding and Archbishop John Ireland the serious problems that would result from the immigrants living together for too long a time in nationality groups. Here they spoke their own language, printed and read their own newspapers, and preserved their national customs. They had little chance of learning American ways of living and, therefore, they found it difficult to adjust themselves to life in the New World.

Furthermore, the tenement houses which they called home were frequently so overcrowded and unsanitary that both the faith and the health of the immigrants suffered.

Bishop Spalding and Archbishop Ireland felt that the faith, the health, and the citizenship of the immigrants would benefit if they could be moved from the large cities of the East to the wide open spaces of the West.

Immigrant settlements. After the Civil War many enlightened bishops and priests worked on plans to settle immigrants, especially the Irish, on farms in the West. In 1876 Archbishop Ireland (then Bishop of St. Paul) established the St. Paul

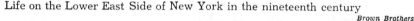

Life on the Lower East Side of New York in the nineteenth century

Catholic Colonization Bureau. He selected a tract of land in Minnesota and arranged with the railroad company that owned the land to give him the sole right for three years to bring in settlers. He built a church, appointed a pastor, and then widely advertised the settlement especially among the Irish of the East.

Later in 1879, the Catholic Colonization Association of the United States was established in Chicago under the leadership of Archbishop Ireland and Bishop Spalding, who became its first president. In this project, the railroad companies and the land agents showed a fine spirit of cooperation.

In all these colonization projects every effort was made to induce the immigrants to leave the crowded cities of the East and to go West where they could enjoy clean healthful surroundings. Besides material assistance, Catholic churches and schools were built and priests were appointed to care for the spiritual needs of the immigrants.

Cardinal Gibbons. No one worked harder than Cardinal Gibbons of Baltimore to make good Americans of the immigrants. He did everything in his power to show them the meaning of our American institutions. At the same time, he endeavored to show all Americans, Catholics and non-Catholics, that the Church is not a "foreign" church, but that it belongs to every country, America included. He wanted Americans to see and understand that Catholicism as a religion fosters and protects the free institutions of this country.

Like a true son of the Catholic Church, he always acted on the principle that the bonds of religion bind every Catholic to the Holy Father and at the same time strengthen the bonds of patriotism that bind him to the President of the United States.

In order to aid the many Catholic immigrants who came to our shores, the Bishops of the United States established the Bureau of Immigration as a part of the National Catholic Welfare Conference.

This Bureau meets and helps immigrants at the various ports where they enter the United States. It refers immigrants to the various agencies in the Catholic dioceses in which they will live, and serves as a clearing-house for problems

Cardinal Gibbons

connected with immigration.

The main purpose of the Bureau is to protect the Catholic immigrant's faith.

The Bureau has offices in New York, Washington, and Texas.

Through its contacts in foreign countries, the Bureau is enabled to protect immigrants upon arrival in America, to reunite separated families, and to assist the foreign-born of all nationalities.

These activities show how the Church always has the welfare of her people at heart, and is helping immigrants to become good American citizens.

As a result of such agencies as the Bureau of Immigration, the lot of the immigrant is much improved over what it was many years ago when the great tides of people began to flow into our country from Europe.

Terms to know

immigrant	bigotry	emigrate
immigration	cooperatives	immigrate
"new" immigrants	credit unions	Nativists
"old" immigrants	tenement houses	Know-Nothings
race	British Isles	militia
creed	Scandinavia	overpopulated
nationality	slum districts	cultural heritage
riots	policies	nineteenth century

How well have you read?

1. The Church states that a good Catholic is a good citizen.
2. Does the Church mean, therefore, that the Church and the state should be united? Give reasons for your answer.
3. Who were the Nativists and the Know-Nothings? Discuss their real purpose.
4. Discuss the work of Archbishop John Ireland, Bishop John England, Bishop John Lancaster Spalding, Bishop Matthias Loras, and Archbishop John Hughes for the immigrants.
5. Discuss the advantages and disadvantages of national parishes.

Test yourself

Match Column I with Column II.

Column I

...1. "old" immigrants
...2. German immigrants
...3. Scandinavians
...4. "new" immigrants
...5. Indians

Column II

a. only *real native* Americans.
b. Norwegians, Swedes, and Danes.
c. people from Great Britain, Germany, Ireland, and Scandinavia.
d. people from southern and eastern Europe.
e. Catholic Central Verein of America.
f. Catholic Colonization Association of the United States.

CHAPTER II

OUR IMMIGRATION POLICY—CHRISTIAN OR PAGAN?

Are we Christians? For a long time the door of America stood open. People from all lands were welcome. Millions entered and found in the United States a land of refuge and opportunity. It is true that there were several movements to save America from the foreigner and that during these times the cry "America for Americans" was heard on all sides. But for the most part, Americans for many years lived these noble words inscribed on the base of the Statue of Liberty:

Give us your tired, your poor,
Your huddled masses yearning
   to breathe free,
The wretched refuse of your
   teeming shore.
Send these, the homeless, tempest-tossed to me!
I lift my lamp beside the golden door.

Since 1882, however, our reputation for welcoming the poor, the oppressed, and the ambitious is not so commendable. Some persons and groups of persons began to fear that too many immigrants were coming to our shores at one time. They thought that the task of Americanizing this large number of newcomers would be impossible.

In this chapter we will learn how (1) Immigrants Become Citizens; (2) Immigration Is Restricted; and (3) Contributions of the Immigrants.

1. Immigrants Become Citizens

In the last chapter we learned that the fears of the so-called "Native" Americans were more imaginary than real. Both the Irish and the Germans who came in such large numbers fitted into the patterns of American life without too much difficulty. As long as there were wide open spaces in the West, Americanization was not a real problem.

Americanization. Every immigrant who wishes to be useful to his adopted country must become a loyal citizen. To be a good citizen, he must learn the English language, the ideals of our government, and the rights and duties of a citizen. The United States does not want to make all Americans alike; therefore she does not believe that the immigrants should be absorbed in the mass. She believes that the immigrant should share his customs and traditions rather than forget and discard them, that he should be trained to take an intelligent part in American political life, and that he should be helped to fit himself into American social ways and habits. That is Americanization.

Many agencies were established to help Americanize the adult immigrant. Many schools, churches, and clubs conducted evening classes. At times factories held special classes during the noon hour or after work. Here the immigrant had an opportunity to learn our language, our history, our ideas of government, as well as the duties of a good citizen. Other helps for self-education are the library, the radio, the newspaper, lectures, and contacts with true Americans.

Americanizing children. To Americanize the children of immigrants is an easy task. At school they are taught how to speak, read, and write our language. They also learn our history and our ideas of government. In a very short time they are Americans at heart. They love their new land.

Knowing that the healthy development of a nation depends upon a united people, the Catholic Church endeavors to teach the immigrant as well as the native citizen the principles of American citizenship. Many of her colleges and organizations conduct classes for these new Americans. The National Catholic Welfare Conference has

This Americanization class is learning how to vote

published material on this subject, such as *The Civic Catechism, Fundamentals of Citizenship,* and the Bureau of Immigration of The N.C.W.C. also helps immigrants who come to this country. The Church also encourages social work under the direction of Catholic organizations especially in immigrant areas.

We all have the duty to help in the work of Americanizing the immigrant. We can do this if we are *tolerant.* That is if we are patient, understanding, and sympathetic and do not act as if we think ourselves better. This will be easy if we remember that we all are immigrants or the descendants of immigrants. America is what it is today because of the energy, the abilities, the ambition, and the ideals of our immigrants in the past.

Naturalization. To become a citizen of the United States an immigrant must go through a procedure called *naturalization.* This process requires that the immigrant fulfill four conditions. They are:

1. He must be at least eighteen years of age.

2. He must have lived five years in the United States.

3. He must pass a simple test in American history and government.

4. He must take an oath of allegiance to the United States.

Swearing in applicants for citizenship papers

When he takes the oath of allegiance to the United States he says:

"I do hereby declare on oath that I will support and defend the Constitution and laws of the United States of America against all enemies, foreign and domestic, and that I will bear true faith and allegiance to the same, so help me God."

These are serious words. Since we are all citizens of the United States, these words also apply to us. Read the oath thoughtfully, then ask yourself how faithful you have been in living up to it.

2. Immigration is Restricted

As time went on and people from other countries continued to come in large numbers, many Americans thought that something should be done to control and regulate immigration. Some claimed that it was impossible to Americanize the immigrants when they came so rapidly. Others feared that the immigrants would take the jobs of Americans or that they would lower our standards of living. Still others were of the opinion that Chinese and Japanese could not be fitted into the pattern of American life.

First restrictions. Our first laws restricting immigration affected "undesirables" and Orientals. In 1882 Congress passed a law forbidding insane, diseased, or criminal *aliens* to enter the United States. This same law excluded paupers and those that might stir up revolt or trouble.

After gold was discovered in 1849, many Chinese came to California. Later, Chinese laborers were brought to the United States to work on the continental railroad. At first these immigrants from the Orient were welcome. After the Civil War, the Chinese came in such large numbers and they were willing to work for such low wages that the people of California became alarmed. They petitioned Congress to keep the Chinese from coming to their state. In 1882, therefore, Congress passed a law which forbade the immigration of Chinese to the United States. Only Chinese students and merchants were permitted to come to our country under certain conditions for a short period of time.

About the year 1900, the people of California became excited over the large number of Japanese who were buying and leasing farm and fruit lands. They asked to have the Japanese excluded. President Theodore Roosevelt did not want to offend the Japanese, so in 1907 he made a "Gentleman's Agreement" with Japan. Under this agreement Japan promised to keep her laborers from coming to the United States. At the same time we promised not to pass an exclusion act against the Japanese. Japan kept her promise. Our immigration law of 1924, however, excluded Japanese as well as Chinese and all members of the yellow race.

Later restrictions. In the beginning of the nineteenth century, demands came from many parts of the

Japanese workers planting trees in California

United States for the restriction of immigration. There were, however, just as many people who thought that we should keep up our glorious tradition of being a harbor of refuge for the persecuted and downtrodden of all lands. Finally, in 1917, those in favor of restriction had their way. Congress passed a law which required a "Literacy Test." All immigrants desiring to live permanently in the United States had to be able to read English or some other language. This law had far-reaching effects. Now only those immigrants who had some education could enter the United States.

Results of World War I. After World War I, war-stricken Europe was in a very bad condition. Most of the countries were ruined financially. Heavy taxes were unavoidable. Since it was hard to get a job, it was feared that many of the people would want to come to the United States to escape the heavy taxes and to have an opportunity for employment. It was felt that the United States was in no position to receive large numbers of immigrants. Her returning soldiers would need jobs. Many of her own workers were now jobless due to the slowed-down conditions following the War. To protect the country from a deluge of immigrants that would be larger than the United

States could handle, Congress passed the "3% Quota Law" in 1921. This reduced immigration considerably but it did not satisfy all.

Finally in 1924, a law was passed by Congress which excluded all immigrants from Asia and limited the total of all other newcomers to 150,000 a year.

This legislation is often called the "2% Quota Law" because between 1924 and 1929 any country could send to the United States as many immigrants as equalled 2% of the number of people of that nation who lived in the United States in 1890. This law favors immigrants from western and northern Europe, and discriminates against the others.

There is no limit placed on the number of immigrants that may come to the United States from any country in North or South America. Out of respect for China who was our ally in World War II, Congress passed a law permitting Chinese to come to the United States on the quota basis.

Restriction of immigration — how Christian? It is always important to keep out undesirables and those who would destroy our government or way of life. Many people, however, think it is unwise to restrict immigration as America has done since 1924. First of all, our nation has become and still is great because of the contributions of people from many lands. Thinking men and women feel that it is not Christian nor democratic to deny certain people the right to settle in America. Furthermore, Europe, as well as some Asiatic countries, is overcrowded. Living conditions in these countries are becoming more cramped year after year. There are many, however, who continue to fight for restriction of immigration because they feel that a still larger influx of immigrants would cause more unemployment. Others insist that we have no room for a larger population.

None of these reasons really excuses us from helping the distressed of other countries. An increased population would not only increase employment because of the added necessities, it would also make us greater in the eyes of other countries. Then, too, the number of people per square mile in the United States is about one third of the number per square mile in Europe.

We are Christians or followers of Christ. Christ gave reasons for a heavenly reward when He said: "For I was a stranger and you took Me in," and again, "What you have done to these the least of My brethren, you have done to Me." The real test of charity is not only to feed the hungry and to clothe the naked, but to give the needy a chance to get a new start in life. Christ will reward our nation according to its charity, justice, and mercy.

Should America once more live the inscription on the base of the Statue of Liberty? Should she give the needy of the world a chance to get a new start in life?

3. Contributions of the Immigrants

The gifts of the immigrants are many and varied. Without their strength and numbers the United States could never have grown so rapidly. The vast influx of immigrants during the nineteenth century made possible the development of the West, the progress of our industries, the construction of canals, railroads, and highways. Their alert minds and strong arms have helped to make our country great.

No other nation has ever had the wonderful opportunity the United States has had to develop and enrich herself from the heritage of all lands and peoples. The immigrants brought with them their characteristics, their customs, their abilities, their ideals, and their love of music and art. For over a hundred years there has come to our shores a continuous stream of intelligent and alert people, eager to use the opportunities which the land of the free had to offer them.

Culture and civilization. The culture and civilization of Europe which the immigrants brought with them to the new world have been reshaped into new ways of living. Even the characteristics of these people from the old world have undergone a change. When people of many nationalities live together they learn from one another and benefit by the contributions of each nation.

People born in America lived side by side with people from other lands. Their children played together and when they grew up, married. As time went on there were in America men and women who were part English, German, Irish, or some other nationality. As the people of different nationalities continued to intermarry there came into being the typical American— one whose blood comes from many nationalities.

Each of these nationalities contributed much to the true American character. The shrewdness, quick wit, and ready humor of the Irish, plus the lightheartedness and quick temper of the Italians have been modified by the law-abiding qualities of the English and the industry, thrift, and dependability of the Germans and Scandinavians.

Later immigrations of Slavs and people from southern and eastern Europe added other characteristics. These people were simple, docile, and calm. Furthermore, they had a strong bond of family life and a reverence for authority.

Immigration caused an enormous growth in the Catholic Church. Practically all the Irish, about half of the Germans, and almost all of the people from southern and eastern Europe were Catholics.

Before long even the religious tone of the nation was changed for the better. The simple Catholic faith of the Germans tempered the sad and gloomy character of Puritanism. Later the childlike faith and trust of most of the people who came from southern and eastern Europe further helped to replace the coldness and fear of the Puritan idea of religion with the warmth and love of Catholicism.

The immigrants brought not only themselves, their religion and their labor, but they brought many other valuable gifts to America. Their literature, their songs, their dances, their games, their ways of cooking, and their ideas about education, science, art, and music have made our national life richer.

Contributions of immigrants from the British Isles. The thirteen colonies were settled chiefly by people from Great Britain. As these early immigrants were too busy setting up a new nation in America, most of the cultural and scientific contributions were made later by people from other nations.

Since the majority of the early settlers were English, our language, our form of government, and our system of courts were patterned on those of England. The influence, however, of the early Scotch-Irish and German immigrants, who had pushed into the interior, helped to establish the idea of equality before the law and representation based upon population.

Many of our industries, especially the cotton mills and iron-works, were organized and developed by the English immigrants.

Some outstanding persons of English descent are George Washington, the first President of the United States; Richard Hoe, the in-

Scene in an American law court. Identify judge, witness and jurors

ventor of the rotary printing press; and Louise Imogen Guiney, a Catholic poet. Alexander Graham Bell, the inventor of the telephone; Patrick Henry, a leading patriot; and Andrew Carnegie, a great philanthropist and steel maker, were of Scotch-Irish descent. Elihu Yale, a leading American educator; and Thomas Jefferson and Abraham Lincoln, both great Presidents of the United States, were of Welsh descent.

Irish immigrants. The Irish, because of their ability to manage people, soon climbed to the top of several professions. Many of them became successful businessmen, politicians, and lawyers. Others swelled the ranks of the priesthood. The warm human touch of the Irish made them successful as teachers, salesmen, foremen, contractors, and leaders of labor unions. Likewise, their imagination, humor, and keen insight into human nature made them successful in journalism and literature.

Both Archbishop John Ireland and Bishop John England, two great leaders of the early Church in America, were born in Ireland. A few of the many notable Americans of Irish descent are Cardinal Gibbons, who labored so untiringly for the upbuilding of a strong Catholicism and a strong America; John Barry, "Father of the American Navy"; Robert Fulton, inventor of the steamboat; Alfred E. Smith, a staunch Catholic, former governor of New York and candidate for President of the United States; George P. A. Healy, the portrait painter; Augustus Saint-Gaudens, a famous sculptor; Victor Herbert, a musician and composer; and Catholic poets like Father Abram Ryan, Father John B. Tabb, Arthur J. Riley and Joyce Kilmer. Christopher Colles, an engineer, planned the waterworks system of New York.

Contributions of the German and Scandinavian immigrants. The Germans and Scandinavian immigrants turned many of the waste lands in the West into thriving farms and prosperous towns. The keen interest of the Germans in a sound school system led to a modified form of the Prussian system of education being introduced into the United States. In fact German remained in the curriculum of many American school systems un-

Father Abram Ryan

An old gymnasium of a German Turnverein in Brooklyn

til World War I. One of the most unique and lasting of the German contributions to American education was the kindergarten.

These immigrants taught us many things. They were skilled in mechanics, furniture making, science, and medicine. It was the German immigrants who raised our standards in medicine by bringing to the United States the trained pharmacist.

Many of the Germans were trained musicians. The *Turnvereins* or clubs formed among the German immigrants in America did much to keep alive their national love of music and sports.

Our American observation of Christmas grew from German customs. In Puritan New England, Christmas was not celebrated. Even after the middle of the nineteenth century places of business throughout the United States closed on Christmas only in the German sections of the cities. In the southern part of the United States Christmas was a day of rowdyism. It was celebrated in a manner similar to that of Hallowe'en, while in parts of the West and Midwest it was celebrated like the fourth of July.

The religious observance of Christmas in this country originated with the German immigrants. The Germans also introduced the Christmas tree and giving gifts.

Christmas tree in a modern home

Some famous Americans of German descent are Reverend Isaac T. Hecker, founder of the Paulists and originator of the *Catholic World* magazine; Walter Damrosch, musical composer and conductor; Baron Von Steuben, organizer and drill master of Washington's army; Admiral Chester W. Nimitz, Dwight D. Eisenhower, President of the United States; and Charles P. Steinmetz, a noted scientist.

Among the Scandinavians, John Ericsson, the inventor of the iron-clad *Monitor*, and Professor A. J. Carlson, one of America's greatest scientists, were born in Sweden. Jacob Riis, who fought for better living conditions in America, was from Denmark.

Contributions of the "new" immigrants. Many of these later immigrants overcame the difficulties and discrimination which confronted them and became leaders in industry, business, professions, and government.

Columbus, an Italian, was the discoverer of America. Many early missionaries were Italians. Father Mazzuchelli, an Italian, was one of the greatest pioneers of the Northwest. Father Venuta, an apostle of Italian immigrants, and Mother Cabrini, a canonized saint, labored unceasingly for the good of the Italian immigrants.

Brumidi, an Italian and a Catholic, has been called the "Michaelangelo of the Capitol" because of his frescos in the Capitol. Of the many Italian immigrants renowned for their sculpture, Attilio Piccirilli holds first place today. Ciseri, an Italian Catholic, organized the first orchestra in the United States.

John Ericsson

In Italian opera and music we have Arturo Toscanini, conductor, and Enrico Caruso, the great singer. Joe DiMaggio, a prominent baseball player, is just one of the many descendants of Italian immigrants who has won fame in American sports, while Vincent Impelliteri is the mayor of New York City.

The many musicians among the later immigrants from Germany and the eastern countries of Europe made possible our famous opera houses and concert halls. These countries furnished leaders in all lines: poets, artists, scientists, and statesmen. The Jews have given us some of our leading bankers, lawyers, and merchants.

The Slavic Countries. Of the many Slavic peoples that have come to the United States to live about one-half have come from Poland, Bohemia, and Croatia. People from each of these nations as well as from the other Slavic nations have become leaders in America. A few of these are Pulaski and Kosciusko, fighters for freedom in the American Revolution; Leopold Stokowski, a famous conductor of the Philadelphia Symphony Orchestra; Artur Rodzinski, a famous conductor of the New York Philharmonic Symphony Orchestra; Michael Pupin, a great American scientist; Igor Sikorsky, an airplane builder; and Rudolph Friml, composer of light operas.

Immigrants or their descendants from practically every nation have risen to the top. Among the Americans of Jewish descent who have

Artur Rodzinski

become famous are Haym Solomon, a banker of Philadelphia who spent his fortune to further the American cause during the Revolutionary War; Walter Lippmann, newspaper columnist; Eddie Cantor, comedian; Herbert H. Lehman, one time governor of New York; and Albert Einstein, a refugee from Nazi Germany, and an eminent mathematician.

Immigrants have influenced our menus. Even the method of preparing food in America has been enriched by the achievements of the nations from which our immigrants have come. In practically every large city of the United States one can find restaurants which provide Italian spaghetti and ravioli, foreign cheeses; German dishes such as wieners, sauerkraut, *hasenpfeffer*, coffee cake, cole slaw, potato

Herbert Lehman

clude recipes for dishes from all nationalities.

Then too, the very language we Americans speak has grown out of the language of the immigrants. *Cigar, gala, barbecue, alfalfa,* are derived from Spanish terms. *Bush leaguer,* used in American baseball slang, originated from the German. *Bouillon* and *bouquet* are French. How many other words can you think of that we have borrowed from other nations?

The Church and the immigrant. During the latter part of the nineteenth century the Catholic Church in America practically doubled its membership as a result of immigration. There were Catholics among the English colonists in America, but their numbers were few. The first great increase in the membership of the Catholic Church in the United States came with the purchase of Louisiana in 1803. About one hundred thousand Roman Catholics were added to the population of the United States at that time. With the annexation of Texas and with the acquisition of our southwestern states through the Mexican Cession other members were added.

salad, dill pickles, and pumpernickel. Scattered throughout these cities are the typical Chinese restaurants. Again one can find many little Bohemian shops that provide their famous pastry which includes delicious cakes. Then, too, eating places conducted by Czech and other Slavic peoples provide such native dishes as roast goose and duck, pork and dumplings, and cakes with almonds and poppy seeds. Dumplings and crullers are popular in Polish restaurants. From the Dutch communities we can obtain Edam cheese, smoked beef, rusks, rye bread, and currant bread. To this day French cooking is held in high esteem. Omelettes, croquettes, and French wines are on almost all menus in America's largest hotels and restaurants. In fact American cookbooks today in-

None of these additions, however, could begin to compare with the influx of Catholics into the United States after 1840. After this time, Catholic religious orders, especially in Germany, sent scores of men and women to open schools, hospitals, and charitable institutions in the United States. During the persecutions in Germany many priests immigrated to the United States.

The Catholic Church in the United States could never have grown so rapidly without this large number of immigrants. The immigrants were happy to find the Catholic Church already established in this country and did all in their power to further develop her churches and institutions.

On the other hand these immigrants were fortunate to have the Church. Her bishops and priests were on hand from the very beginning to aid them in adjusting themselves to life in a new country and to encourage them to become "Americanized."

Word study

Christian	Puritanism	aliens
citizen	*Turnverein*	Orient
"Native" Americans	influx	distressed

How well have you read?

1. Would you say that the immigration policy in America is Christian?
2. Should the United States follow the pattern for happiness set up by Christ and make the Works of Mercy part and parcel of her life as a nation?
3. Should America go further and reject the materialism of the world that ignores God for the almighty dollar and pleasure, and pattern her ideals on the Beatitudes?
4. Find and discuss the contributions made by the immigrants from the nations represented in your classroom.
5. Discuss the benefit of the Church to the immigrants and the benefit of the immigrants to the Church.

Test yourself

I. Arrange the following measures restricting immigration in the order in which they took place.

...2% Quota Law
...Literacy Test
...Chinese Excluded
...Gentlemen's Agreement

...Chinese permitted after World War II
...3% Quota Law

II. Each of the items below is associated with either the "old" immigrants or the "new" immigrants. Arrange two columns on your paper. Head the first column "Old" Immigrants and the second "New" Immigrants. Then copy each item in the proper column.

religious observance of Christmas
our form of government
slow to become Americanized
easily Americanized
our language
organized first symphony orchestra
custom of giving gifts at Christmas

developed waste lands of United States
leading bankers and merchants
artists and musicians
trained pharmacists
made possible our opera houses and concert halls

1. The United States has much more land and many more resources than she needs for her population. Christian charity should prompt her to aid the overcrowded nations of Europe and Asia.

2. God intended the goods of the earth to be shared by all.

3. Christ said, "As long as you did it for one of these, the least of my brethren, you did it for me" (Matt. 25:40).

4. The real test of charity is not only to feed the hungry and to clothe the naked, but to give to the needy a chance to get a new start in life. We, as a nation, should practice charity, justice and mercy to all regardless of race, color, creed, or nationality.

5. An immigrant is a person who enters a country, not his own, to live there permanently.

6. The only native Americans are the Indians.

7. Every person, other than Indians, in the United States is an immigrant or a descendant of immigrants.

8. Most of the immigrants before 1880 came from the British Isles, Germany, and Scandinavia.

9. The majority of immigrants after 1880 came from southern and eastern Europe.

10. Immigrants came to the United States for many reasons, chiefly to better their condition and to be free from religious and political persecution.

11. Archbishop John Hughes organized the Irish Emigrant Society to protect and aid the immigrants.

12. Bishop Joseph Cretin of St. Paul and Bishop Matthias Loras of Dubuque helped many immigrants to settle in Iowa and Minnesota.

13. The Star-Spangled Banner party was a secret organization to prevent foreigners and Catholics from holding any political office.

14. This party was dubbed the Know-Nothings because its members always answered "I don't know."

15. The Catholic Colonization Association of the United States was established under the leadership of Archbishop John Ireland and Bishop John L. Spalding.

16. The purpose of this colonization project was to induce the immigrants to leave the crowded cities of the East to go West.

17. Cardinal Gibbons worked untiringly for the Americanization of the immigrants.

18. Immigrants should not be absorbed by the masses. They should share their customs and traditions.

19. America is what it is today because of the energy, the abilities, the ambition, the ideals, and the contributions of the immigrants.

20. The process of naturalization requires that the immigrant fulfill four conditions.
    a. He must be at least eighteen years of age.
    b. He must have lived five years in the United States.
    c. He must pass a simple test in American history and government.
    d. He must take an oath of allegiance to the United States.

Something to do

1. Make a map, chart, or graph comparing the "old" immigration with the "new" immigration. Be sure to show:
   a. countries from which they came
   b. Dates
   c. Approximate numbers
   d. Occupations
   e. Section of the United States in which they settled
2. Prepare and hold a panel discussion or a round table discussion on the question: *"How Christian is the Immigration Policy of the United States?"*
3. Make a chart showing the gifts of the immigrants from the different countries of Europe to the United States.
4. Make a graph showing the nationalities represented in your class.
5. Give an illustrated lecture which will tell the story of immigration. Use for this purpose either slides or charts that have been made by members of the class.

6. Prepare and present to the class a report on one of the following:

Carl Schurz
Michael Pupin
Albert Einstein
Isaac T. Hecker

Cardinal Gibbons
Leopold Stokowski
Bishop Matthias Loras
Archbishop John Ireland

John Ericsson
Mother Cabrini
Costanzo Brumidi
Joe DiMaggio

MASTERY TEST

I. Multiple-Choice Test

Number your paper from 1 to 15. Behind each number write the letter found before the word or group of words which best completes the statement.

1. Most of the Irish immigrants who came here after 1840 were
   a. skilled laborers
   b. unskilled laborers
   c. artists
   d. engineers

2. After 1880 immigration from northern and western Europe
   a. increased slightly
   b. increased rapidly
   c. decreased
   d. was excluded

3. After 1880 most of the immigrants came from
   a. southern and eastern Europe
   b. southern and western Europe
   c. northern and western Europe
   d. northern and eastern Europe

4. The Scandinavian immigrants settled chiefly in the
   a. Western states
   b. North Central states
   c. Eastern states
   d. Southern states

5. The *Literacy Test* requires that no immigrant be admitted to the United States unless he knows how to
   a. read English
   b. read his native language
   c. read some language
   d. speak English

6. There is no restriction on immigrants from
   a. Europe
   b. North and South America
   c. Asia
   d. Japan

7. The *Gentlemen's Agreement* was made with
   a. China   c. Japan
   b. Italy   d. England
8. An immigrant becomes a citizen of the United States when he
   a. applies for his second papers
   b. enters the country
   c. takes the oath of allegiance
   d. applies for his first papers
9. The largest number of Catholic immigrants before 1860 came from
   a. Germany
   b. Ireland
   c. Italy
   d. France
10. Most of the "new" immigrants were from
    a. Catholic countries
    b. Protestant countries
    c. countries with no religion
    d. Communist countries
11. The bigotry of the Know-Nothings was directed chiefly against
    a. German Catholic immigrants
    b. Irish Catholic immigrants
    c. all immigrants
    d. Italian Catholic immigrants
12. The first immigrant restrictions were against the people from
    a. Europe   c. China
    b. Japan   d. South America
13. The only *native* Americans are
    a. Nativists
    b. Indians
    c. Early colonists
    d. Puritans
14. The reasons which brought the immigrants to the United States during the nineteenth century were
    a. very different from those of the sixteenth-century colonists
    b. not very different from those of the sixteenth-century colonists
    c. different from the sixteenth century colonists
    d. same as those of the sixteenth century colonists
15. The *Irish Emigrant Society* was founded by
    a. Archbishop John Ireland
    b. Bishop John L. Spalding
    c. Archbishop John Hughes
    d. Bishop Matthias Loras

True-False Test

The italicized word or phrase in each item below makes the statement true or false. If the statement is true, write "True" on the line to the right; if the statement is false, make it true by writing the correct word or phrase on the line to the right for the one italicized.

1. The Irish Emigrant Society was established by *Cardinal Gibbons*.   1..........
2. The majority of the "old" immigrants came from *southern and eastern Europe*.   2..........
3. The first people to be excluded from the United States were the *Chinese*.   3..........
4. Most of the Irish immigrants settled in the *West*.   4..........
5. A large number of the German immigrants were *skilled* workmen.   5..........
6. The German immigrants as a rule were not attacked by the *Ku Klux Klan*.   6..........

222

7. The "new" immigrants were used to *high standards* of living.

7..............

8. Most of the "new" immigrants were *Protestants*.

8..............

9. The first president of the Catholic Colonization Association of the United States was *Archbishop Ireland*.

9..............

10. *Cardinal Gibbons* worked untiringly for the Americanization of the immigrants.

10..............

11. The United States believes that the immigrants should *discard* their customs and traditions.

11..............

12. *Americanization* means helping the immigrant to fit into American social and political life.

12..............

13. *Americanization* is the process by which a foreigner becomes a citizen of the United States.

13..............

14. The 2% Quota Law favors immigrants from *southern* Europe.

14..............

15. Since World War II *Japanese* are admitted on a quota basis.

15..............

16. The fear that a larger influx of immigrants into the United States would cause more unemployment and would tend to overpopulate the United States is a *poor and unchristian* reason for restricting immigration.

16..............

17. The immigrants are responsible for the *slow growth* of the United States during the nineteenth century.

17..............

18. Many of the cotton mills and iron works of the United States were organized and developed by the *Germans*.

18..............

19. Two great leaders of the Early Church in America who were *born in Ireland* are Archbishop Ireland and Bishop England.

19..............

20. Elihu Yale was a noted educator of *English* descent.

20..............

21. The *Scandinavians* were skilled in mechanics, science, and medicine.

21..............

22. Our opera houses and concert halls were made possible by immigrants from *England and Ireland*.

22..............

23. The influx of Catholics into the United States after 1840 almost *doubled* the membership of the Catholic Church in America.

23..............

24. The Catholic Church in America did *little* to Americanize the immigrants.

24..............

25. *Many* of the immigrants from southern and eastern Europe have become leaders in the United States.

25..............

Essay Test

Compare the "old" and the "new" immigrants as to countries from which they came, regions in which they tended to settle, ways in which they tended to earn a living, and some contributions they have made to American life.

Mary's Angelus

HISTORY. In the early times Catholic people began to say three Hail Marys in honor of Our Lady in the evening about sunset. Later the custom arose of ringing a bell in the evening to remind people to say these prayers. Soon a bell was rung in the morning and at noon as well, at each of which times the people said three Hail Marys. Next it became customary to say a short verse before each of the three Hail Marys.

THE DEVOTION. The name "Angelus" reminds us of the Angel who appeared to Our Lady at the Annunciation.

The devotion consists of saying three prayers in honor of Our Lord's having become Man, each of which is followed by a Hail Mary. The devotion ends with a prayer in honor of Our Lord. These prayers are usually said at the ringing of the Angelus bell in the morning, at noon, and in the evening. In Eastertime the prayer "Queen of Heaven, Rejoice," is recited instead of the ordinary Angelus prayers.

Prayer

THE ANGELUS

V. The angel of the Lord declared unto Mary.
R. And she conceived of the Holy Ghost. Hail Mary, etc.
V. Behold the handmaid of the Lord.
R. Be it done unto me according to thy word. Hail Mary, etc.
V. And the Word was made flesh.
R. And dwelt among us. Hail Mary, etc.
V. Pray for us, O Holy Mother of God.
R. That we may be made worthy of the promises of Christ.

Let us pray

POUR FORTH, we beseech Thee, O Lord, Thy grace into our hearts, that we to whom the Incarnation of Christ, Thy Son, was made known by the message of an angel, may by His passion and cross be brought to the glory of His resurrection, through the same Christ Our Lord. Amen.

REGINA CAELI

(Said during Eastertide, instead of the Angelus)

V. Queen of heaven, rejoice, Alleluia.
R. For He whom thou didst deserve to bear, Alleluia.
V. Hath risen as He said, Alleluia.
R. Pray for us to God, Alleluia.
V. Rejoice and be glad, O Virgin Mary! Alleluia.
R. Because our Lord is truly risen, Alleluia.

Let us pray

O God, who by the resurrection of Thy Son, Our Lord Jesus Christ, has vouchsafed to make glad the whole world, grant, we beseech Thee, that, through the intercession of the Virgin Mary, His Mother, we may attain the joys of eternal life. Through the same Christ Our Lord. Amen.

The faithful who at dawn, at noon, and at eventide, or as soon thereafter as may be, devoutly recite The Angelus, or at Eastertide the Regina Caeli, with the appropriate versicles and prayers, or who merely say the Hail Mary five times, may gain an indulgence of 10 years each time; a plenary indulgence on the usual conditions if they persevere in this devout practice for a month (see "The Raccolta," the official book of indulgenced prayers, page 232).

DEVOTIONAL GIFTS OF MARY. The Angelus is one of seven great devotions given to us through Mary. The other great devotions are the Hail Mary, the Rosary, the Miraculous Medal, the Scapular, the First Saturday Devotion, and the Little Office of the Blessed Virgin Mary. Through these devotions you appeal to Mary for the graces which, as Mother of God, she obtains to help you save your soul.

Courtesy of Rev. J. B. Carol, O. F. M.

UNIT SIX

SELFLESS COURAGE—PRICE OF PROGRESS

UNIT SIX

SELFLESS COURAGE—PRICE OF PROGRESS

THE UNITED STATES that fought the Civil War was very different from the United States that came into being at the close of the Revolutionary War. Through natural increase, conquest, purchase, annexation, and immigration the four million people who had made up the population of the United States in 1790 increased to a little over thirty-one million. Settlement reached the Pacific. Steamboats plowed all large rivers and lakes, while canals, roads, and railroads linked the East with the West.

Within the space of one hundred years great changes took place in the American way of living and working. While people from Europe and the eastern states moved farther and farther westward and the United States added territory after territory to its original domain, a flood of inventions brought about changes on the farm, in the factory, in the office, and in the home.

Civilized man had always endeavored to develop better ways of travelling, communicating, working, and living. With the discovery of electricity, oil, rubber, and steel many new inventions were made possible.

Inventions, like all progress, are brought about by the sharing of ideas. God gave His gifts of the earth to all men. God, likewise, expects men to share spiritual, intellectual, and social goods with one another.

During this period of rapid growth and development, education, literature, art, and music were not neglected. Writers like Irving, Longfellow, Emerson, and Whittier, who were forerunners of writers such as Louisa M. Alcott, Mark Twain, and James Whitcomb Riley, were at their best. Stephen C. Foster, Dan Emmett, and Edward MacDowell headed the list of musicians. The greatest sculptor of the period was Augustus St. Gaudens, while John S. Sargent, George Innes, and John LaFarge were the outstanding artists of the 19th century.

CHAPTER I

SCIENCE AND INVENTION IMPROVE TRANSPORTATION AND COMMUNICATION

Looking ahead. While the frontier was being pushed westward, great achievements in communication and transportation were made. Men seemed determined to improve the methods of communication and transportation already in use.

In this chapter we shall meet men of determination and perseverance — men who refused to become discouraged by difficulties or failure. At times these men were forced to suffer cold, hunger, and even ridicule in their attempts to better transportation and communication so that various sections of our country might be developed. The topics in this chapter are: (1) American Genius Improves Communication; (2) American Genius Improves Comfort and Safety of Railroads; (3) American Genius Speeds Up Transportation on Roads.

1. American Genius Improves Communication

In LEADERS OF FREEDOM we learned how the canals, the National Road, the steamboat, and the steam railway improved means of travel and trade. Up to this time there was no easy method of sending news. The Pony Express was slow and uncertain. Sometimes the weather interfered and sometimes the news carriers failed to reach their destination. Until about the middle of the nineteenth century messages could be carried no faster than man could travel by foot, by horseback, by stagecoach, or by rail. As soon as men began to realize the practical value of electricity, a period of important inventions which greatly improved and speeded up communication took place.

The electric telegraph. Among these inventions was that of the telegraph — the result of American genius and perseverance. Even though others knew that electricity could be sent through a wire, Samuel F. B. Morse was the first to show how it could be made to transmit messages.

Like Fulton, Morse was an artist, but he was an artist who also had a keen interest in science.

It was in 1832, while Morse was returning from Europe after having spent three years of further study in art, that he conceived the idea of a recording telegraph. While he was on the ship *Sully*, he conversed

The first telegraph

with some passengers who were scientists. Being keenly interested in science, Morse asked many questions about electricity and its possibilities. Finally, he became absorbed in the fact that electricity passes almost instantly over a length of wire.

Then Morse conceived the idea that if electricity passed over wires messages could be sent from place to place by means of opening or closing the circuit. The idea set Morse on fire. He immediately made a rough plan of his idea in a series of drawings. Later he worked out an alphabet of dots and dashes by means of which he could spell out words.

When he was once more at home, he was tempted to give up his profession of art and to devote all his time to developing the telegraph.

But he found that that was impossible, for he had to support his three motherless children.

Morse's experiments. Morse, therefore, continued to paint and endeavored to develop the telegraph in his spare moments. While he was busy with his experiments, he earned so little that he had hardly enough money to support his children. Often, he himself went hungry. His work was hindered and delayed because most of the time he was too poor to buy materials for his experiments.

In 1835 he secured a teaching position at New York University. Here, while he was giving lessons in art, his mind was constantly on his invention. During the course of 1836 he took into his confidence Leonard D. Gale, who helped him to improve his apparatus. Alfred

Samuel F. B. Morse
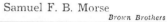

Vail, one of Morse's students, persuaded his father to advance money for the experiment. Finally, after six years of hard work, Morse succeeded in sending a message a short distance.

Again Morse found himself facing an impossible task, for he needed an experimental telegraph line to further the improvement of his invention. He travelled to Washington to ask Congress for $30,000 to build such a line from Washington to Baltimore. Most of the members of Congress were not in sympathy with the experiment. They thought it was impractical: that it would be of no use and that Congress would only be throwing away a large sum of money.

Success at last. Morse spent six more years of agony and waiting before the bill for the $30,000 passed the House of Representatives by a majority of six votes. But Morse's worries were not over. The bill still had to pass the Senate. On the last day of the session of Congress, Morse sat in the gallery all day long hoping that any minute the bill would come up for discussion. It was shortly before midnight, the hour when Congress closed, that Morse finally decided that there was no more hope. He returned to his hotel. He thought that all he had done those seven years in developing the telegraph was futile. Now he felt that his last hope of proving to the world what could be done was gone. Heartbroken, he retired for the night.

The next morning Miss Annie Ellsworth, the daughter of his friend, the commissioner of patents, informed him that the bill had been passed at midnight without discussion or revision. On receiving this unexpected news, Morse was overcome with joy. He promised Miss Ellsworth that she could choose the first message to be sent over the first telegraph line to be operated.

Finally on May 24, 1844, the telegraph line was in readiness. Morse sat at a table in the Capitol at Washington, prepared to send the first message. Miss Ellsworth handed him the fitting words which she had chosen. Morse tapped out the words: "What hath God wrought!" Vail, his assistant, forty miles away in Baltimore, received the momentous words instantly and sent them back correctly to Morse. The telegraph was a success!

Sending the first telegram

Value of the telegraph. Soon telegraph lines connected all the large centers of population in the Eastern United States. Even before the building of the first transcontinental railroad, the Atlantic and Pacific coasts were connected by telegraph.

The telegraph made possible the safe handling of trains. It supplied the modern newspaper with current news from all parts of the world. It enabled merchants and businessmen to keep in touch with the markets, crops, and other business conditions in distant parts of our country.

Morse, after his years of suffering and poverty, saw the telegraph span the continent. Then in 1872 he died — a man honored by most of the great nations of the world.

The Atlantic cable. Several years after the invention of the electric telegraph another American, Cyrus W. Field, got the idea of extending telegraph lines across the Atlantic Ocean. He thought that it could be done by means of submarine cables.

Several short cables had been laid before this. About the middle of the nineteenth century, a cable was laid between England and the continent. Later another made possible the transmission of messages between England and Ireland. But the problem of sending messages over a long stretch of water such as the Atlantic Ocean had not been solved.

The idea of Cyrus W. Field to lay a cable two thousand miles long on a deep ocean bed seemed a tremendous undertaking. Many

Cyrus Field   *Brown Brothers*

thought it impossible. Others said it would be a foolish adventure. Field, nevertheless, succeeded in persuading some businessmen not only of its advantages, but also of its possibility. Soon the Atlantic Telegraph Company was organized to lay a cable from Newfoundland to Ireland. It was not, however, until 1866 that a really successful cable was laid. The story of laying the Atlantic cable is one of skill, courage, and perseverance.

In 1857 the first attempt to lay the cable was made. Two warships, large enough to carry the bulky cable, were fitted up with machinery for laying it. Finally in June of that year the two ships set out from Ireland. The cable was slowly let down. It had been laid across almost four hundred miles when the cable broke. Half a million dollars was lost!

Field was not discouraged. The next year he tried another plan. This time he had the cable reeled out from two ships starting in mid-ocean. One sailed towards Ireland, the other towards Newfoundland. Again the cable broke. It was spliced, but broke again. Miles of cable were lost, but Field refused to give up.

Another attempt. During the summer of 1858 a third attempt was made. This time the task was accomplished in eight days. The first message was exchanged between Queen Victoria of England and President Buchanan of the United States. The message was: "Europe and America are united by telegraph. Glory to God in the highest; peace on earth and good will to men."

The cable had been safely landed. Everywhere there were celebrations. But Field's triumph was short-lived. After about a month the messages became faint and hard to understand. Then they stopped altogether. The cable could not resist the tremendous pressure of the ocean. Again the cable seemed to be a failure!

Field, nevertheless, did not lose faith. It worked once. He was convinced that it would work again. Even though forced by the bankruptcy of his company and the outbreak of the Civil War to abandon his idea for some time, he refused to be discouraged.

As soon as the War was over Field made ready to renew his attempt. A heavier cable was constructed and the *Great Eastern*, the largest ship in existence, was secured to lay it. In July, 1865, the big ship set out on her westward course. All went well for about a week. Two-thirds of the distance had been covered and about twelve hundred miles of cable had been laid. This time success seemed certain. Then suddenly, without warning, the cable snapped and sank to the bottom of the ocean. The men tried to raise it but all efforts were in vain. Still Field's faith in the success of the cable never wavered.

Finally in 1866 the *Great Eastern* with a heavy cable left the Irish coast. Slowly and steadily it moved across the Atlantic Ocean letting down the cable as it went. This time there was no mishap. After two weeks the great ship slowly made her way into a small harbor of Newfoundland. The cable was carefully dragged ashore. After years of heartbreaking delays and failures, Field achieved success and the ocean had been successfully spanned.

The cable which had been lost was recovered, and a new one spliced to it. In less than a year two cables had been laid across the Atlantic. Soon submarine cables were laid in all parts of the world. Important messages could now be flashed across thousands of miles in a few moments.

Speaking over wires. Alexander Graham Bell was not a scientist. He was a teacher. For years he taught deaf and dumb people. Then, one day, an idea came to him. He thought that if signals could be sent by electricity, then the actual sound of words over wires charged with electricity should be possible. He became so absorbed with the idea that he gave up teaching and devoted all his time to the experiment.

He had to solve many problems. First, he needed a steady current of electricity. It took him a long time to solve this problem. He also had to find a way to send the sound waves of the voice. His greatest problem, however, was the obtaining of enough money to carry on his experiments. Sometimes he had little or nothing to eat but he kept to his task.

For years he experimented. Then one day Thomas Watson, his assistant, heard clearly over the experimental telephone the words, "Mr. Watson, come here, I want you." Watson rushed up the stairs to tell Bell the good news. Together the two men labored to improve the invention. Finally after years of hard work, they succeeded in making an instrument that transmitted words very clearly and distinctly.

Bell secured a patent for his invention but he found that the people were not interested in it. They called it a "toy" and found no practical use for it.

Bell's success. In 1876 a Centennial Exposition was held at Philadelphia to celebrate the hundredth

The end of the Atlantic Cable is hauled ashore in Newfoundland

Bettmann Archive

The first telephone message: "Watson, come here. I want you."

anniversary of the signing of the Declaration of Independence. Bell had his telephone on exhibition. As it was on a table in an out-of-the-way corner few people noticed it. One day Don Pedro, the Emperor of Brazil, entered the hall. Don Pedro had met Professor Bell and esteemed his work with the deaf. He examined the telephone. He put the receiver to his ear; Bell spoke into the transmitter. In amazement Don Pedro cried, "It talks!" Others gathered, among them Sir William Thomson, one of the greatest electrical scientists in England. Upon examining the telephone, he claimed it to be the most important thing he had seen in America.

Soon the telephone was the most popular article at the fair. Everybody was talking about it. Even newspapers published columns about it. Nearly a year passed, however, before anyone attempted to put it into public use.

Growth of the telephone. As the years went on many improvements were made. Transmitters and receivers were made to carry the voice more distinctly, a way was found of sending more than one message over a wire at the same time, automatic switchboards were invented, and long-distance calls were made possible.

In 1915 the wires stretched across the continent. New York and San

Francisco were linked by telephone for the first time. The message on this occasion was that which had been sent across the wires forty years before: "Watson, come here. I want you." In order to obey that message Watson would have had to travel some three thousand miles, for this time Bell spoke from Boston to San Francisco, where Watson was.

No longer is the telephone a luxury. It is found in almost every American home. It speeds up business; it adds to the convenience, the pleasure, and the welfare of people throughout the world. Although telephones are found in all parts of the world, more than half of them are installed in the United States.

Like Morse, Bell was one of the few inventors who lived long enough to see the success of his work.

A boy inventor. Today it is possible for crews on ships at sea and for men in stations on land to speak to each other across large bodies of water without the use of wires. This is made possible through wireless telegraphy, the invention of Guglielmo Marconi, an Italian and a Catholic.

Marconi was born at Bologna, Italy, before Bell invented his telephone. As a boy he became interested in electricity and read every-

Alexander Graham Bell speaks into an early telephone

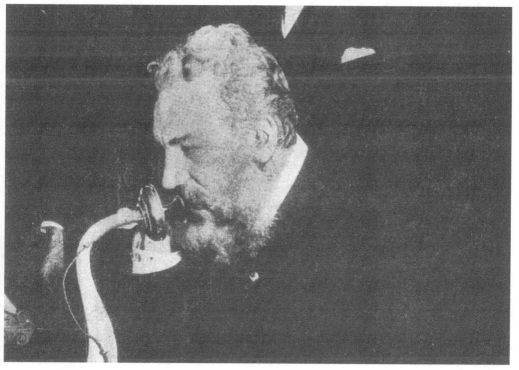

thing that he could find on the subject. He set up a laboratory at home where, in 1896, he succeeded in sending messages from one room to another without the aid of wires. He was at this time only nineteen years of age. He continued to experiment until he was able to reach more distant points.

Then he went to England where his invention was tested. Here he was successful in sending messages over the English Channel, a distance of twenty miles. This was considered a great achievement but it did not satisfy Marconi. He dreamed of sending wireless messages across the Atlantic Ocean. Other scientists thought it impossible, but Marconi went ahead and made plans for an experiment between England and Newfoundland.

He built a very powerful transmitter on the western coast of England. Then with two assistants he set sail for America. Before doing so, however, he arranged that on a certain date at a given time the Morse signal for the letter "S" should be transmitted to Newfoundland.

The first transatlantic signal. On December 12, 1901, in a little shack in Newfoundland shortly after noon Marconi received the expected signal. At first it was faint, then suddenly there were three clicks in his receiving set. It was the message he had expected — the Morse Code for "S". Marconi called his assistant to listen. Again and again they heard the three little ticks. Sound had leaped across the Atlantic! Marconi's invention had proved to

Marconi scanning a message from an early wireless telegraph

Brown Brothers

be a success. Now there remained for Marconi the task of building powerful transmitting and receiving stations on both sides of the ocean.

Marconi had the usual experiences of most inventors. Few appreciated the value of wireless. At first its main use was at sea. England soon equipped her warships with wireless instruments. Ships so equipped could be informed of coming storms and other dangers. Ships in difficulty could send out distress signals.

The value of wireless. The first example of the value of wireless in saving lives at sea took place in January, 1909. The passenger ship *Republic*, outbound from New York, collided with another ship in the fog off the coast of New England. Water immediately poured into the hold of the *Republic* and it began to sink. Realizing the danger, the wireless operator on board the sinking ship sent out his distress signal. Instantly the message was picked up at the wireless station at Nantucket. Ships at sea equipped with wireless were notified of the distress of the *Republic*. Within twelve hours one of these ships reached the *Republic*. As a result of wireless, over a thousand people were rescued before the ship finally sank.

From then on, wireless became an important means of communication, especially at sea. Today the United States government requires all ships carrying fifty or more persons including the crew

to contain wireless equipment.

Wireless telegraphy was not to be the final word in communication. Marconi's invention was later developed into a wireless telephone and the radio. That, however, is a story for the next book, GUARDIAN OF FREEDOM.

The rotary press. By the middle of the eighteenth century there were a few small local newspapers. These early newspapers were usually weeklies and contained very little real news. The newspapers of the first part of the nineteenth century were more numerous and contained important news. Their editorials, which were usually written by important men, did much to influence people and events.

The printing of these newspapers was still a slow and tedious job. Each line of type had to be set by hand and the heavy "chases" had to be changed for each page.

During the nineteenth century two inventions greatly speeded up the printing of newspapers, books, and magazines. One was that of Richard M. Hoe. In 1846 Richard M. Hoe completed a new kind of printing press. Because this new machine made use of a cylinder it was called the rotary press. The type was arranged on a cylinder drum which resembled a small barrel. The paper was shoved under the drum as it turned round and round. This new invention made it possible to print over a thousand pages an hour. This was a great improvement over the old type of press which could never produce

A rotary press in operation about 1880

more than four hundred pages an hour.

The linotype. Until 1885 typesetting was a slow process. Each line had to be set letter by letter. In that year Ottamar Mergenthaler invented the linotype. This new machine was very much like the typewriter which had been invented in 1868 by C. L. Shoales. By touching keys similar to those of a typewriter a linotypist was able to set type very rapidly. These two inventions, the rotary press and the linotype, made it possible for the public to receive news more quickly. Daily papers could also be sold much cheaper.

As newspapers became larger and more numerous, they began to mold public opinion. Some newspapers printed material which proved interesting but which was harmful to the morals of the people. Other newspapers gave incorrect information and bad advice. On the whole the newspapers had both a good and a bad influence upon their readers.

It is important that we weigh the opinions found in our newspapers today. More than that, we should seek for the truth so that we may overcome the harmful influence of misguided publishers.

2. American Genius Improves Comfort and Safety of Railroads

Fast trains, swiftly-moving auto-

The first linotype

mobiles, huge motor trucks, and zooming airplanes have become so much a part of our daily lives that we seldom stop to think about them. Yet, many of these methods of carrying people and goods are not yet in existence a hundred years.

Before 1850 not a single railroad line crossed the Appalachian Mountains. By the time the Civil War broke out most of the large cities such as New York, Chicago, and St. Louis were well connected by railroads, while several short lines ran north and south. In fact it is said that by 1860 the railroad mileage in the United States exceeded that of all Europe.

In Unit Four we read about the construction of the first continental railroad. By 1884 three other railroads crossed the United States to connect the East with the West.

Improving the railroads. As railroads increased in number they were steadily improved. In the early days a person who travelled several hundred miles had to change trains frequently. This was due to the way the rails had been laid. When the first railroads were built the distance between the rails ranged from three to six feet. Not all trains, therefore, could be used on every track. After much work and planning this situation has been remedied. Today all roads use a "standard gauge," that is, all rails throughout the United States are laid the same distance apart.

Other improvements such as those which would affect the safety, comfort and convenience of the passengers were made on railroads. The wooden rails of the early railroads were replaced first by iron and later by heavy steel ones. Strong roadbeds of crushed rocks were made so that heavy trains could pass safely over them. After the telegraph was invented the railroad used it to arrange the movement of trains. In this way the number of wrecks was cut down and railway travel and transportation became safer.

The airbrake. One of the greatest improvements at this time was the airbrake. The brakes on the early trains were so arranged that all the cars could not be stopped at one time. Trainmen had to apply the brakes one at a time. It took a thousand feet to stop a train going at twenty-five miles an hour. Furthermore, the coaches were

Bettmann Archive
Braking an early train

Other improvements. Soon automatic couplers replaced the link-and-pin system, and block signals were introduced. These latter control the movement of trains and prevent collisions. They require trains to halt unless the track ahead is clear.

As time went on passengers were able to travel with comfort as well as safety. Comfortable coaches with better springs and new methods of heating and lighting added to the pleasure of travelling.

Pullman cars bring more conveniences. Another great improvement was the Pullman car which was built in 1864 by George M. Pullman. The first trains had no sleeping cars. People slept as well as they could sitting in a coach. Later one railroad company devised a way for people to lie down when

small and light; consequently, wrecks were frequent.

A bad wreck near Schenectady, New York, convinced many that improved brakes were a necessity. George Westinghouse, a passenger at the time of the wreck, decided that there must be some way of setting the brakes of a train so that all the cars would stop at the same time. Westinghouse set to work to find such a method. Before long he was successful in inventing a brake operated by compressed air. The airbrake, as the new invention was called, was first tried in 1868. This brake enabled an engineer to stop in a very short distance a heavy train going at high speed. The new airbrake gave such perfect control over long trains travelling at great speed that is was soon adopted by all railroad companies.

Pullman interior, 1890
Brown Brothers

travelling at night. This new sleeping car had three bunks one above the other. Each bunk had a rough straw mattress but no bedding.

In 1858 George Pullman decided to make a better sleeping car. He experimented with a day coach. This he turned into a sleeper with two berths one above the other, in each section. This first Pullman car was much higher than the other coaches. It was so much higher that changes had to be made in the bridges and station platforms. These changes were made, and the Pullman cars became popular.

Gradually the number of Pullman cars increased. Further improvements were made, and luxuries were added until the Pullman car became what it is today. These modern sleepers have not only berths, but single and double bedrooms, roomettes, and drawingrooms.

Then the Pullman Palace Car Company was organized to build not only sleepers, but also dining cars, parlor cars, and club cars. Today Pullman cars are equipped to give all the comfort and convenience of a modern hotel.

In recent years stream-lined trains, diesel and electric locomotives, air-conditioning, and refrigeration have brought about greater speed, comfort, and convenience in the transportation of people and goods.

3. American Genius Speeds Up Transportation on Roads

For many years railroads did not have to worry about competition.

Towards the close of the nineteenth century, however, came the greatest rivals of the railroad — the automobile, the bus, and the truck.

The automobile. The problem of producing a horseless carriage occupied the minds of men for a number of years. As early as 1769 Nicholas Joseph Cugnot, a French military officer, built a carriage for guns which was driven by steam. Early in the nineteenth century some steam-driven carriages were built in England. The first horseless carriages appeared in the United States towards the end of the nineteenth century. These were moved by steam.

About this time the first electric automobile was built in the United States. Neither the steam nor the electric automobile was very successful. The steam engine, which

A horseless carriage

241

needed a large supply of fuel to keep it going, was found to be impractical. The drawback of the electric car was its batteries. These had to be recharged frequently. Long trips under these conditions could not be taken without great inconvenience and expense.

American automobiles. The invention of the modern automobile began with the invention of the small gasoline engine by Daimler, a German scientist, in 1886. This engine was then used a few years later in France to make the first automobile driven by gasoline.

Towards the close of the nineteenth century several Americans experimented with the building of horseless carriages. Among these inventors were George Seldon, Charles Duryea, Elwood Haynes, and Henry Ford. But the credit for making the first successful automobile in the United States is given to Charles Duryea, who took out a patent for the first practical gasoline-driven car in 1892. George B. Seldon had succeeded in building such a car in 1879, but because he lacked financial aid he did not have it patented until 1895. A year later Elwood Haynes and Henry Ford each produced a gas-driven automobile.

The first cars to appear on the road caused considerable trouble. They were slow and unable to weather the rough and muddy roads. There were no gasoline stations along the way, nor were there garages to call upon in case of a breakdown.

Henry Ford. Until about 1910 few automobiles were in use. They were so expensive that only wealthy people could afford to own them. In 1903 Henry Ford became tremendously interested in producing an automobile that would be within the means of ordinary people. To do this, he organized the Ford Motor Company. He immediately set to work to devise a way to turn out inexpensive cars and at the same time to make enough profit to continue and expand his business.

Ford soon solved the problem by introducing mass production and standardized parts. He arranged to have the parts that make up an automobile made separately in large quantities. He then had these parts assembled in one place. Each machine made a single kind of screw, bolt, bar, wheel, fender, or some other part of the car. These were called *standardized* parts. Sometimes they were also called *interchangeable* parts, because they could be changed from one Ford auto to another. This was possible because each part turned out by a certain machine was exactly like every other part turned out by that machine.

As the body of the automobile traveled down the assembly line between two rows of workers, each man put on a certain part such as a screw, a nut, a fender, a wheel, or the like. This method of mass production reduced the cost of production and made it possible for the automobile owner to replace worn-out or broken parts at a low cost.

The Model-T. The small Model-T Ford soon appeared on American streets and highways. Other automobile manufacturers, who had been turning out expensive cars, noticed the success of Ford's experiment. Quickly they adopted his method of mass production. Year after year improvements have been made until today there are many moderate priced cars on the market. Their upkeep is simple and reasonably inexpensive. The automobile is no longer considered a luxury.

Although Europe was the first to invent the automobile, our democratic way of life made it possible for the United States to sweep ahead in production. Today over thirty million cars are registered in the United States. Each year four to five million new cars are produced. At the present time the horse is almost as strange a sight on our streets and highways as the gas-driven car of fifty years ago.

Better roads. The invention of the automobile created a demand for better roads. Counties, states, and the federal government have all cooperated in the building of roads and highways. Every year millions of dollars are spent to build and maintain well-surfaced roads. Improvements have been made until today a great network of hard-surfaced highways stretches from one

A modern highway for high-speed traffic

Brown Brothers

end of the United States to the other.

Among these hard-surfaced roads are many superhighways designed for speed and safety. The most famous of these is the Lincoln Highway which connects New York with San Francisco.

Trucks and buses. Shortly after 1900 automobile manufacturers became aware of a market for trucks. In 1904 the first motor truck came into use. About 1915 motor trucks could be seen moving over our highways both day and night. Today there are over seven and a half million registered trucks travelling the highways of the United States.

At first it was feared that the cheap operation of trucks might ruin the freight business of the railroads. Some small railroads were forced out of business because of the competition. But it soon was found that the truck was more profitable for short hauls, while the railroad was more economical for long-distance hauling of bulk merchandise.

Most of the hauling in out-of-the-way places where railroad service is inadequate has been taken over by motor trucks. There is a place for both in the United States, and frequently trucks can and do serve as feeders to the railroads.

The "jitney" of 1910 which was

This woman and her little boy are getting into a jitney bus

A fast mail train, about 1875

nothing but an ordinary automobile used to carry passengers, soon gave way to a much larger vehicle known as a bus. The number of buses steadily increased until today there are in operation in the United States almost two hundred thousand motor buses for the public use and over twenty thousand buses for school service. Regular bus lines operate in all parts of the United States. Some carry on a transcontinental business. With the development of rapid transportation — better, larger, faster, and safer trains, automobiles, trucks, and buses — the United States has become a nation on wheels.

Postal service. The development of rapid transportation and communication speeded up postal service. In the early days most of the important letters were sent by special messengers. The regular mail was carried by slow and lumbering stagecoaches.

In 1860 the Pony Express was established as a quicker way of sending news from Missouri, where railroad service ended, to Sacramento, California. Relay riders on fleet horses were able to make the trip over dangerous trails and roads in ten days. This was just half the time required by the stagecoach to cover the same distance.

With the development of the railroad Federal Postal Service grew in efficiency. Gradually private mail carriers were forced out of business. Even the Pony Express ceased operating in 1861 when the first telegraph wires connected New York and California.

In 1896 the Post Office Department extended free delivery of mail to the rural areas. This is known as rural free delivery or simply R.F.D. Thirty-three years before, during the Civil War, free delivery of mail had been begun in the cities.

The extension of the railroad, together with the development of the postal system, has made possible the frequent delivery of mail to even the most remote regions of our country. Do you know of any other services which the Post Office Department offers the people?

Word study

invention	inventor	progress
achievements	genius	perseverance
tremendous	submarine	luxury
telegraph	wireless	cable
rotary press	opinions	standard gauge
mass production	standardized parts	interchangeable parts
steam engine	gasoline engine	federal

How well have you read?

1. Discuss the characteristics which men like Morse, Bell, and Field possessed that enabled them to persevere in spite of difficulties and obstacles.
2. Show how some inventors chose the welfare of the group rather than their own personal gain.
3. Discuss in how far the telegraph has aided the railroad and how the railroads have aided the postal system.
4. Prepare a report on the lives of the inventors studied in this chapter. Did their earlier lives prepare them in any way for the work they were to do?

Test yourself

Before each item in Column I write the letter found before the item in Column II which best matches it.

Column I	Column II
....1. Alexander Graham Bell	a. first low priced automobile
....2. Richard M. Hoe	b. typewriter
....3. George Westinghouse	c. improved sleeping cars
....4. Charles Duryea	d. Atlantic cable
....5. Samuel F. B. Morse	e. telephone
....6. Guglielmo Marconi	f. airbrake
....7. C. F. Shoales	g. small gasoline engine
....8. Daimler	h. rotary printing press
....9. George M. Pullman	i. wireless telegraphy
...10. Cyrus W. Field	j. first gasoline-driven automobile
	k. telegraph

CHAPTER II

AGRICULTURAL AMERICA BECOMES AN INDUSTRIAL NATION

A glance backward and forward. About the middle of the eighteenth century machinery began to be used in industry. In LEADERS OF FREEDOM we learned how the invention of the spinning jenny, the flying shuttle, and the power loom transferred spinning, weaving, and other crafts from the home to the factory. At first this industrial awakening was confined to England. Englishmen had invented these machines, therefore England forbade anyone to send them out of the country. Punishment was inflicted upon those who even attempted to send drawings of such machines out of England.

Regardless of all these precautions, machinery soon found its way to the United States. Again in LEADERS OF FREEDOM we learned how Samuel Slater came to America, set up a mill at Pawtucket, and constructed from memory the necessary machinery. Before the middle of the nineteenth century, hundreds of other mills and factories were established in the Northern states. Shortly after Slater built his mill at Pawtucket, Eli Whitney, an American, invented the cotton gin. We read about the great influence of this machine in Unit Four.

In this chapter we shall learn how: (1) Inventions Help Industry to Grow and Develop, and (2) Inventions and the Growth of Industry Change Our Ways of Living.

1. Inventions Help Industry to Grow and Develop

During the nineteenth century new inventions hastened the industrial growth of our country.

The sewing machine. Even though the invention of machines brought about the transfer of the making of cloth from the home to the factory, clothes were still sewed by hand at home or in small shops. This was not only a slow and tiresome process but also an expensive one.

Various attempts had been made to produce a machine that would sew. Walter Hunt discovered the principle of the lock-stitch and built a machine for his experiment. Just as he was about to enjoy success, he grew tired of his work and abandoned the idea.

Some time later a machinist, Elias Howe, knowing nothing of Hunt's experience, became interested in the problem. He became so absorbed in the idea that he could think of nothing else. But, like most of the great inventors, he, too, was poor. He earned only nine dollars a week and had to support his wife and three children. At this time a friend, George Fischer, who believed in Howe's idea, offered to help him.

Howe's work. Night after night, Howe worked at his experiment, even though all his first efforts failed. Then one night on his way home from the workshop, he got the idea of the lock-stitch. He figured that the lock-stitch could be made if he put the eye of the needle in the point and used a wheel to move the threaded needle up and down while another thread was run under the cloth by means of a bobbin. Then, each time the threaded needle went down, the two threads would lock together to make a

Howe's first sewing machine

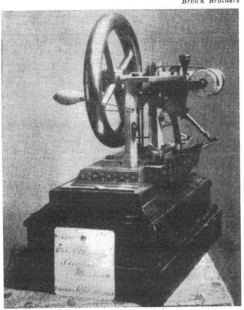

stitch. He set to work at once to invent such a machine.

Finally, Howe completed his machine, but he had no money with which to obtain a patent. Again Fischer came to his rescue and paid all the expenses. The patent was secured in September, 1846.

Howe's sewing machine. Disappointment was in store for Howe. When he put his machine on the market, he could find no buyers. The tailors to whom he showed his machine were surprised and interested, but they would not buy it. Many of them feared that it would put them out of work; others thought it too expensive. When Fischer learned how the machine had been rejected, he refused to give Howe any further aid. He had invested some two thousand dollars in the invention and could not afford to do more.

Howe was disappointed, for he had spent many years of his life on the invention and during those years he and his family had suffered from extreme want. Howe did not give up. He went to England to try his luck but there, too, he failed to sell his invention. Shortly after Howe's return from England, his wife died from the hardship of their utter poverty. Howe was so poor that he had only the one suit of clothes which he wore in the shop. He actually had to borrow clothes to wear to his wife's funeral.

After his wife's death, Howe learned that some men were using his idea in making sewing machines. Howe obtained the aid of George

Brows Brothers

Elias Howe

W. Bliss, a man of means, and brought the men to court for ignoring his patent rights. The case dragged on until 1854 when finally it was decided in Howe's favor. From that time on, anyone who wished to make sewing machines had to pay Howe twenty-five dollars on every machine. Such a sum of money was known as a *royalty*.

Howe's determined fight for his patent rights gave the sewing machine a great deal of publicity. This aroused public interest and soon Howe found a ready market for his machine.

Uses of the sewing machine. At first sewing machines were used only in homes. Later they were introduced into factories where they were operated by power. Through these power-operated machines the wholesale production of garments

was made possible. As the years went on, the sale of the machines increased. Howe became a wealthy and famous man. Several foreign governments conferred honors on him.

Then, too, there were constant improvements made on the sewing machine. Soon Howe's machine could be used for the sewing of carpets, straw goods, and leather goods. Even the shoe industry found it helpful. In the years that followed many men shared their ideas, and Howe's slow, clumsy machine was converted into special models run at a terrific speed by electricity.

Chief among those who improved the sewing machine was Isaac M. Singer. He also did much to bring the sewing machine within the means of the average home. The sewing machine has been a blessing

Modern sewing machines

Brown Brothers

249

to our country in many ways. It has made it possible for even the poorest of our people to buy shoes and clothing.

From iron to steel. As the number of machines increased, more and better metals were needed. Up to about the middle of the nineteenth century iron was used to make vessels, rails, locomotives, and implements of all sorts. But iron proved to be too brittle and too expensive for the newly-invented machines. A stronger and cheaper material was needed for America's fast-growing industries.

Centuries before, men had discovered that if they burned the impurities out of iron and added other materials to strengthen it they could make steel which was tougher and stronger than iron. This was just the metal that was needed for the new machines. But the process of producing steel was so slow and expensive that it could not be used on a large scale. A quick and inexpensive method of manufacturing steel was needed. That method was soon discovered by accident.

William Kelly. One day William Kelly, an iron-worker in Kentucky, noticed that when a draft of air was blown into the glowing mass of molten iron a white hot flame flared up. This burned away the impurities and at the same time produced sufficient heat to keep the iron molten. Kelly was delighted with the discovery. He thought that if he could build a furnace so that air could be forced through it, the slow process of refining iron by means of charcoal would be ended.

He set to work immediately and built a *converter*, or kettle-shaped vessel with holes in the bottom. Through these holes blasts of air were forced into the molten iron, Kelly, like most other inventors, struggled along in poverty. Iron workers made fun of him. They thought that the idea of making iron hotter with blasts of cold air was ridiculous. Even his customers did not trust his new method of refining iron.

Before Kelly's process became well known, Sir Henry Bessemer, an Englishman, made the same discovery. Although Kelly and Bessemer deserve an equal share in the new discovery, it was Bessemer who made the process popular. It is by his name, then, that the process is known.

Sir Henry Bessemer

A Bessemer converter in action.
A stream of air forced through molten iron removes impurities

The Bessemer process. By this new process steel was refined in twenty-minutes and work that formerly required three months was completed in less than an hour. Since good steel could be made quickly and in large quantities, it could be sold cheaply. Later the open hearth furnace was discovered. This was a somewhat slower and more expensive process, but it produced steel of a better quality.

Steel is stronger than wood or iron, and it is superior to stone in the construction of buildings. It was also found to be suitable for so many purposes that soon it was in great demand. To supply these rapidly growing demands, American iron and steel mills needed an abundant supply of iron ore and plenty of cheap fuel.

God has blessed America with both of these. The enormous iron ore deposits in Minnesota, Michigan, and Wisconsin supplied the iron ore; the rich coal fields of Pennsylvania provided the fuel; and the Great Lakes made possible cheap transportation of iron ore to the great steel mills in the cities located along the southern edge of the Great Lakes.

Growth of the steel industry. The rapid growth of the steel industry in the United States was largely brought about by Andrew Carnegie. Little did Andrew Carnegie

251

dream of the fortune that lay ahead of him, when he, as a poor Scotch boy just thirteen years of age, was brought to the United States by his parents. Little did he dream that always, above all his wealth and success, he would treasure the memory of his parents and of his days of poverty. On one occasion this rich man born of poor parents said:

> I was born in poverty, and would not exchange its sacred memories with the richest millionaire's son who ever breathed. Give me the life of the boy whose mother is nurse, seamstress, washerwoman, cook, teacher, angel, and saint, all in one, and whose father is guide, exemplar, and friend. These are the boys who are born to the best fortune.

Today, all great nations of the world are using more and more steel which has become the basic metal of our modern world. It is steel that shelters us, that helps to feed and clothe us, that makes possible our industries, and that provides means of communication and transportation. Our is truly the Age of Steel.

A new source of power. Falling water and steam had been used to run machinery for some time, when a third source of power was discovered. Although men had known of petroleum, or crude oil, for a long time, they made little use of it until the second half of the nineteenth century. Perhaps this was because there was no quick way of obtaining petroleum in quantities.

In 1859, E. L. Drake decided to bore a well in western Pennsylvania. He hired an experienced salt-well driller and his two sons. These men began this project the following May. They found the drilling to be a slow process, but they did not give up. They finally reached rock seventy feet down into the earth. Still they felt that there was little hope of striking oil. Then, on August twenty-eighth, a black oily liquid began to rise in the pipe. Drake immediately connected a pump which he had ready. By October the well was yielding over twenty barrels of oil a day.

When news of the oil well spread, thousands of people rushed to western Pennsylvania to buy land. Before long the upper valley of the Allegheny River was dotted with oil wells.

Kerosene. Many of the inexperienced people were surprised when they saw the oil come from the ground — a thick dark liquid with an unpleasant smell. Then, too, they were astonished to find that in the process of refining the oil gave off a pale liquid called kerosene. They also found that this new oil produced a much better flame for lighting than that of a candle or whale oil. Soon they began to use the oil for heating purposes. The natural gas which they often found while drilling for the oil was used to light houses and streets and to provide fuel for homes and factories.

The refining of petroleum quickly became an important industry. Then, shortly after the first oil well

The first oil well. The famous Drake well at Titusville, Pennsylvania

was drilled, the gasoline engine was invented. It could not burn crude oil, therefore the men experimented until they found a way to separate petroleum into many substances such as benzine, gasoline, and naphtha gas.

Today, it would be impossible to run many of our machines, autobiles, and motor vehicles without oil. Oil is also used to grease every wheel that turns, and it even runs our diesel engines. It has become so important that nations go to war to gain possession of territories rich in oil.

Electricity, another source of power. Besides oil, electricity is also important to our modern age. Although no one knows what electricity is, man has known some of its effects. The first practical use of electricity, however, came with the invention of the telegraph. After that, scientific students in various countries tried to find a way in which to harness its power. In the early part of the nineteenth century Michael Faraday, an Englishman, and Joseph Henry, an American, discovered the principles of the dynamo, or electric generator.

It was not until after the Civil War that scientists found a use for the dynamo. Soon they used electric motors to run automobiles and streetcars, to move heavy articles, to dig ditches, and to do other similar work. But the scientist had still another problem — the use of electricity as power to run industrial plants.

That problem was solved in time by Thomas Alva Edison, the electrical wizard. He constructed huge dynamos and placed them in central power stations. The thousands of volts that could then be produced were carried from the central power stations by heavy cables to distant places. The use of the central station made it possible to build factories at a great distance from water power or from coal mines.

Electrical development. Large power stations were constructed throughout the United States wherever swift flowing water could be found to turn the wheels of the generators which produced electricity. In some rivers where there

Thomas A. Edison

were no natural falls, huge dams were built to raise the level of the water and to create artificial waterfalls.

Hundreds of men, including persons from many countries in Europe, as well as people from the United States, have helped to develop the use of electricity.

Edison, the electrical genius. Outstanding among the inventors who have harnessed the might of electricity and made it our servant is Thomas Alva Edison. He was born in Milan, Ohio, in 1847.

As a young boy Edison showed a great interest in science. At about the age of ten or eleven years, he became greatly interested in chemistry and persuaded his mother to allow him to set up a laboratory in the cellar. Two or three years later, he obtained a job as a newsboy on a train in order to earn money to carry on his experiments. He was allowed part of a baggage car in which to keep the newspapers, magazines, candy, and other articles which he sold on the train. He moved his laboratory from home to this baggage car. There, when he was not selling papers and articles, he continued his experiments. Not content with that, he bought a small printing press and published a weekly newspaper called the Weekly Herald. At one time his news sheet reached a sale of five hundred copies. All went well, until one day a bottle of phosporous fell on the shelf, broke, and set fire to the baggage car.

At the next station the conductor

threw the boy and all his equipment off the train. Edison's railroad days came to an end.

At fifteen Edison learned telegraphy. Sometime before the baggage car episode, Edison had saved the life of a station agent's child. In gratitude the father offered to teach the boy telegraphy. Edison, who had a deep interest in electricity, eagerly accepted the offer.

He then obtained employment as a telegraph operator. For the next five years or so, his work as telegraph operator took him to different parts of the United States. But Edison was not satisfied with merely tapping the keys. He was determined to know how the instrument worked and why. Before long he had invented many improvements in telegraphy.

Edison's career. In 1869 he decided to try his fortune in New York. Early one morning he arrived in that city without even enough money to buy breakfast. He went immediately to the Western Union Telegraph Company to put in his application for work. At the same time, he obtained permission to sleep in the battery room of the Gold Indicator Company until he could get a position. This company operated the electric tickers used to transmit the prices of stocks and bonds.

While waiting for a reply to his application, he spent his days studying the operations of the Gold Indicator Company. A few days after his arrival, an accident in the central transmitting system stopped the operation of machines in the offices of about three hundred customers. Everyone was in a state of confusion and did not know what to do. Edison calmly offered to find the difficulty and to make the proper adjustment. The president of the company accepted his offer.

About two hours later Edison had all the machines back in operation again. The grateful president asked him if he could accept the position of superintendent with a salary of three hundred dollars a month. For a moment Edison was dazed. Then he managed to stammer out his acceptance. This was the beginning of Edison's real career. He stayed with the company for some time and made improvements in the electric tickers which are used to record the price of stocks and bonds in the stock exchange.

Edison's research. The money Edison earned as superintendent, together with $40,000 which he received from inventions, was used to build a laboratory at Menlo Park, New Jersey. Here Edison labored day and night in order to find new uses for electricity. It was at Menlo Park in 1877 that he invented the phonograph which startled the world. The phonograph was Edison's "pet" invention.

Once an admirer of Edison asked him if his inventive ideas just flashed into his mind. Edison who frequently worked and studied day and night replied: "Genius is two per cent inspiration and ninety-eight per cent perspiration."

When Edison got a new idea on a subject, he read everything he could find which was related to it. Then he made hundreds and sometimes thousands of tests in order to find the best device for the purpose. **The electric light.** One of the best examples of Edison's method of experimenting and testing was his invention of the electric light. Other men had experimented with lighting before Edison. An electric light called the arc light was in use for street lighting at the time. It was not too satisfactory, because it created a great deal of heat and did not burn smoothly. Furthermore, it was not suitable for homes and offices. Edison was sure that he could invent a lamp that would produce a steady light for a long period. He was certain that such a light could be produced by passing an electrical current through a substance that would become white hot without breaking or burning up.

Edison set out to find that substance. One after another he tried metals, minerals, and vegetable substances. In all, he experimented with about ten thousand substances. During that time Edison hardly ever took time to eat his meals. Usually he ate what he could while he continued to work. At times he went without sleep for long hours. Seldom did he take more than four hours of sleep.

Edison tests the first electric lamp.
This light burned continuously for over forty hours

The dynamo room in the first Edison electric light plant, New York

At last on October 21, 1879, he succeeded by using a charred cotton thread. Edison described how for forty hours he watched the lamp burn. When the light finally burnt out Edison was elated.

Already $40,000 had been spent on the experiment and this was only the beginning. He was confident that he could find a substance that would make the light burn a hundred hours. He began a relentless search for a filament which would burn for many days.

Bamboo fiber proved to be better than all other filaments. Then Edison began a search for the best bamboo. Men were sent to all parts of the world to find specimens.

Japanese bamboo was adopted after a long search which cost about $100,000. Bamboo was used for a number of years.

Edison, however, continued to experiment with other filaments in order to bring the electric light to perfection. Finally in 1910 the present filament of drawn tungsten wire was invented. This was further improved in 1913. The inside frosted bulb was not introduced until 1925. Tungsten lights burn from one to two thousand hours. Can you imagine what the world would be like without electric lights?

Other inventions. Among the numerous inventions of Edison are the moving picture camera and projector which led to the modern motion picture industry. Before his death in 1931, Edison had taken out two thousand five hundred patents in the United States and twelve hundred in other countries.

During the First World War Edison gave patriotic service to our country. When his country called upon him for aid, he left his business affairs in the hands of his managers for two years. During that time he worked on special problems, especially some related to submarines, for the Navy Department. He also helped out industries and the government by perfecting processes for making carbolic acid, benzol, and other products previously obtained from European countries.

The secret of Edison's success

The first motion picture camera
Bettmann Archive

was his unbounded patience, his active imagination, and his ceaseless industry. Edison was never known to be discouraged.

Rubber, an essential of modern life. The automobile, the bicycle, and many of our modern conveniences would probably not have been possible if a way of treating rubber had not been discovered. Rubber itself had been known to civilized man since the days of Columbus. At the time of the discovery of America, Columbus found the Indians in Haiti playing a game with balls made of the dried sap from certain trees. Later Europeans accidentally discovered that this material would erase pencil marks. Since the material came from the Indies and could be used for rubbing, it was called India rubber.

The Indians knew how to dry rubber, but no one knew how to cure it so that it would not be affected by temperature changes. Men in Britain, France, and America had experimented with rubber but no one could find a way to keep it from melting and becoming sticky in the summer and from cracking and becoming stiff in winter.

Charles Goodyear. When Charles Goodyear heard of the problem he felt sure that God had called him to solve it. He was certain, therefore, that God would crown with success his efforts to find a way to perfect rubber. With the spirit of a crusader consecrated to an important cause, he set to work on the problem of perfecting rubber.

Goodyear spent many years of his life experimenting with raw rubber. Most of these experiments were carried out on his kitchen stove. Again and again he tried to find a way to keep rubber from becoming sticky in warm weather and brittle in cold weather. He mixed various chemicals with raw rubber. On several occasions, he thought he had solved the difficulty, but his hope was shattered.

In 1836 when he found that nitric acid would cure rubber he was confident that at last he had discovered the secret. He and a partner set to work to manufacture rubber articles. His first order was from the government for a large number of mailbags. Once again his efforts met with failure. By the time the order was completed and ready for delivery, the first bags had rotted from their handles.

Goodyear continues his work. At this Goodyear's friends lost faith in him, but his patient wife stood by him through every difficulty. She had labored hard to feed and clothe their children, for Goodyear's experiments kept them poor. More than once, she had experienced hunger and had seen her children go hungry. Never, however, did she reproach her husband nor doubt his success. Even though Goodyear and his family lived in dire poverty during these years, his own gentleness and tenderness made his family cling to him. They were willing to bear any sacrifice for his sake. Their love and affec-

Charles Goodyear

tion for him was deep even though each failure cast him into the debtor's prison and they were forced to depend upon charity.

In spite of all difficulties, Goodyear continued his experiments. Then one cold day in 1839, he accidentally made the important discovery. He had mixed sulphur with raw rubber and was boiling it on the kitchen stove when he happened to drop a lump of it on the red hot top of the stove. Instantly it vulcanized, that is, it no longer became sticky and it did not crack. He exposed other pieces that had been mixed with sulphur. They too kept their hardness and elasticity. He then experimented with different degrees of heat until he produced a rubber that could not be affected by heat or cold.

Goodyear had discovered the

formula which made rubber serviceable under all conditions of heat and cold, but his trials were only beginning. He had the secret, but he was not believed. Then, too, he was so poor that he would gratefully accept food at any time from a neighbor. Finally, Goodyear felt it his duty to sell the furniture and other household articles, to beg, to borrow, and, if need be, to go hungry rather than to let the discovery be lost to the world. With this spirit he was able to persevere in spite of suffering, disappointment, poverty, and defeat.

In order to advertise the uses of vulcanized rubber he made and wore a complete suit of rubber clothes. It is said that one of Goodyear's neighbors described him to a stranger in the following words: "You will know him when you see him; he has on an India rubber cap, stock, coat, vest, and shoes, and an India rubber purse without a cent in it."

Results of Goodyear's work. Goodyear lived twenty-one years after he discovered the process of vulcanizing rubber. Before he died in 1860 he had taken out about sixty patents on rubber products. Most of the last years of his life were spent on trying to protect his patent rights. He was involved in so many law-suits that he died a poor man. It was others who made fortunes on his inventions. But Goodyear's whole aim was to make his discoveries of still greater service to mankind. He was indifferent to money. In his book on rubber he wrote:

The writer is not disposed to repine and say that he has planted and others have gathered the fruits. The advantages of a career in life should not be estimated exclusively by the standard of dollars and cents, as is too often done. Man has just cause for regret when he sows and no one reaps.

The process of vulcanization was responsible for the innumerable uses of rubber that play so important a part in our daily lives. This process became especially valuable after automobiles were invented. It also led to the development of the great rubber industry in the United States.

The growth of industry began in the United States when the Industrial Revolution reached this country towards the end of the eighteenth century. The inventions and

Modern rubber factory

discoveries of the nineteenth century helped to make the United States the greatest industrial nation in the world.

2. Inventions and the Growth of Industry Change Our Ways of Living

Agriculture still remains the basic industry of the United States even though today less than twenty-five per cent of our people are engaged in farming. Though we have less farmers now than ever, we are able to feed all of the people in the United States and a large number of the people of other countries as well. American farmers also produce large quantities of raw materials, such as cotton, wool, and hides. This is possible because inventions have brought about easier and quicker ways of planting and harvesting while the large-scale use of machinery has made it possible to produce vast quantities with less help.

Discoveries and inventions aid the farmer. The discovery of ways of refining oil, making steel, and using electricity aided the farmer as well as industry. These made possible the invention of many machines which have not only lightened work on the farm but have increased production of foods and raw materials.

In the early 1800's the wooden tools of colonial days gave way to iron and steel plows, rakes, harrows, and hoes. As time went on other improvements were made. A horse-drawn hayrake which was able to do the work of eight or more men came into use around 1820. The sulky plow on which the farmer rode while he plowed his fields was in use as early as 1844. This made the work of the farmer much easier.

McCormick's reaper. As the frontier moved westward machines were needed to cultivate the prairie lands. These fertile lands yielded grain in abundance. But much of this grain was going to waste because the harvesting could not be completed on time by the slow hand methods of the day.

There was great need of a harvesting machine. Although a number of men in Europe and America attempted to construct a reaper, no one was successful until 1831. In that year Cyrus McCormick completed a reaping machine. For fifteen years his father, Robert McCormick, had tried but had never succeeded in making a reaper that would work. Cyrus, after watching his father time after time, got an idea. He set to work. With the help of a faithful slave, he patiently carried out his experiments.

At the end of three years his reaper was finished. It was just the time of the harvest. After receiving permission from a nearby farmer, he drove his reaper into the field of wheat ready for cutting. The first field was rough and hilly, therefore the machine worked badly.

The first trial. McCormick decided to give the reaper a fairer trial. He drove into the neighboring field which was level. The reaper worked well. By the end of the day six acres of grain had been well cut. This was almost ten times as much grain as

The first McCormick reaper. How did this machine change farm life?

one man could cut with a scythe.

McCormick secured a patent in 1834, but he sold only two reapers during the first ten years. The machine was not adapted to Virginia hills. McCormick had enough vision and business genius to see that. He decided to go West where sometime before he had noticed the rolling prairies with their fertile soil well suited to the growing of wheat. He set up his factory in Chicago. His keen business sense told him that farmers would not have money to pay cash. He therefore offered to give them credit with the understanding that they were to pay him after the harvest time. Before long McCormick was selling reapers as fast as he could build them.

Other farm inventions. The reaper or harvester was the first great farm labor-saving device. Today, on large grain farms, harvesting is done by combines. This machine cuts the grain, threshes it, and puts it into sacks.

After the invention of the chilled steel plow in 1869, many other improvements were made on the plow. In time a plow was invented that would not only cut the furrow, but would break up the clods of ground. Later, other machines such as seeders, corn planters, cutters, huskers, and shellers helped to relieve farm life of its drudgery.

The next step forward was to substitute a tractor engine for horses. The invention of the gasoline engine and its successful use in the automobile suggested the idea of gas-driven machines for planting and harvesting.

New machinery made it possible to plant larger crops. Most farmers then purchased more land in order to get the full value out of their machinery. As the size of the farms steadily grew larger, many farmers found that it would pay to devote all their land to a single crop such as wheat, corn, or cotton. In this way the farmer gradually became a business man who depended upon his profits for his living.

Inventions improved on the farm. Besides machinery for planting and harvesting, there were machines for milking and separating the cream. Power likewise drove the butter churn, pumped the water, and sawed the wood. Automobiles and trucks soon came to be regarded as a necessity.

Inventions have also improved the farmer's home. Hot and cold running water, electric lights, and electrical appliances such as washing machines, sweepers, toasters, and the like are found in many rural homes.

Problems of the farmer. Soon difficulties began to plague the farmer. These problems centered around

Steam engines and threshing machines at work in Dakota, 1870

prices. If the price of crops was high the farmer received a great deal of money and was prosperous. On the other hand, if the price was low there were sure to be hard times. Frequently, the farmers had to pay high prices for the things they needed, while they received next to nothing for their farm produce.

The farmers also felt that the railroad leaders did not understand the problems of farm life. At first the farmer considered the railroad his friend. After a time he was convinced that the railroad was a greedy monster because it charged extremely high and unfair rates to move farm produce to market. As farmers seldom had much ready cash they often had to borrow money to buy farm equipment. When prices were low and the railroad rates were high, the farmers could not pay the interest on their loans. In this way many a farmer, unable to meet his payments, lost not only his machinery, but his farm also.

The Granges. Farmers began to feel that they might succeed in overcoming some of these problems if they banded together.

In 1867, they formed the Grange, which is the oldest farmers' organization. At first the growth of the Grange was slow. But after the panic of 1873 the Granger Movement gradually increased. Farmers began to realize that by uniting they could make their influence felt.

In the early stages of its develop-

ment the Grange had no intention of meddling in political affairs. It did get action, however, by uniting the farmers. It has men appointed to state offices who would protect the interests of the farmers. In this way the farmers were able to have laws passed that compelled the railroad and grain elevators to give them fair rates for hauling their products and storing their grain. In time they were able also to secure favorable terms on their bank loans.

By working together through the Grange the farmers also learned the value of marketing their crops in groups and of not depending upon single money crops. Even though the Grange declined after about ten years because of poor financial undertakings, the farmers did succeed in arousing public interest in their problems.

The Farmers' Alliance. After the decline of the Grangers, another important society was organized. This was known as the National Farmers' Alliance. Organized in 1879, it soon claimed thousands of farmers among its members. Its aims and policies were chiefly those of the Grangers. Among other things, this organization fought for free and unlimited coinage of silver, for income tax, for popular election of senators, and for government control of railroads.

Like the Grange, the Farmers' Alliance also provided its members with an opportunity for social gatherings and other forms of entertainment.

The Greenback Party. Many farmers, especially in the West, in an attempt to better their conditions, joined political parties. Among these was the Greenback Party. One of the purposes of this party was to keep in use large amounts of paper money which had been issued by the United States during the Civil War.

We can see the reason for this demand of the farmers if we know the difference between "cheap" and "dear" money. Anything becomes cheap when there is plenty of it.

That is just what can happen to the paper dollar or the so-called greenback. First of all, the paper dollar has no value in itself, and secondly its value changes. This is not the case with gold dollars. Their value seldom changes. At times we get very little for the paper dollar. If we can get a great deal for the dollar we say money is "dear," that is, the dollar is a good one. If we get very little for the dollar, we say money is "cheap," that is, the dollar is a poor one. "Hard" is often used for "dear" and "soft" for "cheap."

The farmers wanted Congress to issue more paper money so that prices would go up. Then, they would get more money for their produce. In this way they would be better able to pay their debts.

In 1875 the government had announced that it intended to call in all greenbacks and redeem them in gold. The Greenback Party was organized not only to protest against the calling in of paper dollars but to endeavor to get more greenbacks printed. When the government finally announced that it would redeem paper dollars in gold few people turned them in. This gave the country a fixed standard to carry on business because the paper dollar was now of equal value with the gold dollar. This did not satisfy the farmers because they were interested in getting "cheap" dollars.

Free silver. From the earliest days of our history, Congress provided for free or unlimited coinage of both gold and silver. This meant that anyone could take either gold or silver to the mint and have it coined into money. In 1837 an ounce of gold was worth sixteen times as much as an ounce of silver. Congress, therefore, fixed the ratio between gold and silver at sixteen to one, which meant there had to be sixteen times as many grains of pure silver in a silver dollar as there were grains of pure gold in a gold dollar. Both gold and silver dollars were coined.

After the discovery of gold in California, the output of this precious metal became so abundant that it soon grew cheaper than silver at the ratio of sixteen to one. The silver miners at this time found that they could get more money for their metal when they sold it to jewelers or silversmiths than when they brought it to the mint. For almost twenty-five years, no silver was sent to the mint and silver dollars began to disappear.

The Crime of 1873. In 1873 Congress passed new coinage laws. At the time the principal countries of Europe were beginning to use only a single standard as the basis for the coinage of their money. That was the gold standard. As silver dollars had been practically unknown for over twenty years, Congress put the United States on the gold standard. The new law, therefore, put silver dollars out of circulation.

At the time there was no objection to the new law. Soon other silver mines were discovered in Colorado, Montana, Nevada, and Utah. As more and more silver was mined it decreased in value. When the miners could no longer get a high price for silver from the silversmith, they took it to the government mint to be coined. But this could not be done, for the law of 1873 did not provide for the making of silver dollars. The miners and others then began to clamor for the restoration of the free coinage of silver. They demanded that the law of 1873 be repealed. The West loudly condemned the act and called it the "Crime of 1873."

The Bland-Allison Act. In response to this demand, Representative Richard P. Bland of Missouri introduced a bill for the free coinage of silver. Senator Allison of Iowa suggested some slight changes. Although many thought that the unlimited coinage of silver was unwise, Congress passed the Bland-Allison Act in 1878. Instead of free coinage of silver the law now required the government to buy not less than two million dollars' worth and not more than four million dollars' worth of silver a month. The Bland-Allison Act remained in force for twelve years.

In 1890, to further satisfy miners, farmers, and workers from the West and South, Congress passed the Sherman Free Silver Act. The new law required the government to buy twice as much silver as it had been purchasing under the Bland-Allison Act. Instead of coining all this silver, the government stored it in the treasury. When early in 1893 a severe panic, about which we will read in GUARDIAN OF FREEDOM, started, President Cleveland demanded the repeal of the Sherman Free Silver Act.

Inventions aid business. Besides bringing about changes in agriculture and industry, the invention of machines has brought about many improvements in offices and business houses. Not long after the invention of the typewriter other office time-saving devices came into use. Among these were adding machines and dictaphones. Today nearly all office work is done with such machines. One of the greatest time-saving devices in the office was and still is the telephone. It brings all parts of our country close together. To the modern businessman the telephone is essential.

Then, too, in by-gone days all type was set by hand. The invention of the linotype with all its improvements has made possible the rapid setting of type. Machines turn out some sixty thousand papers in one hour. These machines do all the work. They print, cut, fold, and count the numerous papers. Inventions in the field of printing have made possible vast numbers of newspapers, magazines, and books.

Machines affect home life. The influence of machines upon the life of the American people has been great also. Machines have changed not only our ways of living but also our place of living. Although these changes have brought about great benefits they have also introduced certain evils.

Through inventions, the candle, the kerosene lamp, and the gas jet which were used in the American home were gradually replaced by electric lights and lamps. The fireplace, the gas stove, and the base burner in time gave way to steam, hot air, and hot water heating systems. Hot and cold running water has been installed in most city homes and in a large number of rural homes. In addition electrical appliances have lightened the labor of housework and have added immeasurably to the convenience and enjoyment of home life. Among these are electric washing machines, irons, refrigerators, clocks, toasters, heaters, and fans. Other luxuries of city and farm life which a large percentage of American families enjoy are the automobile, the telephone, the radio, and the television.

Movement from the land. As more and more farm machinery came into use, fewer persons were needed to do the work. At the same

Brown Brothers

A Parlor Stove

time industry gradually developed to great proportions. Factories were in need of many hands to keep the machines in operation in order to speed up production. These conditions, together with the improvement of transportation and communication, led many farmers to move to the city. This movement, though slight at first, gradually led to the settlement of large groups of people around the industrial centers. As more people left the farms and more immigrants came to the United States, it was possible for manufacturing to increase. With the growth of manufacturing, commerce increased, and with the increase of both manufacturing and commerce cities grew rapidly.

Many people abandoned the rural areas because of the advantages they could enjoy in the city. Among these were greater religious, educational, social, and recreational opportunities. Churches were conveniently located; public libraries carried a variety of reading matter; and regulated factory hours gave the people more leisure for educational, cultural, and recreational purposes.

Problems of the Machine Age. Although the changes brought about by the Machine Age were of some benefit, they did create tremendous problems. For one thing the United States changed in a very short time from a nation of small towns and farms to one of large cities and enormous farms. Such rapid growth was not too good. It brought about conditions in which extremes of poverty and riches existed side by side. Millions of Americans were poorly sheltered, poorly clothed, and poorly fed in spite of increased production and all the conveniences of modern life. Many of our farmers, as well as the Europeans who flocked to the cities, were unskilled laborers and consequently they could earn only a low wage. Often they did not have enough money to house, feed, and clothe themselves properly. Much less could they afford to give their children a good education or the comforts of life.

Soon these people found themselves herded together in wretched tenement houses in the slum sections of our large cities. Whole families were crowded into one or two dark and dingy rooms. Living together under such conditions they lost their sense of the dignity of human life and their respect for the rights and property of others.

The children suffered not only physically but also morally. Denied a decent home life, they often pilfered to get what they wanted. From this small beginning they gradually drifted downward until they finally became hardened thieves and murderers. It was not long before the slums of the cities with their wretched homes and lack of necessities of life were notorious breeding places of vice and crime.

Weakening of the family. The changes brought about by the Machine Age created problems even in the better sections of the large cities. One of the most serious of these was the weakening of family ties. Fathers and mothers, as well as their growing children, found employment outside the home. They also found the many opportunities for commercialized recreation outside the home more inviting. Consequently, parents drifted from their children and broke the ties of intimate family life.

Another factor in the breakdown of the family was that of rearing children under city conditions. Because large cities were so congested, even in the better sections, it was difficult for parents with many children to find a suitable home with plenty of sunshine and fresh air. Even today when tenement houses are being replaced with apartments there is little chance of securing a home for a large family.

Formerly most of the work was done at home. Today, with the increase of conveniences, canning, the making of clothes, and other similar tasks are done in factories. This has tended to lessen the work of the housewife but it has increased expenses. As expenses increased, families decreased in size for every child meant an extra mouth to feed. At the present time the ordinary family consists of one, two, or frequently no children.

We have seen that the characteristics of city life—crowded living conditions, low wages, fear of unemployment, the tendency to consider luxuries as necessities, and the manifold opportunities for occupation and entertainment outside the home — have all contributed to the weakening of family life. In the United States family life is tottering. That is very serious for everyone knows that any nation is as strong as its family life.

Word study

lock-stitch	royalty	vulcanize
invested	petroleum	slums
patent rights	filament	reaper
ready market	cure rubber	Granges
telegraphy	free coinage	Granger
unskilled labor	plow	laboratory
Granger Movement	combine	alliance

How well have you read?

1. Discuss how the principle of "interchangeable parts" in manufacturing works in articles used in the classroom such as eversharp pencils, fountain pens, lockers, pencil sharpeners and other articles.
2. Discuss with your classmates the characteristics you think are essential for an inventor or for success in any worthwhile undertaking.
3. Discuss the effects of industrial growth on the family.
4. To what extent were the natural resources of the United States responsible for the progress our country made during the nineteenth century.

Test yourself

On the line(s) behind each item below write the name or names of the person or persons associated with the invention or discovery. The number of lines behind each name designates the number of names needed. Score: 10 points.

sewing machine	. . . .	. . . .
steel	. . . .	. . . .
oil	. . . .	
dynamo	. . . .	
phonograph	. . . .	
electric light	. . . .	
rubber	. . . .	
reaper	. . . .	

CHAPTER III

EDUCATIONAL AND CULTURAL PROGRESS KEEP PACE WITH INDUSTRY

How far progress? During the rapid and prosperous growth of the United States, our people did not forget to interest themselves in the finer things of life, such as education, literature, music, and art. Last year we read about the development of the public school system and the progress of culture in the eighteenth century. In this chapter we shall study: (1) Catholic Education Develops in the United States, and (2) Cultural Progress during the Nineteenth Century.

1. Catholic Education Develops in the United States

In LEADERS OF FREEDOM we read about Horace Mann and his efforts to establish the American Public School System. We also learned how he started the first school for the training of teachers in the United States. Horace Mann was not alone in the struggle for free public schools. He received much help from DeWitt Clinton, Governor of New York, and Henry Barnard, Commissioner of Education from 1838 to 1849 in Connecticut and later in Rhode Island. Together Horace Mann and Henry Barnard laid a firm foundation for a system of free education for the children of all classes of people in the United States.

All schools religious schools. Up to the time of Horace Mann, practically all schools were parish or church schools. Each denomination conducted its own schools. Each wanted religion to be a part of the progress of education. Horace Mann also believed that children should be taught religion, but he did not know how this could be done in schools attended by children of every creed. He finally planned a public school system in which no religion was to be taught. The Catholic Church in America then decided to found parish schools according to the recommendation made by the First Provincial Council of Baltimore in 1829.

Parochial schools. The greatest problem in the foundation of parochial schools was that of supporting them. The Catholics were called upon to build and to support their schools. This required much sacrifice on the part of the Catholics for they were already obliged to pay taxes for the support of the public schools. Many non-Catholics believed that the Catholics should in justice be allowed to use a portion of the taxes to support Catholic education. Others thought that it would be undemocratic to use public taxes for private schools.

The Catholic Church received from Jesus, the Redeemer of mankind, the authority to teach. She recognizes the right of the state to provide for the education of its citizens, but she strongly emphasizes the fact that the state has neither the right to forbid the spiritual training of its citizens nor the right to force individuals to attend a certain type of school. Catholic education has always insisted that the right to educate one's children is a right given by God to parents.

This right of parents was upheld by the United States Supreme Court on June 1, 1925. The government of the State of Oregon attempted to pass a law which would require parents to send their children to public schools. The Supreme Court in its decision proclaimed that the direction of the education of their children was a fundamental right of parents.

Beginning of parochial school system. From the establishment of our nation Catholics have always had to fight for their rights in education. Archbishop John Hughes, whom we met in our Unit on immigration, again fought for the rights of his people. Before the establishment of the public school system, the State of New York had given grants of money to schools conducted by various churches to be used especially for the education of poor children.

Through the influence of Horace Mann, the Public School Society, a private organization, was given control of the taxes apportioned to education. Grants which had been given to religious schools were stopped and all the money received as taxes was used for the support of the public schools.

Archbishop Hughes believed that such a practice was unfair. He believed that Catholics, as well as the other denominations that conducted their own schools, should receive a just share of the taxes for the purpose of educating their children according to the dictates of their conscience. He claimed that they should share in public funds not because they were Catholics or members of some other church, but because they were also citizens of the United States. In his fight for justice Archbishop Hughes even carried the case to the state legislature.

Although the Archbishop's efforts to obtain funds for the support of Catholic education failed, he did succeed in getting objectionable-textbooks and sectarian religion removed from the public schools for at least a time.

Establishment of Catholic schools. When the Archbishop saw that it was useless to carry the case further, he put all his zeal and energy into the establishment of a Catholic school system in his diocese. He called together all the clergy of his diocese and urged them to build parish schools. He also took upon himself the task of finding teachers for these schools. He hoped that in time it would be possible for his people to withdraw their children from the public schools.

Several religious orders responded to the Archbishop's plea for teachers. Among the first to answer the call were the Sisters of Charity, an American community founded by Mother Seton. It was these same Sisters of Charity who had started the first free Catholic school in Baltimore. Two other communities of women that answered the Archbishop's plea were the Sisters of Mercy who did fine work in Pittsburgh, and the Religious of the Sacred Heart who had opened the first free school west of the Mississippi under the direction of Mother

Mother Seton

Duchesne. The religious community of men that responded was that of the Brothers of the Christian Schools. This community was founded by St. John Baptist de la Salle.

From the very beginning religious orders of men and women have played an important part in the growth and development of Catholic education in America. It was really through the self-sacrificing zeal and devotion of these consecrated men and women that the parochial school system was made possible.

The First Plenary Council of Baltimore in 1852 and the Second Plenary Council of Baltimore in 1866 again sent out a plea for the establishment of Catholic schools. As a result of the pleadings of these councils and the zealous efforts of the clergy and many teaching communities of religious, the parochial school system was well under way before the close of the nineteenth century.

Catholic higher education in America. As time went on the Catholic Church took not only an interest but a leading part in providing for her members a high school and college education. It was not, however, until after 1900 that a high-school education became general. During the nineteenth century, high-school training was for the most part conducted in academies or tuition schools. By the time the parochial school system was firmly established in our country, there were four universities, five colleges, and two seminaries in the United

States for the higher education of Catholic youth.

Chief among the universities was The Catholic University of America which was established in Washington, D. C., in 1888. This University has become the center of Catholic higher education. When Pius XI sent out a letter in which he pleaded for someone to work out a program for training in good citizenship, The Catholic University responded wholeheartedly. The Commission on American Citizenship was established. The purpose of this Commission is to form good staunch Catholics and loyal citizens.

2. Cultural Progress During the Nineteenth Century

Although there were some literary selections written in America before and during the Revolutionary War, American literature and art as such did not become important until the early years of Jackson's administration. It was then that Washington Irving, William Cullen Bryant, James Fenimore Cooper, and Nathaniel Hawthorne wrote the classics that still hold a prominent place in the world of literature today.

American writers. William Cullen Bryant is our first great nature poet. In his poems *To a Fringed Gentian,* and *To a Waterfowl* he helps us to see the beauty and power of God in the flower, the bird, the forest, and the field. Always Bryant showed a deep, unfaltering trust in God. *Thanatopsis,* a poem written when he was only seventeen years of age, shows his interest in so serious a topic as death.

James Fenimore Cooper and Washington Irving are also famous American writers. Cooper was in love with the sea, the forest, and the frontier. Because of his gift of story-telling Cooper was able to write tales of the sea and stories of the frontier which still fascinate American boys and girls. His *Leather-stocking Tales,* which are exciting stories of frontier life, vividly portray the Indian and the pioneer. Irving, like Cooper, was a charming story-teller. As he travelled about, he wrote sketches of what he heard and saw. These, together with other stories, he published in a book called the *Sketch Book.* His humor and his use of American ideas and people in stories such as *Rip Van Winkle* and *Sleepy Hollow* have endeared him to the people of our country. Irving is considered America's first man of letters and the father of the American short story.

Hawthorne and others. America's leading novelist of the time was Nathaniel Hawthorne. Even though the gloominess and loneliness of his early life is seen in many of his writings, he is, nevertheless, one of America's greatest story-tellers. Hawthorne's *Tanglewood Tales* and *Grandfather's Chair* are some of the best tales that have ever been written, while *The Scarlet Letter* and *The House of Seven Gables* won great fame for him.

Other writers of the nineteenth

Brown Brothers

Nathaniel Hawthorne

life. Two of these which were and still are popular are "The Barefoot Boy," and "Snowbound."

The most outstanding work of Oliver Wendell Holmes is *The Autocrat of the Breakfast Table,* while the "Wonderful One-Hoss Shay" is his best-known comical poem. Among his more serious poems are "Old Ironsides" and the "Chambered Nautilus."

Although Emerson wrote several short poems, he won fame through his essays. His best-known poem is "Concord Hymn."

The most beautiful poem of James Russell Lowell is the "First Snowfall." His "Bigelow Papers" are a series of humorous poems directed against the politicians of his day, while the "Vision of Sir Launfal" pictures for us the religious side of Lowell's character.

century who were outstanding were Henry Wadsworth Longfellow, Ralph Waldo Emerson, John Greenleaf Whittier, James Russell Lowell, Oliver Wendell Holmes, and Edgar Allan Poe. Most of these writers influenced the lives of the people by the high moral tone of their writings.

Henry Wadsworth Longfellow is known as the children's poet of America. He told his stories about the affairs of everyday life so simply and with such vividness and color that he will ever remain one of America's best loved poets. Some of his poems are "The Village Blacksmith," "The Children's Hour," "Hiawatha," "Evangeline," and "Paul Revere's Ride."

Whittier, like Longfellow, is best known for his poems on everyday

Edgar Allen Poe

Brown Brothers

Most outstanding of all American writers of the time was Edgar Allan Poe. Besides giving us some excellent poetry like "The Raven" and "Annabel Lee," he also helped to make the short story popular.

The most famous of America's historians were George Bancroft, William Prescott, Francis Parkman, and John Gilmary Shea, the last of whom was a Catholic.

After the Civil War. After the Civil War, writers like Louisa May Alcott, who glorified home life in her stories *Little Women* and *Little Men;* Bret Harte, a clever writer, who vividly portrayed life in the Far West in *The Luck of the Roaring Camp* and *The Outcasts of Poker Flat;* and Joel Chandler Harris, who brought to life Negro folklore in his Uncle Remus stories, helped further the cultural growth in America.

The most distinguished writer of this period was Samuel L. Clemens who is better known as Mark Twain. His two stories, *Huckleberry Finn* and *Tom Sawyer*, will always be favorites with the boys and girls of America.

Another writer who understood and loved children was Father Francis J. Finn, a Jesuit. His books *Tom Playfair, Sunshine and Freckles,* and *Fairy of the Snows* became so popular that they were translated into many languages.

Edward Everett Hale won fame through his story *A Man Without a Country,* while Thomas Bailey Aldrich, another writer of the period, related his childhood experi-

Brown Brothers

Mark Twain

ences in *The Story of a Bad Boy.*

After the Civil War the literature of America changed. It was no longer as imaginative and idealistic as it had been. It became more realistic, that is based more on fact than on ideas. This came about partly because America was changing from an agricultural to an industrial and commercial country.

Father Abram Ryan wrote such serious poems as "The Conquered Banner" and "The Sword of Robert Lee." Father John B. Tabb, on the other hand, depicted the joy of life in most of his poems. Those on Our Lady are among his best.

Walt Whitman is often called the "poet of democracy." His greatest poem, "O Captain, My Captain," was written upon the assassination of Abraham Lincoln. "Little Orphan Annie" and "The Raggedy

Man," poems of James Whitcomb Riley, abound with humor and pathos and are still loved by young and old. Another poet of this period who has given the American people two of their favorite poems, "Little Boy Blue" and "Wynken, Blynken, and Nod," is Eugene Field. As a writer for children, he is outstanding.

Progress in art. A definite style in American art did not develop until after the Civil War. Painting took on an American tone much earlier than sculpture. Benjamin West, about whom you read in LEADERS OF FREEDOM, was the first American portrait painter. The most noteworthy painters of the nineteenth century were Sargent, LaFarge, Abbey, Inness, and Whistler.

John S. Sargent, considered America's greatest portrait painter since 1876, achieved fame through his magnificent murals. Some of them which illustrate the pageant of religion as found in the Bible may still be seen in the Boston Public Library. Like Sargent, John LaFarge and Edwin Abbey were also renowned painters of murals. Both have painted literary and historical events with charm and accuracy. Abbey told in color the story of Sir Galahad from infancy to death. "The Story of the Holy Grail" in the Boston Public Library is considered his masterpiece. La-

Whistler's Mother

Farge, who is the father of the Jesuit, Father John LaFarge, was also famous for his work in glass and his landscape paintings.

George Inness, whose love for the American landscape is seen in all his paintings, was America's greatest landscape painter. James McNeill Whistler, a master of color, has given America many fine portraits, landscapes, and etchings. The best known of his works is the picture popularly called "Whistler's Mother."

Sculptors and architects. The greatest of American sculptors was Augustus Saint Gaudens. His statues and memorials are found in many of our large cities. Among his most outstanding works are his monuments of General Sherman and Admiral Farragut in New York City and his bronze statue of Lincoln in Chicago.

Early architects, like early artists, imitated the style of the Old World. A distinctly American type of architecture did not appear until late in the nineteenth century.

An outstanding architect was Benjamin H. Latrobe, who designed the Catholic Cathedral in Baltimore, and the famous Thomas Viaduct, still in use on the B & O Railroad.

Music in America. As in the other arts, America did not produce much of her own music in the early days.

Thomas Viaduct

During the years before the Civil War most of the music developed out of the life and activities of the people. The pioneers, the Negroes, the sailors, the forty-niners, the boatmen, and the cowboys sang at their work. These songs became the folk music in America. Outstanding among all these are the Negro Spirituals which were the religious songs of the slaves.

Then, too, many of the immigrants, especially the Germans, brought with them a love of music. Wherever they settled in large numbers, an interest in music grew rapidly.

It was not, however, until after the days of Reconstruction that American composers made their appearance. The songs of Stephen Foster, rich in the love of plantation life are familiar to every American. His "My Old Kentucky Home," "Old Black Joe," and "Way Down Upon the Swanee River," along with Dan Emmett's "Dixie," have won great popularity.

Most distinguished of American musicians is Edward MacDowell. Much of his charming music has a distinctly Indian background. Every pianist is familiar with his "Woodland Sketches" and his "Indian Suite."

Theodore Thomas, a famous conductor of music, did much to develop the musical taste of America, especially in New York and Chicago, while Lowell Mason, a composer, encouraged musical education in the schools.

During the rapid growth and industrial development of America, our people did not entirely neglect the fine things of life. On the contrary, they carried with them into the fields of education, literature, art, and music the enterprising spirit that has become characteristic of America. By the close of the nineteenth century, then, America was famous not only for her industrial development but also for her cultural growth.

Terms to study

free public schools	education	cultural progress
religious schools	college	prose
parochial schools	university	poetry
essay	literature	folklore
sculptor	architect	mural
sculpture	skyscraper	folk music

How well have you read?

1. Discuss with your classmates the possibility of having public schools which are at the same time religious schools.
2. Why did Archbishop Hughes try to secure a share of the public funds for Catholic schools? Was he justified in his efforts?
3. Discuss the statement: "The home is no longer the center of recreation."

Test yourself

Divide your paper into four columns. Above the first write *Education*, above the second *Literature*, above the third *Art*, and above the fourth *Music*. Then write each of the following names in the proper column.

Walt Whitman	James Whitcomb Riley	Augustus Saint Gaudens
Henry Barnard	Theodore Thomas	Archbishop John Hughes
Mark Twain	Edward MacDowell	Father Francis J. Finn, S.J.
John S. Sargent	James Russell Lowell	James Fenimore Cooper
Horace Mann	Nathaniel Hawthorne	James McNeil Whistler
John LaFarge	Louisa May Alcott	Henry Wadsworth Longfellow
Stephen Foster	George Inness	

REVIEW OF UNIT SIX

Minimum essentials

1. God gave his gifts of the earth to all men.

2. God expects all men to share spiritual, intellectual, and social goods with one another.

3. The many inventors of the nineteenth century brought about a period of rapid growth and development.

4. Some of the outstanding inventors of this period are:

Inventor	Invention	Date
Samuel F. B. Morse	Electric telegraph	1844
Cyrus W. Field	Atlantic Cable	1866
Alexander Graham Bell	Telephone	1876
Guglielmo Marconi	Wireless telegraphy	1895
Richard M. Hoe	Rotary press	1846
Ottmar Mergenthaler	Linotype	1885
George Westinghouse	Airbrake	1869
George M. Pullman	Pullman cars	1864
Gottlieb Daimler	Gas engine	1886
Charles Duryea	Automobile (gasoline)	1892
Elias Howe	Sewing machine	1846
Thomas Alva Edison	Electric light	1879
Thomas Alva Edison	Phonograph	1877
Charles Goodyear	Vulcanized rubber	1839
Cyrus McCormick	Reaper	1835

5. The invention of the automobile created a demand for hard-surfaced roads.

6. Most famous of the highways in the United States is the Lincoln Highway.

7. Free delivery of mail began in the cities during the Civil War. This service was extended to the rural areas in 1896.

8. Motor trucks and motor buses operate side by side with railroads.

9. Steel is iron with most of the carbon removed. It is much stronger than iron.

10. Henry Bessemer and William Kelly discovered the process of making steel.

11. The abundant natural resources with which God has blessed America have helped industry to grow and develop.

12. Petroleum and electricity are important sources of power.

13. Agriculture is still the basic industry of the United States even though only 30% of our people are engaged in farming.

14. The large scale use of farm machinery has made possible the production of large quantities with little help.

15. The discovery of ways of refining oil, making steel, and using electricity has aided both the farmer and industry.

16. The reaper, or a machine for cutting grain, was the first great farm labor-saving device.

17. The Grange is the oldest organization of farmers.

18. Another organization of farmers was the Farmers' Alliance established in 1879.

19. Both of these organizations of farmers succeeded in arousing interest in the problems of farmers.

20. Money is called "cheap money" when we get little for the dollar. It is considered "dear money" when we get a great deal for a dollar.

21. Inventions of time-saving devices such as the adding machine, the typewriter, the dictaphone, and the telephone aided business.

22. The development of industry and commerce caused cities to grow rapidly.

23. The Machine Age
   a. changed the United States into a nation of large cities and enormous farms.
   b. caused a quick shifting of population from farms to cities which created problems such as
      1) slums which became dens of vice and crime
      2) congested conditions which made it hard to rear a large family
      3) commercialized recreation which helped to break down family ties.

24. The American system of free public schools was established by Horace Mann.

25. Another outstanding American educator of the time was Henry Barnard.

26. The State does have the right to provide for the education of its citizens.

27. The State does not have the right to force individuals to attend a certain type of school. Neither does the State have the right to forbid religious training of its citizens.

28. The right to educate one's children is a right given by God to parents. The Supreme Court of the United States upheld this right of parents in its decision of the Oregon Case on June 1, 1925.

29. Archbishop Hughes rightly claimed that Catholics should receive a just share of taxes to run their schools not because they are Catholics but because they are citizens.

30. The establishment of parochial schools was strongly urged by both the first and second Plenary Councils of Baltimore.
31. Some outstanding writers of the nineteenth century were: William Cullen Bryant, Washington Irving, James Fenimore Cooper, Nathaniel Hawthorne, Henry Wadsworth Longfellow, Ralph Waldo Emerson, John Greenleaf Whittier, James Russell Lowell, Oliver Wendell Holmes, Edgar Allan Poe, Louisa May Alcott, Bret Harte, Joel Chandler Harris, Samuel L. Clemens (Mark Twain), Father Francis J. Finn, S.J., Edward Everett Hale, Thomas Bailey Aldrich, Father Abram Ryan, Father John B. Tabb, Walt Whitman, James Whitcomb Riley, and Eugene Field.
32. Some outstanding artists of this period were: John S. Sargent, John LaFarge, Edwin Abbey, George Inness, James McNeill Whistler, Augustus Saint Gaudens.
33. A few musicians were: Stephen Foster, Edward MacDowell, Theodore Thomas, and Dan Emmett.

Something to do

1. Prepare and present a pageant or a series of slides showing the progress of inventions and their influence upon man's ways of living. This could also be carried out using just one invention such as the automobile or the railroad.

2. Make a sectional frieze on inventions. Divide the class into five groups. Let each group be responsible for one section of the frieze, as —

   a. Improvements in transportation
   b. Improvements in communication
   c. Improvements in industry
   d. Improvements in farm machinery
   e. Inventions which have improved urban and rural living.

3. The idea in No. 2 above could be worked out to show the educational and cultural progress of the nineteenth century. Divide the class into five groups. Let each group be responsible for one section of the frieze, as —

   a. Educational developments
   b. Prose writers
   c. Poets
   d. Artists and sculptors
   e. Musicians

4. Learn and sing more songs composed by Stephen Foster.

5. Choose one invention such as the telephone, cable, phonograph, or electric light. On a map of the world show from which countries the raw materials needed for that article are obtained.

6. Prepare and give a report on one of the following.

   Elias Howe
   Thomas Alva Edison
   Henry Ford
   Stephen Foster
   Archbishop John Hughes
   Augustus Saint Gaudens
   Louisa May Alcott

7. Make an illustrated chart showing the uses of electricity.
8. Make a scrapbook or chart showing all the labor-saving devices that inventions have brought to the farm, to the home, or to the factory.

TEST ON THE ENTIRE UNIT

I. Completion Test

Number a sheet of paper from 1 to 13. Select the correct word or phrase from the list below and write it behind the number of the statement that it completes.

1. A cheap and quick process of making steel was discovered by.......... and.........
2. The .... helped bring the city and the country together.
3. The sewing machine was invented by ....
4. .... found a way to manufacture low-priced automobiles.
5. The chief material needed in the manufacture of machinery is ....
6. The invention of the .... revolutionized the clothing industry.
7. .... invented the electric light and the phonograph.
8. Marconi invented the ....
9. The first means of rapid communication between America and Europe was the ....
10. The .... was passed to satisfy the silver miners of the West.
11. The invention of the automobile created a demand for .... roads.
12. The abundant .... with which God blessed America have helped industry to grow and develop.
13. Two very important sources of power are .... and ....

Henry Ford	petroleum	Atlantic Cable
William Kelly	hard-surfaced	automobile
Thomas Alva Edison	steel	natural resources
wireless telegraph	electricity	sewing machine
Henry Bessemer	Elias Howe	Bland-Allison Act

II. Essay Questions

1. What are the advantages and the disadvantages of living in a large city?
2. How have the conditions found in our large cities affected family life?
3. What two factors have made possible the rapid industrial growth of the United States?

III. Matching Test

A. Number your paper from 1 to 15. Behind each number on your paper write the letter found before the item in Column II which was invented by the person whose name is written behind that number in Column I.

Column I

... 1. Cyrus McCormick   a. electric telegraph
... 2. Thomas Alva Edison   b. typewriter
... 3. Samuel F. B. Morse   c. reaper
... 4. Charles Goodyear   d. phonograph
... 5. Charles Duryea   e. rotary press
... 6. Cyrus W. Field   f. Atlantic cable
... 7. Richard M. Hoe   g. automobile

B. Do the same with these.

... 8. Alexander Graham Bell   h. vulcanized rubber
... 9. Gottlieb Daimler   i. telephone
...10. Ottmar Mergenthaler   j. Pullman cars
...11. George Pullman   k. wireless telegraphy
...12. Guglielmo Marconi   l. sewing machine
...13. George Westinghouse   m. gasoline engine
...14. Elias Howe   n. airbrake
...15. C. L. Sholes   o. linotype

C. Match the following in the same manner.

... 1. William Cullen Bryant   a. "Hiawatha"
... 2. James Fenimore Cooper   b. "The Raven"
... 3. Washington Irving   c. "Old Black Joe"
... 4. Archbishop John Hughes   d. "Rip Van Winkle"
... 5. Henry Wadsworth Longfellow   e. "Leather-stocking Tales"
... 6. Edgar Allan Poe   f. parochial school system

D. Do the same with these.

... 7. Stephen Foster   g. "To a Waterfowl"
... 8. John S. Sargent   h. "Sunshine and Freckles"
... 9. Louisa May Alcott   i. "O Captain, My Captain"
...10. John Gilmary Shea   j. historian
...11. Mark Twain   k. "Indian Suite"
...12. Father Francis J. Finn, S.J.   l. a sculptor
...13. Edward MacDowell   m. "Little Women"
...14. Walt Whitman   n. "Huckleberry Finn"
...15. Augustus Saint Gaudens   o. painter of murals

THE DECLARATION OF INDEPENDENCE

Reasons for Declaration.

When, in the course of human events, it becomes necessary for one people to dissolve the political bonds which have connected them with another, and to assume among the powers of the earth the separate and equal station to which the laws of nature and of nature's God entitle them, a decent respect to the opinions of mankind requires that they should declare the causes which impell them to the separation.

Rights given by the Creator.

We hold these truths to be self-evident: That all men are created equal; that they are endowed by their Creator with certain inalienable rights; that among these are life, liberty, and the pursuit of happiness. That to secure these rights, governments are instituted among men, deriving their just powers from the consent of the governed; that, whenever any form of government becomes destructive of these ends, it is the right of the people to alter or to abolish it, and to institute a new government, laying its foundation on such principles, and organizing its powers in such form, as to them shall seem most likely to effect their safety and happiness. Prudence, indeed, will dictate that governments long established should not be changed for light and transient causes; and accordingly all experience hath shown that mankind are more disposed to suffer, while evils are sufferable, than to right themselves by abolishing the forms to which they are accustomed. But when a long train of abuses and usurpations, pursuing invariably the same object, evinces a design to reduce them under absolute despotism, it is their right, it is their duty, to throw off such government and to provide new guards for their future security. Such has been the patient suffering of these colonies, and such is now the necessity which constrains them to alter their former systems of government.

The tyranny of the British King.

The history of the present king of Great Britain is a history of repeated injuries, and usurpations, all having in direct object the establishment of an absolute tyranny over these states. To prove this, let facts be submitted to a candid world.

1. He has refused his assent to laws the most wholesome and necessary for the public good.

2. He has forbidden his governors to pass laws of immediate and pressing importance, unless suspended in their operation till his assent should be obtained, and, when so suspended

he has utterly neglected to attend to them.

3. He has refused to pass other laws for the accommodation of large districts of people, unless those people would relinquish the right of representation in the legislature— a right inestimable to them and formidable to tyrants only.

4. He has called together legislative bodies, at places unusual, uncomfortable, and distant from the repository of their public records, for the sole purpose of fatiguing them into compliance with his measures.

5. He has dissolved representative houses repeatedly for opposing with manly firmness his invasions on the rights of the people.

6. He has refused for a long time after such dissolutions to cause others to be elected; whereby the legislative powers, incapable of annihilation, have returned to the people at large for their exercise: the state remaining, in the meantime, exposed to all the dangers of invasion from without and convulsions within.

7. He has endeavored to prevent the population of these states; for that purpose obstructing the laws for naturalization of foreigners; refusing to pass others to encourage their migration hither, and raising the conditions of new appropriations of lands.

8. He has obstructed the administration of justice by refusing his assent to laws for establishing his judiciary powers.

9. He has made judges dependent on his will alone for the tenure of their offices and the amount and payment of their salaries.

10. He has erected a multitude of new offices and sent hither swarms of officers to harass our people and eat out their substance.

11. He has kept among us, in times of peace, standing armies without the consent of our legislature.

12. He has affected to render the military independent of and superior to the civil power.

13. He has combined with others to subject us to a jurisdiction foreign to our constitutions and unacknowledged by our laws, giving his assent to their acts of pretended legislation.

14. For quartering large bodies of armed troops among us;

15. For protecting them by a mock trial from punishment for any murders which they should commit on the inhabitants of these states;

16. For cutting off our trade with all parts of the world;

17. For imposing taxes on us without our consent;

18. For depriving us in many cases of the benefits of trial by jury;

19. For transporting us beyond seas to be tried for pretended offenses;

20. For abolishing the free system of English laws in a neighboring province, establishing therein an ar-

bitrary government, and enlarging its boundaries so as to render it at once an example and fit instrument for introducing the same absolute rule into these colonies;

21. For taking away our charters, abolishing our most valuable laws, and altering fundamentally the forms of our government;

22. For suspending our own legislatures and declaring themselves invested with power to legislate for us in all cases whatsoever.

23. He has abdicated government here by declaring us out of his protection and waging war against us.

24. He has plundered our seas, ravaged our coasts, burnt our towns and destroyed the lives of our people.

25. He is at this time transporting large armies of foreign mercenaries to complete the work of death, desolation, and tyranny already begun, with circumstances of cruelty and perfidy scarcely paralleled in the most barbarous ages and totally unworthy of the head of a civilized nation.

26. He has constrained our fellow citizens taken captive upon the high seas to bear arms against their country, to become the executioners of their friends and brethren, or to fall themselves by their hands.

27. He has excited domestic insurrection amongst us, and has endeavored to bring on the inhabitants of our frontiers the merciless Indian savages, whose known rule of war-

fare is an undistinguished destruction of all ages, sexes, and conditions.

In every stage of these oppressions we have petitioned for redress, in the most humble terms; our repeated petitions have been answered only by repeated injury. A prince whose character is thus marked by every act which may define a tyrant is unfit to be ruler of a free people.

Attempts to avoid separation from Britain.

Nor have we been wanting in attentions to our British brethren. We have warned them, from time to time, of attempts by their legislature to extend an unwarrantable jurisdiction over us. We have reminded them of the circumstances of our emigration and settlement here. We have appealed to their native justice and magnanimity; and we have conjured them by the ties of our common kindred to disavow these usurpations, which would inevitably interrupt our connection and correspondence. They, too, have been deaf to the voice of justice and sanguinity. We must, therefore, acquiesce in the necessity which denounces our separation, and hold them, as we hold the rest of mankind, enemies in war; in peace, friends.

Freedom declared.

We, therefore, the representatives of the United States of America, in general congress assembled, appealing to the Supreme Judge of the World for the rectitude of our intentions, do, in the name and by the authority of the good people of these colonies solemnly publish and declare that these united colonies are, and of right ought to be, free and independent states; that they are absolved from all allegiance to the British crown, and that all political connection between them and the state of Great Britain is, and ought to be, totally dissolved; and that as free and independent states they have full power to levy war, conclude peace, contract alliances, establish commerce, and to do all other acts and things which independent states may of right do. And for the support of this declaration, with firm reliance on the protection of Divine Providence, we mutually pledge to each other our lives, our fortunes, and our sacred honor.

JOHN HANCOCK

NEW HAMPSHIRE:
Josiah Bartlett. Wm. Whipple, Matthew Thornton.

MASSACHUSETTS BAY:
Samuel Adams, John Adams, Robert Treat Paine, Elbridge Gerry.

RHODE ISLAND:
Stephen Hopkins, William Ellery.

CONNECTICUT:
Roger Sherman, Samuel Huntington, William Williams, Oliver Wolcott.

NEW YORK:
Wm. Floyd, Philip Livingston, Francis Lewis, Lewis Morris.

NEW JERSEY:
Richard Stockton, John Witherspoon, Francis Hopkinson, John Hart, Abraham Clarke.

PENNSYLVANIA:
Robert Morris, Benjamin Rush, Benjamin Franklin, John Morton, George Clymer, James Smith, George Taylor, James Wilson, George Ross.

DELAWARE:
Caesar Rodney, George Read, Thomas M'Kean.

MARYLAND:
Samuel Chase, William Paca, Thomas Stone, Charles Carroll of Carrollton.

VIRGINIA:
George Wythe, Richard Henry Lee, Thomas Jefferson, Benjamin Harrison, Thomas Nelson, Jun., Francis Lightfoot Lee, Carter Braxton.

NORTH CAROLINA:
William Hooper, Joseph Hewes, John Penn.

SOUTH CAROLINA:
Edward Rutledge, Thomas Heyward, Jun., Thomas Lynch, Jun., Arthur Middleton.

GEORGIA:
Button Gwinnett, Lyman Hall, George Walton.

THE CONSTITUTION OF THE UNITED STATES

Preamble

WE THE PEOPLE of the United States, in Order to form a more perfect Union, establish Justice, insure domestic Tranquillity, provide for the common defense, promote the general Welfare, and secure the Blessings of Liberty to ourselves and our Posterity, do ordain and establish this Constitution for the United States of America.

Article I. Legislative Department
Section 1. Congress
Legislative powers.

All legislative Powers herein granted shall be vested in a Congress of the United States, which shall consist of a Senate and House of Representatives.

Section 2. House of Representatives
1. Election of members.

The House of Representatives shall be composed of Members chosen every second Year by the People of the several States, and the Electors in each State shall have the Qualifications requisite for Electors of the most numerous Branch of the State Legislature.

2. Qualifications.

No Person shall be a Representative who shall not have attained to the Age of twenty-five Years, and been seven Years a Citizen of the United States, and who shall not, when elected, be an Inhabitant of that State in which he shall be chosen.

3. Apportionment.

Representatives and direct Taxes shall be apportioned among the several States which may be included within this Union, according to their respective Numbers, which shall be determined by adding to the whole Number of free Persons, including those bound to Service for a Term of Years, and excluding Indians not taxed, three fifths of all other Persons. The actual Enumeration shall be made within three Years after the first Meeting of the Congress of the United States, and within every subsequent Term of ten Years, in such Manner as they shall by Law direct. The Number of Representatives shall not exceed one for every thirty thousand, but each State shall have at least one Representative; and until such enumeration shall be made, the State of New Hampshire shall be entitled to choose three, Massachusetts eight, Rhode Island and Providence Plantations one, Connecticut five, New York six, New Jersey four, Pennsylvania eight, Delaware one, Maryland six, Virginia ten, North Carolina five,

South Carolina five and Georgia three.

4. Vacancies.

When vacancies happen in the Representation from any State, the Executive Authority thereof shall issue Writs of Election to fill such Vacancies.

5. Officers; impeachment.

The House of Representatives shall choose their Speaker and other Officers; and shall have the sole Power of Impeachment.

Section 3. The Senate

1. Number and election of Senators.

The Senate of the United States shall be composed of two Senators from each State, chosen by the Legislature thereof, for six Years; and each Senator shall have one Vote.

2. Classification.

Immediately after they shall be assembled in Consequence of the first Election, they shall be divided as equally as may be into three Classes. The Seats of the Senators of the first Class shall be vacated at the Expiration of the second Year, of the second Class at the Expiration of the fourth Year, and of the third Class at the Expiration of the sixth Year, so that one third may be chosen every second Year; and if vacancies happen by Resignation, or otherwise, during the Recess of the Legislature of any State, the Executive thereof may make temporary appointments until the next meeting of the Legislature, which shall then fill such Vacancies.

3. Qualifications.

No Person shall be a Senator who shall not have attained to the Age of thirty Years, and been nine Years a Citizen of the United States, and who shall not, when elected, be an inhabitant of that State for which he shall be chosen.

4. President of the Senate.

The Vice President of the United States shall be President of the Senate, but shall have no Vote, unless they be equally divided.

5. Officers of the Senate.

The Senate shall choose their other Officers, and also a President pro tempore, in the Absence of the Vice President, or when he shall exercise the Office of President of the United States.

6. Trial of Impeachments.

The Senate shall have the sole Power to try all Impeachments. When sitting for that Purpose, they shall be on Oath or Affirmation. When the President of the United States is tried, the Chief Justice shall preside: And no Person shall be convicted without the Concurrence of two thirds of the Members present.

7. Judgment on Conviction.

Judgment in Cases of Impeachment shall not extend further than to removal from Office, and disqualification to hold and enjoy any Office of honor, Trust, or Profit under the United States: but the Party convicted shall nevertheless be liable and subject to Indictment, Trial,

Judgment and Punishment, according to Law.

Section 4. Elections and Sessions

1. Elections.

The Times, Places and Manner of holding Elections for Senators and Representatives, shall be prescribed in each State by the Legislature thereof; but the Congress may at any time by Law make or alter such Regulations, except as to the Places of choosing Senators.

2. Meetings.

The Congress shall assemble at least once in every Year, and such Meeting shall be on the first Monday in December, unless they shall by Law appoint a different Day.

Section 5. Rules and Procedure

1. Conduct of business.

Each House shall be the Judge of the Elections, Returns and Qualifications of its own Members, and a Majority of each shall constitute a Quorum to do Business; but a smaller Number may adjourn from day to day and may be authorized to compel the Attendance of absent Members, in such Manner, and under such Penalties as each House may provide.

2. Proceedings.

Each House may determine the Rules of its Proceedings, punish its members for disorderly Behavior, and, with the Concurrence of two thirds, expel a Member.

3. Journal.

Each House shall keep a Journal of its Proceedings, and from time to time publish the same, excepting such Parts as may in their Judgment require Secrecy; and the Yeas and Nays of the Members of either House on any question shall, at the Desire of one fifth of those present, be entered on the Journal.

4. Adjournment.

Neither House, during the Session of Congress, shall, without the Consent of the other, adjourn for more than three days, nor to any other Place than that in which the two Houses shall be sitting.

Section 6. Privileges and Limitations on Members

1. Compensation and privileges of members.

The Senators and Representatives shall receive a Compensation for their Services, to be ascertained by Law, and paid out of the Treasury of the United States. They shall in all Cases, except Treason, Felony and Breach of the Peace, be privileged from Arrest during their Attendance at the Session of their respective Houses, and in going to and returning from the same; and for any Speech or Debate in either House, they shall not be questioned in any other Place.

2. Limitations upon members.

No Senator or Representative shall, during the time for which he was elected, be appointed to any civil Office under the authority of the United States, which shall have been created, or the Emoluments whereof shall have been increased during such time; and no Person holding any Office under the United States, shall be a Member of either House during his Continuance in Office.

Section 7. Method of Passing Laws

1. Revenue bills.

All Bills for raising Revenue shall originate in the House of Representatives; but the Senate may propose or concur with Amendments as on other Bills.

2. Passage of bills.

Every Bill which shall have passed the House of Representatives and the Senate, shall, before it become a Law, be presented to the President of the United States; if he approve he shall sign it, but if not he shall return it, with his Objections to that House in which it shall have originated, who shall enter the objections at large on their Journal and proceed to reconsider it. If after such Reconsideration two thirds of that House shall agree to pass the Bill, it shall be sent, together with the Objections, to the other House, by which it shall likewise be reconsidered, and if approved by two thirds of that House it shall become a Law. But in all such Cases the Votes of both Houses shall be determined by Yeas and Nays, and the Names of the Persons voting for and against the Bill shall be entered on the Journal of each House respectively. If any Bill shall not be returned by the President within ten days (Sundays excepted) after it shall have been presented to him, the Same shall be a law, in like Manner as if he had signed it, unless the Congress by their Adjournment prevent its Return, in which Case it shall not be a law.

3. Veto power of President.

Every Order, Resolution, or Vote to which the Concurrence of the Senate and House of Representatives may be necessary (except on a question of Adjournment) shall be presented to the President of the United States; and before the Same shall take Effect, shall be approved by him, or being disapproved by him, shall be repassed by two thirds of the Senate and House of Representatives, according to the Rules and Limitations prescribed in the Case of a bill.

Section 8. Powers of Congress

The Congress shall have the power:

1. To lay and collect Taxes, Duties, Imports and Excises, to pay the Debts and provide for the common Defense and general Welfare of the United States; but all Duties, Imports and Excises shall be uniform throughout the United States;

2. To borrow Money on the Credit of the United States;

3. To regulate Commerce with foreign Nations, and among the several States, and with the Indian Tribes;

4. To establish a uniform Rule of Naturalization, and uniform laws on

the subject of Bankruptcies throughout the United States;

5. To coin Money, regulate the Value thereof, and of foreign Coin, and fix the Standard of Weights and Measures;

6. To provide for the Punishment of counterfeiting the Securities and current Coin of the United States;

7. To establish Post Offices and post roads;

8. To promote the Progress of Science and useful Arts, by securing for limited Times to Authors and Inventors the exclusive Right to their respective Writings and Discoveries;

9. To constitute Tribunals inferior to the supreme Court;

10. To define and Punish Piracies and Felonies committed on the high seas, and Offences against the Law of Nations;

11. To declare War, grant Letters of Marque and Reprisal, and make Rules concerning Captures on Land and Water;

12. To raise and support Armies, but no Appropriation of Money to that Use shall be for a longer Term than two Years;

13. To provide and maintain a Navy;

14. To make Rules for the Government and Regulation of the land and naval Forces;

15. To provide for calling forth the Militia to execute the Laws of the Union, suppress Insurrections and repel Invasions;

16. To provide for organizing, arming, and disciplining the Militia, and for governing such Part of them as may be employed in the Service of the United States, reserving to the States respectively, the Appointment of the Officers, and the Authority of training the Militia according to the discipline prescribed by Congress;

17. To exercise exclusive Legislation in all Cases whatsoever, over such District (not exceeding ten Miles square) as may, by Cession of particular States, and the Acceptance of Congress, become the Seat of the Government of the United States, and to exercise like Authority over all Places purchased by the Consent of the Legislature of the States in which the Same shall be, for the Erection of Forts, Magazines, Arsenals, dock-Yards, and other needful Buildings;—And

18. To make all Laws which shall be necessary and proper for carrying into Execution the foregoing Powers, and all other Powers vested by this Constitution in the Government of the United States, or in any Department or Officer thereof.

Section 9. Powers Denied Congress

1. The Migration or Importation of such Persons as any of the States now existing shall think proper to admit, shall not be prohibited by the Congress, prior to the Year one thousand eight hundred and eight,

but a Tax or Duty may be imposed on such Importation, not exceeding ten dollars for each Person.

2. The Privilege of the Writ of Habeas Corpus shall not be suspended, unless when in Cases of Rebellion or Invasion the public Safety may require it.

3. No Bill of Attainder or ex post facto Law shall be passed.

4. No Capitation, or other direct, Tax shall be laid, unless in Proportion to the Census or Enumeration herein before directed to be taken.

5. No tax or Duty shall be laid on Articles exported from any State.

6. No Preference shall be given by any Regulation of Commerce or Revenue to the Ports of one State over those of another: nor shall Vessels bound to, or from one State, be obliged to enter, clear, or pay Duties in another.

7. No Money shall be drawn from the Treasury, but in Consequence of Appropriations made by Law; and a regular Statement and Account of the Receipts and Expenditures of all public Money shall be published from time to time.

8. No Title of Nobility shall be granted by the United States: And no Person holding any Office of Profit or Trust under them, shall, without the Consent of the Congress, accept of any present, Emolument, Office, or Title, of any kind whatever, from any King, Prince, or Foreign State.

Section 10. Powers Denied the States

1. General limitations.

No State shall enter into any Treaty, Alliance, or Confederation; grant Letters of Marque and Reprisal; coin Money; emit Bills of Credit; make any Thing but gold and silver Coin a Tender in Payment of Debts; pass any Bill of Attainder, ex post facto Law, or Law impairing the Obligation of Contracts, or grant any Title of Nobility.

2. Powers dependent upon Congress.

No State shall, without the Consent of the Congress, lay any Imposts or Duties on Imports or Exports, except what may be absolutely necessary for executing its inspection Laws: and the net Produce of all Duties and Imposts, laid by any State on Imports or Exports, shall be for the Use of the Treasury of the United States; and all such Laws shall be subject to the Revision and Control of the Congress.

No State shall, without the Consent of Congress, lay any Duty of Tonnage, keep Troops, or Ships of War in time of Peace, enter into any Agreement or Compact with another State, or with a foreign Power, or engage in War, unless actually invaded, or in such imminent Danger as will not admit of Delay.

Article II. Executive Department

Section 1. President and Vice-President

1. Terms of President and Vice-President.

The executive Power shall be vested in a President of the United

States of America. He shall hold his Office during the Term of four Years, and, together, with the Vice President chosen for the same term, be elected as follows:

2. Electors.

Each State shall appoint, in such Manner as the Legislature thereof may direct, a Number of Electors equal to the whole Number of Senators and Representatives to which the State may be entitled in the Congress: but no Senator or Representative, or Person holding an Office of Trust or Profit under the United States, shall be appointed an Elector.

3. Electoral procedure.

The electors shall meet in their respective States, and vote by ballot for two Persons, of whom one at least shall not be an Inhabitant of the same State with themselves. And they shall make a List of the Persons voted for, and of the Number of Votes for each; which List they shall sign and certify, and transmit sealed to the Seat of the Government of the United States, directed to the President of the Senate. The President of the Senate shall, in the presence of the Senate and House of Representatives, open all the Certificates, and the Votes shall then be counted. The Person having the greatest Number of Votes shall be President, if such Number be a Majority of the whole Number of Electors appointed; and if there be more than one who have such Majority and have an equal Number of Votes, then the House of Representatives shall immediately choose by Ballot one of them for President; and if no person have a Majority, then from the five highest on the List the said House shall in like Manner choose the President. But in choosing the President, the Votes shall be taken by States, the Representation from each State having one Vote; a quorum for this Purpose shall consist of a Member or Members from two-thirds of the States, and a Majority of all the States shall be necessary to a Choice. In every Case, after the Choice of the President, the person having the greatest Number of Votes of the Electors shall be the Vice President. But if there should remain two or more who have equal Votes, the Senate shall choose from them by Ballot the Vice President.

4. Date of choosing electors.

The Congress may determine the Time of choosing the electors and the Day on which they shall give their Votes; which Day shall be the same throughout the United States.

5. Qualifications of the President.

No Person except a natural born Citizen or a Citizen of the United States at the time of the Adoption of this Constitution, shall be eligible to the Office of President; neither shall any person be eligible to the Office who shall not have attained to the Age of thirty five Years, and been fourteen Years a Resident within the United States.

6. Vacancy.

In Case of the Removal of the President from Office, or of his Death, Resignation, or Inability to discharge the Powers and Duties of the said Office, the same shall devolve on the Vice President, and the Congress may by Law provide for the Case of Removal, Death, Resignation, or Inability, both of the President and Vice President, declaring what Officer shall then act as President, and such Officer shall act accordingly, until the Disability be removed, or a President shall be elected.

7. Compensation.

The President shall, at stated Times, receive for his Services, a Compensation, which shall neither be increased nor diminished during the Period for which he shall have been elected, and he shall not receive within that Period any other Emolument from the United States, or any of them.

8. Oath of office.

Before he enter on the execution of his Office, he shall take the following Oath or Affirmation: — "I do solemnly swear (or affirm) that I will faithfully execute the Office of President of the United States, and will to the best of my Ability, preserve, protect, and defend the Constitution of the United States."

Section 2. Powers of the President
1. Military and naval.

The President shall be Commander in Chief of the Army and Navy of the United States, and of the Militia of the several States, when called into the actual Service of the United States; he may require the Opinion, in writing, of the principal Officer in each of the executive Departments, upon any Subject relating to the Duties of their respective Offices, and he shall have Power to grant Reprieves and Pardons for Offenses against the United States, except in Cases of Impeachment.

2. Treaties and appointments.

He shall have Power, by and with the Advice and Consent of the Senate, to make Treaties, provided two thirds of the Senators present concur; and he shall nominate, and by and with the Advice and Consent of the Senate, shall appoint Ambassadors, other public Ministers and Consuls, Judges of the Supreme Court, and all other Officers of the United States, whose Appointments are not herein otherwise provided for, and which shall be established by Law; but the Congress may by Law vest the Appointment of such inferior Officers, as they think proper, in the President alone, in the Courts of Law, or in the heads of Departments.

3. Filling of vacancies.

The President shall have Power to fill up all Vacancies that may happen during the Recess of the Senate, by granting Commissions which shall expire at the End of their next Session.

Section 3. Duties of the President

He shall from time to time give to the Congress Information of the State of the Union, and recommend to their Consideration such Measures as he shall judge necessary and expedient; he may, on extraordinary Occasions, convene both Houses, or either of them, and in Case of Disagreement between them, with respect to the Time of Adjournment, he may adjourn them to such Time as he shall think proper; he shall receive Ambassadors and other public Ministers; he shall take Care that the Laws be faithfully executed, and shall Commission all the Officers of the United States.

Section 4. Impeachment

The President, Vice President, and all civil Officers of the United States shall be removed from office on Impeachment for, and Conviction of, Treason, Bribery, and other high Crimes and Misdemeanors.

Article III. The Judicial Department

Section 1. Courts

Supreme and inferior courts.

The judicial Power of the United States shall be vested in one supreme Court, and in such inferior Courts as the Congress may from time to time ordain and establish. The Judges, both of the supreme and inferior Courts, shall hold their Offices during good Behavior, and shall, at stated Times, receive for their Services a Compensation, which shall not be diminished during their Continuance in Office.

Section 2. Jurisdiction

1. Powers.

The judicial Power shall extend to all Cases, in Law and Equity, arising under this Constitution, the Laws of the United States, and Treaties made, or which shall be made, under their Authority; — to all Cases affecting Ambassadors, other public Ministers and Consuls; — to all Cases of admiralty and maritime Jurisdiction; — to Controversies to which the United States shall be a Party; — to Controversies between two or more States; — between a State and Citizens of another State; — between Citizens of different States; — between Citizens of the same State claiming Lands Under Grants of different States, and between a State, or the Citizens thereof, and foreign States, Citizens or Subjects.

2. Jurisdiction.

In all Cases affecting Ambassadors, other public Ministers and Consuls, and those in which a State shall be Party, the supreme Court shall have original Jurisdiction. In all the other Cases before mentioned, the Supreme Court shall have appellate Jurisdiction, both as to Law and Fact, with such exceptions, and under such Regulations as Congress shall make.

3. Trials.

The Trial of all Crimes, except in Cases of Impeachment, shall be by

Jury; and such Trial shall be held in the State where the said Crimes shall have been committed; but when not committed within any State, the Trial shall be at such Place or Places as the Congress may by Law have directed.

Section 3. Treason

1. **Definition.**

Treason against the United States, shall consist only in levying War against them, or in adhering to their Enemies, giving them Aid and Comfort. No Person shall be convicted of Treason unless on the Testimony of two Witnesses to the same overt Act, or on Confession in open Court.

2. **Punishment.**

The Congress shall have Power to declare the Punishment of Treason, but no Attainder of Treason shall work Corruption of Blood, or Forfeiture except during the Life of the Person Attained.

Article IV. The States

Section 1. Official Acts

Full Faith and Credit shall be given in each State to the public Acts, Records, and judicial Proceedings of every other State. And the Congress may by general Laws prescribe the Manner in which such Acts, Records and Proceedings shall be proved, and the Effect thereof.

Section 2. Privileges of Citizens

1. **Privileges.**

The Citizens of each State shall be entitled to all Privileges and Immunities of Citizens in the several States.

2. **Fugitives.**

A person charged in any State with Treason, Felony, or other Crime, who shall flee from Justice, and be found in another State, shall on Demand of the executive Authority of the State from which he fled, be delivered up to be removed to the State having Jurisdiction of the Crime.

3. **Fugitives from labour.**

No person held to Service or Labour in one State, under the Laws thereof, escaping into another, shall, in Consequence of any Law or Regulation therein, be discharged from such Service or Labour, but shall be delivered up on Claim of the Party to whom such Service or Labour may be due. (superseded by Amendment XIII.)

Section 3. New States and Territories

1. **New States.**

New States may be admitted by the Congress into this Union; but no new State shall be formed or erected within the Jurisdiction of any other States; nor any State be formed by the Junction of two or more States, or Parts of States, without the Consent of the Legislatures of the States concerned as well as of the Congress.

2. **U. S. territory.**

The Congress shall have Power to dispose of and make all needful Rules and Regulations respecting the Territory or other Property belonging to the United States; and nothing in this Constitution shall be so construed as to Prejudice any Claims of the United States, or of any particular State.

Section 4. Protection of the States

The United States shall guarantee to every State in this Union, a Republican Form of Government, and shall protect each of them against Invasion; and on Application of the Legislature, or of the Executive (when the Legislature cannot be convened) against domestic Violence.

Article V. Amendments to the Constitution

The Congress, whenever two thirds of both Houses shall deem it necessary, shall propose Amendments to this Constitution, or, on the Application of the Legislatures of two thirds of the several States, shall call a Convention for proposing Amendments, which, in either Case, shall be valid to all Intents and Purposes, as Part of this Constitution, when ratified by the Legislatures of three fourths of the several States, or by Conventions in three fourths thereof, as the one or the other mode of Ratification may be proposed by the Congress; Provided that no Amendment which may be made prior to the Year One thousand eight hundred and eight shall in any Manner affect the first and fourth Clauses in the Ninth Section of the first Article; and that no State, without

its Consent shall be deprived of its equal Suffrage in the Senate.

Article VI. General Provisions
1. Validity of debts.

All Debts contracted and Engagements entered into, before the Adoption of this Constitution, shall be valid against the United States under this Constitution, as under the Confederation.

2. Supremacy of the Constitution.

This Constitution, and the Laws of the United States which shall be made in Pursuance thereof; and all Treaties made, or which shall be made, under the Authority of the United States, shall be the supreme Law of the Land; and the Judges in every State shall be bound thereby, any Thing in the Constitution or Laws of any State to the Contrary notwithstanding.

3. Oath.

The Senators and Representatives before mentioned, and the Members of the several State Legislatures, and all executive and judicial Officers, both of the United States and of the several States, shall be bound by Oath or Affirmation, to support this Constitution; but no religious Test shall ever be required as a Qualification to any Office or public Trust under the United States.

Article VII. Ratification of the Constitution

The Ratification of the Conventions of nine States, shall be sufficient for the Establishment of this Constitution between the States so ratifying the Same.

Done in Convention by the unanimous consent of the States present, the seventeenth day of September, in the year of our Lord one thousand seven hundred and eighty-seven, and of the Independence of the United States of America the twelfth.

In witness whereof, we have hereunto subscribed our names.

GEORGE WASHINGTON,
President and Deputy from Virginia.

NEW HAMPSHIRE:
John Langdon, Nicholas Gilman.

MASSACHUSETTS:
Nathaniel Gorham, Rufus King.

CONNECTICUT:
William Samuel Johnson,
Roger Sherman.

NEW YORK:
Alexander Hamilton.

NEW JERSEY:
William Livingston, David Brearly,
William Patterson,
Jonathan Dayton.

PENNSYLVANIA:
Benjamin Franklin,
Thomas Mifflin, Robert Morris,
George Clymer,
Thomas Fitzsimons,
Jared Ingersoll, James Wilson,
Gouverneur Morris.

DELAWARE:
George Read,
Gunning Bedford, Jr.,
John Dickinson,
Richard Bassett, Jacob Broom.

MARYLAND:
James McHenry,
Daniel of St. Thomas Jenifer,
Daniel Carroll.

VIRGINIA:
John Blair, James Madison, Jr.

NORTH CAROLINA:
William Blount,
Richard Dobbs Spaight,
Hugh Williamson.

SOUTH CAROLINA:
John Rutledge,
Charles Cotesworth Pinckney,
Charles Pinckney, Pierce Butler.

GEORGIA:
William Few, Abraham Baldwin.

Attest: WILLIAM JACKSON,
Secretary.

AMENDMENTS

I. Freedom of Religion, Speech, and the Press; Right of Assembly (1791)

Congress shall make no law respecting an establishment of religion or prohibiting the free exercise thereof; or abridging the freedom of speech or of the press; or the right of the people peaceably to assemble, and to petition the Government for a redress of grievances.

II. Right to Bear Arms (1791)

A well regulated Militia, being necessary to the security of a free State, the right of the people to keep and bear Arms, shall not be infringed.

III. Quartering of Troops (1791)

No Soldier shall, in time of peace be quartered in any house, without the consent of the owner, nor in time of war, but in a manner to be prescribed by law.

IV. Search (1791)

The right of the people to be secure in their persons, houses, papers, and effects, against unreasonable searches and seizures, shall not be violated, and no Warrants shall issue but upon probable cause, supported by Oath or affirmation, and particularly describing the place to be searched, and the persons or things to be seized.

V. Jury Trial (1791)

No person shall be held to answer for a capital, or otherwise infamous crime, unless on a presentment of indictment of a Grand Jury, except in cases arising in the land or naval forces, or in the Militia, when in actual service in time Of War or in public danger; nor shall any person be subject for the same offense to be twice put in jeopardy of life or limb; nor shall be compelled in any Criminal Case to be a witness against himself, nor be deprived of life, liberty, or property, without due process of law; nor shall private property be taken for public use, without just compensation.

VI. Rights of the Accused (1791)

In all criminal prosecutions, the accused shall enjoy the right to a speedy and public trial, by an impartial jury of the State and district wherein the crime shall have been committed, which district shall have been previously ascertained by law, and to be informed of the nature and cause of the accusation; to be confronted with the witnesses against him; to have compulsory process for obtaining Witnesses in his favor, and to have the Assistance of Counsel for his defense.

VII. Suits at Common Law (1791)

In suits at common law, where the value in controversy shall exceed twenty dollars, the right of trial by jury shall be preserved, and no fact tried by a jury shall be otherwise re-examined in any Court of the United States than according to the rules of the common law.

VIII. Excessive Bail and Punishments (1791)

Excessive bail shall not be required, nor excessive fines imposed, nor cruel and unusual punishments inflicted.

IX. Rights Reserved to the People (1791)

The enumeration in the Constitution, of certain rights, shall not be construed to deny or disparage others retained by the People.

X. Powers Reserved to States and People (1791)

The powers not delegated to the United States by the Constitution, nor prohibited by it to the States, are reserved to the States respectively, or to the people.

XI. Suits Against States (1798)

The Judicial power of the United States shall not be construed to extend to any suit in law or equity, commenced or prosecuted against one of the United States by Citizens of another State, or by Citizens or Subjects of any Foreign State.

XII. Election of President and Vice-President (1804)

The Electors shall meet in their respective states, and vote by ballot for President and Vice-President, one of whom, at least, shall not be an inhabitant of the same state with themselves; they shall name in their ballots the person voted for as President, and in distinct ballots the person voted for as Vice-President, and they shall make distinct lists of all persons voted for as President, and of all persons voted for as Vice-President, and of the number of votes for each, which lists they shall sign and certify, and transmit sealed to the seat of the government of the United States, directed to the President of the Senate; — The President of the Senate shall, in presence of the Senate and House of Representatives, open all the certificates and the votes shall then be counted; — The person having the greatest number of votes for President, shall be the President, if such a number be a majority of the whole number of Electors appointed; and if no person have such majority, then from the persons having the highest numbers not exceeding three on the list of those voted for as President, the House of Representatives shall choose immediately, by ballot, the President. But in choosing the President, the votes shall be taken by states, the representation from each state having one vote, a quorum for this purpose shall consist of a member or members from two-thirds of the states, and a majority of all the states shall be necessary to a choice. And if the House of Representatives shall not choose a President, whenever the right of choice shall devolve upon them, before the fourth day of March next following, then the Vice-President shall act as President, as in the case of the death or other constitutional disability of the President. The person having the greatest number of votes as Vice-President shall be the Vice-President, if such number be a majority of the whole number of Electors appointed, and if no person have a majority, then from the two highest numbers on the list the Senate shall choose the Vice-President; a quorum for the purpose shall consist of two-thirds of the whole number of Senators, and a majority of the whole number shall be necessary to a choice. But no person constitutionally ineligible to the office of President shall be eligible to that of Vice-President of the United States.

XIII. Abolishment of Slavery (1865)

Neither slavery nor involuntary servitude, except as punishment for crime whereof the party shall have been duly convicted, shall exist within the United States, or any place subject to their jurisdiction.

Section 2. Enforcement

Congress shall have power to enforce this article by appropriate legislation.

XIV. Citizenship (1868)

Section 1. Citizens

All persons born or naturalized in the United States, and subject to the jurisdiction thereof, are citizens of the United States and of the State wherein they reside. No State shall make or enforce any law which shall abridge the privileges or immunities of citizens of the United States; nor shall any State deprive any person of life, liberty, or property, without due process of law; nor deny to any person within its jurisdiction the equal protection of the laws.

Section 2. Representatives

Representatives shall be apportioned among the several States according to their respective numbers, counting the whole number of persons in each State, excluding Indians not taxed. But when the right to vote at any election for the choice of electors for President and Vice-President of the United States, Representatives in Congress, the Executive and Judicial officers of a State, or the members of the Legislature thereof, is denied to any of the male inhabitants of such State, being twenty-one years of age, and citizens of the United States, or in any way abridged, except for participation in rebellion, or other crime, the basis of representation therein shall be reduced in the proportion which the number of such male citizens shall bear to the whole number of male citizens twenty-one years of age in such State.

Section 3. Insurrection

No person shall be a Senator or Representative in Congress, or elector of President and Vice-President, or hold any office, civil or military, under the United States, or under any State, who, having previously taken an oath, as a member of Congress, or as an officer of the United States, or as a member of any State legislature, or as an executive or judicial officer of any State, to support the Constitution of the United States, shall have engaged in insurrection or rebellion against the same, or given aid or comfort to the enemies thereof. But Congress may by a vote of two-thirds of each House, remove such disability.

Section 4. Public Debt

The validity of the public debt of the United States, authorized by law, including debts incurred for payment of pensions and bounties for services in suppressing insurrection or rebellion, shall not be questioned. But neither the United States nor any State shall assume or pay any debt or obligation incurred in aid of insurrection or rebellion against the United States, or any claim for the loss or emancipation of any slave; but all such debts, obligations and claims shall be held illegal and void.

Section 5. Enforcement

The Congress shall have power to enforce, by appropriate legislation, the provisions of this article.

XV. Negro Suffrage (1870)

Section 1. Negro's Right to Vote

The right of citizens of the United States to vote shall not be denied or abridged by the United States or by any State on account of race, color, or previous condition of servitude.

Section 2. Enforcement

The Congress shall have power to enforce this article by appropriate legislation.

XVI. Income Tax (1913)

The Congress shall have power to lay and collect taxes on incomes, from whatever source derived, without apportionment among the several States, and without regard to any census or enumeration.

XVII. Election of Senators (1913)

The Senate of the United States shall be composed of two Senators from each State, elected by the people thereof, for six years; and each Senator shall have one vote. The electors in each State shall have the qualifications requisite for electors of the most numerous branch of the State Legislature.

When vacancies happen in the representation of any State in the Senate, the executive authority of such State shall issue writs of election to fill such vacancies; Provided, That the Legislature of any State may empower the executive thereof to make temporary appointment until the people fill the vacancies by election as the Legislature may direct.

This amendment shall not be so construed as to affect the election or term of any Senator chosen before it becomes valid as part of the Constitution.

XVIII. National Prohibition (1919)

After one year from the ratification of this article the manufacture, sale, or transportation of intoxicating liquors within, the Importation thereof into, or the exportation thereof from the United States and all territory subject to the jurisdiction thereof for beverage purposes is hereby prohibited.

The Congress and the several states shall have concurrent power to enforce this article by appropriate legislation.

This article shall be inoperative unless it shall have been ratified as an amendment to the Constitution by the legislatures of the several states, as provided in the Constitution, within seven years from the date of submission hereof to the states by the Congress.

XIX. Woman Suffrage (1920)

Section 1. Right of Women to Vote

The right of the citizens of the United States to vote shall not be denied or abridged by the United States or by any state on account of sex.

Section 2. Enforcement

Congress shall have power, by appropriate legislation, to enforce the provisions of this article.

XX. "Lame Duck" Amendment (1933)

Section 1. Terms of President, Vice-President, and Congressmen

The terms of the President and Vice-President shall end at noon on the 20th day of January, and the terms of Senators and Representatives at noon on the 3rd day of January, of the years in which such terms would have ended if this article had not been ratified; and the terms of their successors shall then begin.

Section 2. Sessions of Congress

The Congress shall assemble at least once in every year, and such meeting shall begin at noon on the 3rd day of January, unless they shall by law appoint a different day.

Section 3. Presidential Succession

If, at the time fixed for the beginning of the term of the President, the President elect shall have died, the Vice-President elect shall become President. If a President shall not have been chosen before the time fixed for the beginning of his term, or if the President elect shall have failed to qualify, then the Vice-President elect shall act as President until a President shall have qualified; and the Congress may by law provide for the case wherein neither a President elect nor a Vice-President elect shall have qualified, declaring who shall then act as President, or the manner in which one who is to act shall be selected, and such person shall act accordingly until a President or Vice-President shall have qualified.

Section 4. President Chosen by the House

The Congress may by law provide for the case of the death of any of the persons from whom the House of Representatives may choose a President whenever the right of choice shall have devolved upon them, and for the case of death of any of the persons from whom the Senate may choose a Vice-President whenever the right of choice shall have devolved upon them.

Section 5. Effective Date

Section 1 and 2 shall take effect on the 15th day of October following the ratification of this article.

Section 6. Ratification

This article shall be inoperative unless it shall have been ratified as an amendment to the Constitution by the legislatures of three-fourths of the several States within seven years from the date of its submission.

XXI. Repeal of Prohibition (1933)

Section 1. Repeal of Article XVIII

The eighteenth article of amendment to the Constitution of the United States is hereby repealed.

Section 2. Transportation of Liquor

The transportation or importation into any State, Territory or Possession of the United States for delivery or use therein of intoxicating liquors, in violation of the laws thereof, is hereby prohibited.

Section 3. Ratification

This article shall be inoperative unless it shall have been ratified as an amendment to the Constitution by conventions in the several States, as provided in the Constitution, within seven years from the date of the submission hereof to the States by the Congress.

XXII. Presidential Term of Office (1951)

No person shall be elected to the office of the President more than twice, and no person who has held the office of President, or acted as President for more than two years of a term to which some other person was elected President, shall be elected to the office of the President more than once. But this article shall not apply to any person holding the office of President when this article was proposed by the Congress, and shall not prevent any person who may be holding the office of President, or acting as President, during the term within which this article becomes effective, from holding the office of President or acting as President during the remainder of such term.

INDEX

discovery of silver in, 266

Columbia River, 45, 65, 66, 67

Columbus, 216

commerce, 92

communication, improvement of, 228-246

Compromise of 1850, 100-102

Comstock Lode, 173

Confederate States, 114, 115, 119, 120

Congress, 125

Constitution,
  interpretation of, 22
  and secession, 24, 25
  and slavery, 97
  of Confederacy, 115

Cook, Captain, 65

Cooper, James Fenimore, 273

copper mines, 48

Corby, Father William, C.S.C., 136

Coronado, 52

cotton, 90, 91, 92, 93, 125, 162

cotton gin, 91, 92

couplers, automatic, 240

courts, 213

cowboy, 175-176

"cradle-rocking," 76

Crawford, William, 14, 15

Cretin, Bishop Joseph, 195

Crittenden, Senator, 116

Cumberland, 125

Cumberland River, 132

Custer, General, 180, 181

D

Daimler, 242

Dakotas, 43, 173

Davis, Jefferson, 115

Dawes Act, 180

Declaration of Independence, 24

Delaware, 119

Demers, Father, 71

democracy, 20

Democratic party, 111, 161

Democratic-Republicans, 15, 16, 29

Denver, 172

depression, 31

De Smet, Father, 71-73, 179-180

District of Columbia, 100

Divine Word, Fathers of, 168

Dix, Dorothea, 129

Dominican Sisters of Most Holy
  Rosary, 46

Douglas, Stephen A., 104, 111, 112, 113, 114, 117

draft riots, 134, 135

Drake, Francis, 65

Dred Scott Decision, 107, 108

Drexel, Catherine, 167

Duchesne, Mother Philippine, 78, 272

Duryea, Charles, 242

dynamo, 253

E

Early, General Jubal, 139

East, Civil War in, 133-140

Edison, Thomas Alva, 254-258

education, Catholic, 270-273
  higher, 272-273

Einstein, Albert, 217

Eisenhower, President Dwight D., 216

election,
  of 1824, 14
  of 1828, 16
  of 1832, 30
  of 1844, 56
  of 1860, 114

electric light, 256-257

electricity, 253

emancipation, Catholic Church and, 164

Emancipation Proclamation, 131

Grant, General Ulysses S., 132, 133,
137, 138, 139, 140, 141, 142
President, 159, 160
Gray, Captain Robert, 65
"Great American Desert," 169-170
Great Divide, 44
Great Eastern, 232, 233
Great Lakes, 92
Great Salt Lake, 75
Greenback Party, 265
Guadalupe Hidalgo, 59

H

Hale, Edward Everett, 275
Hamilton, Alexander, 28, 29
Hampton Institute, 162
Harris, Joel Chandler, 275
Harrison, William H., 33
Harte, Bret, 275
Harvey, General, 73
Hawthorne, Nathaniel, 273
Hayes, President, 160
Hayne, Senator, 25, 26-28
Haynes, Elwood, 242
Healy, George P. A., 214
Hecker, Rev. Isaac T., 216
Hendricks, Bishop, 166
Henry, Joseph, 253
Henry, Patrick, 214
Herbert, Victor, 214
Hoe, Richard, 213, 237
Holmes, Oliver Wendell, 274
Holy Family, Sisters of, 165
Holy Ghost, Fathers of, 167
Holy Names, Sisters of, 78
Homestead Act, 170, 176-177
homesteader, life of, 177-178
Hooker, General Thomas, 134
Houston, Sam, 55, 56
Howard University, 162

Howe, Elias, 247-249
Hudson Bay Company, 65, 66
Hughes, Archbishop John, 127, 135,
194-195, 198, 271

I

Idaho, 45, 173
Illinois, 62
Immaculate Conception, dogma of,
62
immigration,
restriction of, 209, 211
immigrants,
"old," 192-199
"new," 200-208
settlements, 203-204
contributions of, 212-219
Impelliteri, Vincent, 217
Independence, Missouri, 48
Indians,
and Lewis and Clark, 43, 44
and Pike, 46
and Santa Fe Trail, 49
in Oregon, 67-73
last stand of, 178
and Father de Smet, 179
become citizens, 180
indigo, 90
industries of West, 45
industry, inventions help, 247
Inness, George, 277
Iowa, 45, 195
Ireland, Archbishop John, 203, 204,
214
Ireland, immigrants from, 194, 197
important immigrants and
descendants, 214
Irish Brigade, 136
iron, 92, 162, 250
Iroquois Indians, 69
Irving, Washington, 273

317